QUEST FOR ECONOMIC EMPIRE

❖

QUEST FOR ECONOMIC EMPIRE

*European Strategies of German Big Business
in the Twentieth Century*

Edited by
Volker R. Berghahn

Berghahn Books
Providence • Oxford

First published in 1996 by
Berghahn Books
Editorial offices:
165 Taber Avenue, Providence, RI 02906, USA
Bush House, Merewood Avenue, Oxford, OX3 8EF, UK

© Volker R. Berghahn 1996

All rights reserved.
No part of this publication may be reproduced in any form or by any means without the written permission of Berghahn Books.

Library of Congress Cataloging-in-Publication Data

```
Quest for economic empire : the European strategies of German business
in the twentieth century / edited by Volker R. Berghahn.
     p.  cm.
  Papers presented at a conference at Brown University.
  Includes bibliographical references and index.

  1. Germany--Foreign economic relations--Europe--Congresses.
2. Europe--Foreign economic relations--Germany--Congresses.
3. Germany--Foreign economic relations--Congresses.  4. Germany-
-Commercial policy--Congresses.  5. Industrial policy--Germany-
-History--20th century--Congresses.  6. Big business--Germany-
-History--20th century--Congresses.  7. Germany--Politics and
government--20th century--Congresses.  8. European Union--Germany-
-Congresses.   I. Berghahn, Volker Rolf.
HF1546.15.E85H67    1995
337.4304'0904--dc20                                       95-38477
                                                              CIP
```

ISBN: 978-1-57181-931-4

British Library Cataloguing in Publication Data
A catalogue record for this book is available from the British Library.

TABLE OF CONTENTS

Preface vii

Introduction
German Big Business and the Quest for a European
Economic Empire in the Twentieth Century
Volker R. Berghahn 1

Chapter 1
Europe in the Strategies of Germany's Electrical Engineering
and Chemicals Trusts, 1919-1929
Harm G. Schröter 35

Chapter 2
The European Strategies of IG Farben, 1925-45
Peter Hayes 55

Chapter 3
Fascism and the Structure of German Capitalism:
The Case of the Automobile Industry
Simon Reich 65

Chapter 4
German Big Business and the Return to the World Market
after World War II
Reinhard Neebe 95

Chapter 5
"Reconquering Our Old Position":
West German Osthandel Strategies of the 1950s
Robert Mark Spaulding, Jr.. 123

Chapter 6
Lowering Soviet Expectations:
West German Industry and Osthandel during the
Brandt Era
Volker R. Berghahn 145

Chapter 7
Strategies of German Big Business in their International
Setting during the 1980s
Margit Köppen 159

Chapter 8
German Industry and the European Union
in the 1990s
Jeffrey J. Anderson 171

Tables 207

List of Contributors 229

Preface

With the end of World War II half a century ago, the period 1939-1945 and the decades leading up to Hitler's war of aggression and extermination continue to be assessed and reassessed by historians and politicians from many different angles. Given the broad public interest, political and military perspectives predominate in debate. In the same way, the question has been raised as to how far there exists a line of continuity between the two "great wars" of the twentieth century, and how far World War II was a repeat performance of the First so that the Allies twice resisted an attempt to establish a *pax Germanica* in which the Reich would reign as the dominant power on the European continent from the Atlantic to the Urals. Some, especially in Germany where the desire to "normalize" the course of German history has grown in recent years, will highlight the discontinuities between 1914 and 1939 and even more so between the first and second halves of this century. Others who are struck by the continuities will, in marshalling the evidence for their view, inter alia point to the map of Europe in 1916/17 and 1941/42 to compare Germany's proclaimed territorial war aims as an indicator of her ambitions. They have little doubt that the powerful and restive nation in the heart of Europe twice in this century aimed to build a large territorial empire. And they also tend to raise the question of where Reunified Germany is headed now.

Given the weight of the German industrial and financial system in Europe today and in the decades since the turn of the century, the European strategies and policies of big business, with their underlying traditions and mentalities, pose some of the most intriguing questions of modern history. What were the aims of German industry and finance in the first half of this century and what are they today? What shifts and changes have there been over time and what accelerated them or slowed them down? What role did German industry carve out for itself in the European as well as the world economies in the past and today? How did it relate to government and to popular movements in the age of mass participation in politics? These are the questions from which the contributors to this volume started their analyses. They were subsequently debated at a conference at Brown University, and this is the place for the organizers to thank the Goethe-Institut Boston and its then director, Dr. Peter Schmidt, for their generous support of this venture. The volume that has now emerged from these joint efforts is not, by any means, the final word on the subject of German big business and Europe in this century. Rather it is an attempt to encourage further work in this underresearched field and to enhance the dialogue between history, economic and business history, political science and historians of mentalities. For while there is obviously a need for hard-nosed quantitative work and for getting the statistics on Germany's role in Europe "straight," it seems no less desirable to bridge the manifest gap between those who deal with structural developments in history and the social sciences and those who believe that societies and their economic systems are shaped by less tangible forces of human perception (and misperception) of the world and who wish to retain the category of agency as a perspective on socioeconomic, political, and cultural change.

So, while we hope that readers will find the articles in this volume intrinsically worthwhile, they also reflect an attempt to highlight the need to connect received notions of economic and business history with those that are concerned with attitudes, traditions of thought, and mentalities, whether in a specific period like World War II or over longer stretches of time.

Providence, R.I. V.R. Berghahn
September 1995

Introduction

❖

GERMAN BIG BUSINESS AND THE QUEST FOR A EUROPEAN ECONOMIC EMPIRE IN THE TWENTIETH CENTURY

Volker R. Berghahn

This volume is concerned with the historical role of German big business in its larger European context and arose in part from the observation of a major irony of modern history. Following the collapse of communism in Eastern Europe and after German reunification, it has become increasingly clear that Germany, which twice in the first half of the twentieth century vainly attempted to establish by force a formal empire stretching from the Atlantic coast to the Ural Mountains and beyond,[1] now at the end of this century finds herself on the verge of acquiring an informal empire of similar dimensions without having fired a single shot. There can be little doubt that reunited Germany – with its powerful industrial and financial sectors, large well-trained population, and situated in the heart of the continent – will occupy a pivotal position not only in the European Union (EU), but also in Eastern Europe. Already the dominant economic factor in Western Europe, German industry and banking, temporary difficulties in the wake of reunification notwithstanding, have no rival

1. See, e.g. F. Fischer, *War of Illusions* (London, 1975); K. Hildebrand, *The Foreign Policy of the Third Reich* (London, 1973).

in the construction of capitalism that is currently and painfully going on in the former Soviet Bloc countries. The British, French, Italians, Americans, and Japanese are potentially serious competitors. Not only have they moved cautiously, fearing the loss of their money in a region that could still experience a major social and political explosion, but also they find themselves at a disadvantage vis-à-vis German business, which after 1945 first maintained and later expanded its many traditional links with the economies of Eastern Europe.

This being the realities, some politicians, intellectuals, and businessmen in France, Britain, Holland, and the former Soviet Bloc countries have been worrying about how the new Germany and its powerful entrepreneurs and bankers might behave in a Europe that still remembers two earlier periods when, backed by its military machine, the Reich tried to establish itself by coercive means as the pre-eminent regional power.[2] In France, a major debate about the old "German Question" has been going on since the late 1980s, if indeed it ever stopped after 1945. In England, feelings, which the British were in the past often too polite to express openly, repeatedly have been articulated and promptly hit the headlines. There was the embarrassing outburst by Nicholas Ridley, the British Trade and Industry Minister, concerning the alleged strategic aims of the Federal Republic within a larger Europe, which made direct reference to the Third Reich. Prime Minister Margaret Thatcher held her intimate consultations at Chequers with a number of eminent British and American historians in order to learn from them whether the new Germany was really any different from the old.

The trouble is that, in trying to answer this question, we quickly discover that we may know much about West German politicians, political culture, and the behavior of the "masses," but we lack information about the behavior of German business in a larger European context in this century. Historians have looked in great detail at the German position from a power-political and military perspective. There are many books on what German diplomats, intellectuals and generals have been doing or dreaming of in this century. Our knowledge of the European strategies of big business, by contrast, is much patchier. The essays in this volume try to fill some of these gaps and hope to stimulate others to enter this neglected field of German history, now that the older concerns with questions of security and military power are, at the end of the Cold War, receding into the background or assuming a different shape.

2. For a good survey of European sentiment on the German Question see R. Fritsch-Bournazel, *Europe and German Unification* (New York, 1992).

There is also the question of whether there is a broader framework within which our topic might be examined. Some analysts have tackled this question with the help of the concept of hegemony, arguing that twice in this century German industry aspired to achieving a hegemonic position but failed and, having succeeded within the EU at the third attempt, is now in the process of obtaining a similar position in the former Soviet Bloc countries. The problem with the concept of hegemony is that it does not capture well the forms that German aspirations in Europe took in the first half of this century. After all, hegemony in its Gramscian definition, as invoked by Andy Markovits and Simon Reich,[3] refers to the more indirect ways and means by which a class or, in this case, a country succeeds in wielding an influence over the fate of another nation by relying not on force, but on gentle persuasion and, to some extent, even on the simple attractiveness of its own model of socio-economic and political organization for those who fall under its spell. Hegemony in this sense is subtle and, above all, more cultural.[4]

Twice in the first half of this century, however, German behavior has been everything but subtle. It has involved instead direct domination, brutal force, and a physical presence in the neighboring states. Although each time the Germans also proclaimed a cultural mission, the intellectual attractiveness of what they offered was invariably weak and repeatedly undermined by the violent methods of occupation and exploitation with which it was pursued.

In light of this experience, hegemony appears to be less suitable as a concept for examining Germany's role in Europe in the first half of this century. This also applies to another notion that can be found in relevant literature. Because the objective of a superior power was to establish its own socio-economic and political system within the region, the Latin term *pax* occasionally has been used. Thus smaller countries are assumed to have lived at various times under a *pax Britannica, pax Americana, pax Sovietica, pax Nipponica*, or *pax Germanica*. Yet again, while the concept of a German peace, defined as the attempt to extend a stable order beyond Germany's national frontiers, may capture aspects of Reich policy within twentieth-century Europe, it says little about the important question concerning the methods by which order was established and maintained.

However, there is a concept that would seem capable of overcoming these drawbacks, i.e. formal and informal empire, as first

---

3. A. Markovits and S. Reich, "Modell Deutschland and the New Europe," *Telos*, 89, Fall 1991, 45-63.
4. See, e.g., J. Joll, *Antonio Gramsci* (London, 1976); G. Williams, "The Concept of 'Egemonia' in the Thought of Antonio Gramsci," *Journal of the History of Ideas* (1959).

developed with regard to British imperial history by John Gallagher and Ronald Robinson.[5] In their influential works the two authors trace the emergence of a formal British empire competing with other European powers in the late-nineteenth-century scramble for colonies – an empire that was ultimately characterized by a direct presence of the metropolitan power in the peripheral territories. They juxtapose this formation with the notion of imperialism of free trade or informal empire, at the same time highlighting even more strongly the economic perspective that they have adopted. Above all, they argued that historians have been too preoccupied with imperialism as formal rule, ignoring in the process that for a long time a larger part of British trade and investments actually went to Britain's informal empire. Thus Gallagher and Robinson compare all previous research on British imperialism with an exercise that tried to judge "the size and character of icebergs solely from the parts above the water-line," when in effect London's policy "followed the principle of extending control informally if possible and formally if necessary."[6] As a result, "the usual summing up of the policy of the free trade empire as 'trade not rule' should read 'trade with informal control if possible; trade with rule when necessary.'" Moreover, they explain why, by the early twentieth century, informal control largely had disappeared from British imperial practice and why formal empires had become the normal form by which the European powers dominated large parts of Africa and Asia.

The subsequent analysis follows this conceptualization of the problem, but adds an explicitly sociological dimension to it. In the German context the ideas of formal and informal empire experienced repeated ups and downs. Yet these shifts were not due to a mysterious anonymous force. Rather they must be related to changing balances of influential socio-economic groups and the outcome of fierce power struggles that occurred between them.

There is another difference that marks the beginning of this century. Although the international developments of the late nineteenth century led to a consolidation of colonial territories, these empires had not yet become synonymous, as was the case later, with the idea of fortress-like blocs whose markets were completely closed off from other nations. Notwithstanding the wave of protectionism that swept all Western countries during the Great Depression of the

---

5. J. A. Gallagher and R. E. Robinson, *Africa and the Victorians* (London, 1961); idem, "The Imperialism of Free Trade," *Economic History Review*, Second Series, 1 (1953), 1-15.

6. J. A. Gallagher and R. E. Robinson, "Imperialism," 13, also for the following. See also M. Doyle, *Empires* (Ithaca, 1986).

1870s and 1880s, the idea of Free Trade and the accessibility of foreign markets continued to be powerful enough before 1914 to preserve a system of international economic exchange that the world abandoned for the next three decades only after 1918. Until then, the flow of goods and people was still largely unencumbered. International commerce was at its peak and, while diplomatic tensions were rising between Britain and Germany before 1914, they continued to be each other's best customers.[7]

FORMAL VS. INFORMAL EMPIRE?

How did the Germans see the future development of the international system around 1900? At a time when existing empires either had not yet been consolidated fully into impenetrable blocs or, seemingly, were on the verge of disintegration from internal weakness, a debate started in Germany concerning the shape of the international map in future decades. Intellectuals and politicians, Reich Chancellor Bernhard von Bülow among them, but also many conservatives in industry predicted a further transformation of existing colonial empires into closed, protectionist entities. Thus with regard to North and South America, they assumed that the Monroe Doctrine would be applied more strictly and the hemisphere be sealed off from the rest of the world.[8] The British, French, and Russian empires were thought to be moving in a similar direction, expanding their preferential tariff systems and cutting out foreign and, above all, German competition.

The decision of the late 1890s to build a huge battle fleet in accordance with a long-term plan, designed by Navy Secretary Admiral Alfred Tirpitz, cannot be understood without this pessimistic vision of the future. The kaiser's navy of more than 60 capital ships was to be used as a power-political lever in negotiating the renewal of trade treaties or distributing the pieces of collapsing empires, like that of Portugal. As Tirpitz never tired of arguing, if no naval power was available, Germany and its booming industries quickly would be suffocated by their rivals. For Tirpitz and his monarch it was a question of life or death, and the creation of strong defenses and a formal German empire were the only answers.[9]

While many more conservative businessmen shared these Social Darwinist and Mahanist views of the future shape of the interna-

---
7. See P. M. Kennedy, *The Rise of the Anglo-German Antagonism* (London, 1980).
8. See, e.g., R. Pommerin, *Der Kaiser und Amerika* (Cologne, 1986).
9. See V. R. Berghahn, *Der Tirpitz-Plan* (Düsseldorf, 1971).

tional system, others were less inward-looking. They feared that Tirpitz's perceptions of the world might become a self-fulfilling prophecy. Huge blocs, surrounded by massive armor and propelled by notions of imperial self-sufficiency, seemed to them to be recipe for destructive wars and, ultimately, for catastrophe. Although they accepted the need for a certain measure of military and naval power, they viewed peaceful trade and diplomatic arbitration of disputes as a better guarantee of continued stability, prosperity, and self-preservation than sharp political rivalries and diplomatic bullying among dangerously armed power blocs. On the British side, the demand to return to concepts of informality could be found in *The Great Illusion*, a bestseller written by a British businessman, Norman Angell.[10] The Hague Peace Conferences of 1899 and 1907 were held to promote arbitration and a reduction of armaments.[11] In Germany, men like Albert Ballin, the director general of the HAPAG shipping line, were deeply troubled by what they saw in the last years before World War I: the spiraling of nationalist protectionism and of a dangerous arms race; and the closing of minds and territories.[12]

It is symptomatic of the profound impact that these two divergent views of the international political and economic system had on the European mind in general and on the German in particular, that the more moderate Social Democrats shared Ballin's nightmares, while their more radical comrades, Vladimir Lenin among them, developed scenarios of bitter rivalries and conflicts between the divergent national-capitalist blocs of highly industrialized and militarized countries.[13] To be sure, the utopias that they expected to emerge from these struggles differed fundamentally from those of the country's conservatives, but their predictions of an era of clashes and wars between large empires were quite similar. The debate among German politicians, intellectuals, and businessmen after the turn of the century was marked by a further split, this time within the camp of the formal imperialists, i.e. those who were pressing for the creation of the German power bloc. Here one faction envisaged the future German empire to be structured like the British one, with large colonial possessions overseas. In particular, they had in mind the acquisition of a Central African belt of lands which, firmly tied to the metropolitan country, would connect Germany's West African territories with her possessions on the East African coast.[14]

10. N. Angell, *The Great Illusion* (London, 1910), originally published in 1909 under the title *Europe's Optical Illusion*.
11. See J. Dülffer, *Regeln gegen den Krieg?* (Berlin, 1981).
12. See L. Cecil, *Albert Ballin* (Princeton, 1967).
13. See H. Bley, *Bebel und die Strategie der Kriegsverhütung, 1904-1913* (Göttingen, 1975); V. I. Lenin, *Imperialism, the Highest Stage of Capitalism* (Moscow, 1966).
14. F. Fischer, *War*, 259ff.

The alternative vision was one of a Central European bloc, a *Mitteleuropa*, whose most ardent advocates could be found in the 1890s among the conservatives in heavy industry and agriculture.[15] They harbored not only deep suspicions of overseas possessions, but also of the socio-economic forces of industrial capitalism that seemed to be pushing for colonies and large navies. Their perceptions of the world are neatly summed up by Otto von Völderndorff, who in November 1897 wrote to his friend, Reich Chancellor Clodwig von Hohenlohe-Schillingsfürst:

> We must keep away from international rivalries (Welthändel); we must confine ourselves to securing our country against the two neighbors (i.e. France and Russia). Greatest parsimony (except for the Army) and a rebuilding of the Reich on the only reliable estate, the rural population. Our industry is not worth much anyway. It is in the hands of Jews; its products are ... 'cheap and bad;' it is a seedbed of Socialism .... Moreover, we are coming too late; all valuable overseas possessions are in the hands of others who hold on to them. We are also not wealthy enough to carry on the great power policies we have embarked upon in 1870.[16]

In the decade before 1914, politicians and businessmen remained divided over whether Germany should try merely to dominate the European continent or whether the country's ambitions should extend to forming a larger colonial bloc. To put it in terms of two key concepts of the time: should a future *Mitteleuropa* stand as an area of German influence on its own, like the Russian continental bloc; or should a *Mittelafrika* be added to it?

This was the question in the Wilhelmine debate over the future of the international system and of Germany's role within it as it had evolved up to 1906. At the same time, the German naval build-up that was to secure an overseas empire began to run into trouble, due to the rapid expansion and reform of England's Royal Navy under Admiral John Fisher.[17] While it became increasingly clear that the kaiser was losing the Anglo-German naval arms race and that all ambitious colonial aspirations had to be abandoned, the idea of *Mitteleuropa* came into sharper focus. The cancellation of Tirpitz's naval program and the renewed emphasis on land forces were perhaps the clearest signs that Germany's earlier imperial designs were put on the back-burner in favor of fostering the country's position on the European continent. Thereafter the debate on formal vs. informal empire in Europe became again the main focus of public

15. H. C. Meyer, *Mitteleuropa in German Thought and Action* (The Hague, 1955).
16. Quoted in V. R. Berghahn, *Germany and the Approach of War in 1914*, 2nd ed. (New York, 1993), 31.
17. Ibid., 56ff., also for the following.

argument among Germany's politicians and businessmen, but it also remained inconclusive.

One reason for this stalemate was that the lands between the Rhineland and the Bosphorus were not colonial territories to be wrung from another power; they were made up of a number of sovereign, non-German states, among which the largest, Austria-Hungary, was moreover the Reich's closest ally. These realities strengthened the hand of the informal imperialists, who argued that there was simply no alternative to a policy of penetrating the region with the help of the country's superior industrial and financial power. In this view, a system of bilateral trading links and preferential tariffs, supported by close diplomatic and dynastic cooperation, would secure the Reich's position in the Balkans and slowly, but effectively, undermine that of the enemies of the Central Powers, notably Serbia and Russia.

One of the more influential organizations advocating this approach to the question of continental empire was the *Mitteleuropäische Wirtschaftstag* (Middle European Economic Diet), founded in 1904 by the economist Julius Wolf as an association of individuals and interest groups wedded to the idea of an informal Central European sphere.[18] Again divisions appeared, also with regard to the boundaries of *Mitteleuropa*.

Some groups, like the *Bund der Industriellen* (Association of Industrialists) took the Central European *Zollverein* (Customs Union) of 1834 and the ideas of Friedrich List, its intellectual father, as their model. Others, like Wolf himself, looked across the Atlantic, postulating that Germany's main problem was that its economic space, compared to that of other powers, was too small. What was needed was the creation of a *Großraum* (literally: great space) stretching from the English Channel to the Balkans.

To those who saw the world through the eyes of a businessman, it was also clear that the booming industries of pre-1914 Germany would have the edge within a *Großraum* that included the Habsburg Empire and the predominantly agricultural regions of southeastern Europe. Not surprisingly, Wolf and others eventually viewed the whole region as one that would receive German manufactured goods in return for the delivery of foodstuffs and raw materials.

There were other similar voices. Robert Kauffmann, the leader of the Young Liberals, demanded a customs union "reaching from [the North Sea island of] Borkum to Baghdad."[19] The *Deutsche Volks-*

---

18. See the materials in R. Opitz (ed.), *Europastrategien des deutschen Kapitals* (Cologne, 1977), 137ff.
19. See V. R. Berghahn, *Germany*, 145, also for the following.

wirtschaftliche Correspondenz (a German business publication) urged the establishment of a "pax Germanica over Asia Minor and the Balkan countries." Albert Ritter published a book in which he put a Central European bloc next to "Greater Russia, World Britannia [and] Pan-America." The secretary general of the *Hansabund*, a liberal pressure group, counseled closer European cooperation to "enable us and our neighboring countries to safeguard our export markets in competition with extra-European states, in particular with the United States of America."

In 1913, Walther Rathenau, the chairman of the *Allgemeine Electricitaets-Gesellschaft* (AEG) and a leading industrialist with an interest in larger strategic and philosophical questions, said: "As regards raw materials, North America is the most fortunate country." In contrast, he thought Germany to be seriously handicapped, for "the more industry becomes tied into a world economy, the more the distant lands have to contribute to its raw materials [and] the more dangerous becomes the fact that we own so little land in the world." Rathenau then mentioned "a possible solution" to this problem, i.e. to work for the creation of a larger Central European trading bloc.[20] His statement is particularly significant because he was head of a company that depended on the world market for the sale of its products. Clearly, he was not thinking in terms of closed autarkic blocs that, armed to the teeth, would exclude each other from their internal markets. The larger territorial and economic entities that he also saw emerging before 1914 were to remain permeable and linked to a multilateral global trading network.

While this remained an influential position in the business community, there were other industrialists whose companies were less dependent on the world market and whose conservative nationalism reinforced their protectionist stance. Just as they were more inclined to favor price-fixing cartels over "cut-throat" competition at home,[21] their attitude toward the evolving pre-1914 world economy – and there is a connection between their notions about the organization of the internal market on the one hand, and of the international system of trade on the other – had become one of hostility by the time war broke out in 1914. Afterward they thought in terms of a German-dominated continental European bloc that would be virtually self-sufficient. In February 1913, Gustav Stresemann, the secretary general of the *Bund der Industriellen* and a leading member of the

---

20. Quoted in R. Opitz (ed.), *Europastrategien*, 204ff.
21. On the German cartel system see, e.g. V. Hentschel, *Wirtschaft und Wirtschaftspolitik im Wilhelminischen Deutschland* (Stuttgart, 1978), 99ff.

National Liberal Party, spoke of a "closed economic area to secure our need for raw materials and our exports." Among the many shades of opinion that inevitably existed in this camp, the Pan-Germans probably occupied the most extreme position in that they envisioned more than merely a closed economy.[22] They agitated for the unification of all German-speaking peoples within a single territorial bloc run by an authoritarian, centralized government. Although they too spoke of a *Mitteleuropa* customs union as "the backbone" of this larger state, they added the idea of German settlements further East and of ruthless Germanization. This thinking introduced biological and ultimately racist concepts into the debate on the future shape of a Germanic empire in continental Europe and on the principles that would hold this large entity together. At the same time it must be stressed that Pan-German ideas were not widely shared within the business community, where questions of empire posed themselves primarily in terms of industrial and commercial penetration and of the methods that would be employed to establish and maintain a German *Mitteleuropa*.

TERRITORIAL EXPANSIONISM AND WAR

We have spent time trying to outline the diverse views on Germany's role as an industrial power in the heart of Europe as they were discussed during the Wilhelmine period because they contain in embryo all the arguments that remained on the agenda between 1914 and 1945. It also should have become clear that the strength of these views was related to the relative power and influence of the various groups in business and politics that articulated them. Consequently, if 1914 represented not a break, but a continuity with earlier thinking about empire in Germany, and if the same positions that have been examined above were promoted thereafter, their success or failure also must be seen in connection with the relative strength or weakness of the forces behind them. The value of such differentiations and of linking ideas to identifiable groups that deploy them in struggles over power and influence within a particular society is stressed here also because it has been challenged again recently as a suitable tool for analyzing the political and economic strategies of German business. At the one end of the spectrum, we find Gerald Feldman who has once more reasserted a more monolithic view of German industry.[23] He sees busi-

---

22. See R. Chickering, *We Men Who Feel Most German* (London, 1984).
23. G. D. Feldman, "Businessmen and Politics in Twentieth-Century Germany" (unpublished MS, 1992), 5.

nessmen as participants in a particular national context. Defending the *Sonderweg* (special path) view of modern German history, he wants the relationship between business and politics to be treated "as an integral element in the evolution of Germany's political culture."

At the other end of the spectrum, Peter Hayes has argued that any attempt to identify industrial factions is bound to fail because there were too many overlaps between branches and groups and individual businessmen that defy such crude categorization.[24] Although apparently most concerned with differences of opinion on domestic politics rather than attitudes toward the world economy, he believes "personal determinants and firm-specific rather than sectoral considerations" to have been "decisive." The only exception he grants is that of Ruhr heavy industry, where he found a "somewhat greater solidarity than [among] its putative rivals, if less than it had been before the war." Later, he added in the same vein that "we need to recognize the distorting effect of the extraordinary phenomenon of the Ruhr." If this is so, it may be just as well to emphasize what also emerges from this volume: there was no uniformity of views when it came to questions of formal or informal empire; nor, however, was there total fragmentation and individualism. There is still an analytical middle way, like the one adopted here.

The debate on the different *economic* conceptions of *Mitteleuropa* – formal or informal, open or closed – unfolded further during World War I. It formed the background to the memorandum that Reich Chancellor Theobald von Bethmann-Hollweg drew up in September 1914 on the basis of submissions he had received from a variety of interest groups, among them the lobbies of industry.

Fritz Fischer, who was the first to discover this document, made it the starting-point of his detailed analysis of the evolution of Germany's aims to the end of the war.[25] The "September Memorandum" also marked the beginning of a renewed and more sharply polarized argument between those who wanted to use the expected German victory to establish a formal continental empire and those who were content with deploying the superior economic weight of the Reich to achieve informal penetration of a Central European sphere, stretching from the Atlantic coast to the Balkans and beyond.

The former faction, including Ruhr steel magnate Fritz Thyssen, blatantly demanded annexation. In the West, Belgium and parts of northern France were to be absorbed by the Reich. In the East, a

---

24. P. Hayes, "Industrial Factionalism in Modern German History," *Central European History*, 29 (1991), 122-31.
25. F. Fischer, *Germany's War Aims in the First World War* (New York, 1967), also for the following.

ruthless territorial revisionism schemed carving out new regions that would become part of Germany. Few people thought of a simultaneous, *Anschluß*-like incorporation of Austria-Hungary. But when it came to discussions about *Mitteleuropa*, not even the most moderate advocates of informal empire had any doubts that Germany would call the tune in this region. Meanwhile, the effectiveness of the Allied blockade began to strengthen the hand of those elements in the larger *Mitteleuropa* movement who, even before 1914, had advocated the establishment of a self-sufficient bloc that would be able to fend for itself in the postwar world, with the British Empire and the United States as the main rivals.

If the September Memorandum also included demands for a *Mittelafrika*, it appears that they were thrown in primarily to appease those sections of the business community which, even during the period of retreat from *Weltpolitik* before 1914, had never abandoned the idea of overseas possessions. Also, once France and Russia had been vanquished, the prospect of acquiring territories in Africa looked much more realistic than it had in the years of repeated diplomatic setbacks before 1914. However, German attention remained fixed on the European continent. This preoccupation also explains why Friedrich Naumann's book *Mitteleuropa*, published in 1915, became an immediate bestseller.[26] In it, the author raised the possibility that, as far as the Reich was concerned, "*Mitteleuropa* and world trade" might be irreconcilable alternatives. That a man who had been a liberal imperialist before the war should put the problem in terms of an either-or indicates a first shift in the balance of forces between the advocates of a closed Germanic *Großraum* and the protagonists of a more loosely organized German sphere that would be a full participant in the world economy. The former gained ground as the war continued. By the spring of 1918, they had won the upper hand. Nothing demonstrated this point more powerfully than the signing of the Treaty of Brest-Litovsk, which resulted in large territories of the former Tsarist empire falling into German hands.

No less significant as a harbinger of future developments were the methods by which this vast enlargement of the German sphere was obtained: the territories in the East were brutally annexed and close to one million German soldiers were moved in to establish a direct military presence.[27] Germany had taken a major step toward building a formal European empire, with the organization of the Balkans and of Western Europe to be settled after final victory in France, which

26. F. Naumann, *Mitteleuropa* (London, 1917). See also P. Theiner, *Sozialer Liberalismus und deutsche Weltpolitik* (Baden-Baden, 1983).
27. See, e.g., J. Wheeler-Bennett, *The Forgotten Peace* (New York, 1939).

Berlin expected to achieve. While more informal arrangements were still conceivable for some parts of a German-dominated Europe, the crucial point is that, for the moment, the hardline imperialists had won the day. This faction had General Erich Ludendorff as its most prominent spokesman who, together with Field Marshal Paul von Hindenburg, had emerged as the virtual dictator of Germany.[28] Since so much of the annexed territories consisted of agricultural lands, it is not surprising that the arguments of the "Ludendorffian" groups should become infused with a heavy dose of Pan-German "blood and soil" ideology. But in staking out his position, Ludendorff also knew that he had the conservative nationalists in heavy industry on his side whose "chief interest was to secure the import of high-grade Ukrainian iron ores and of Caucasian and Ukrainian manganese ores [that heavy industry] needed for steel production."[29]

The ascendancy of the formal imperialists was short-lived. The collapse of the Western Front and the German defeat a few months after the Treaty of Brest-Litovsk threw all dreams of empire, whether formal or informal, into complete disarray. But while the defeat temporarily destroyed Germany's ability to project its power on the European continent, it did not prevent a majority of Germans, including most businessmen, from dreaming of their country's resurgence. The idea of a revision of the Treaty of Versailles, and particularly its territorial provisions, was discussed widely even before the Peace was signed and continued to gain ground thereafter. The question that divided the nation and also the business community was whether revision should be attempted peacefully and through slow negotiation or by force and unilateral action. Still, for the moment it was clear to all but the most radical opponents of the Versailles Treaty that Germany lacked the means actively to resist the Western Allies. The choice was between fulfillment in the hope of obtaining relief that would help to revive German industrial and military power or passive refusal to comply, especially with respect to the payment of reparations even at the price of increasing the chaos in the war-ravaged postwar economy.

WEIMAR REVISIONISM

As to industry, the early 1920s with continuing civil war, run-away inflation, and a badly weakened economy were not a time to take a

28. M. Kitchen, *The Silent Dictatorship* (London, 1976).
29. F. Fischer, *Germany's War Aims*, 483.

strong stand on Germany's role in Europe and the world economy.[30] It was more important to revive the economy, rebuild and modernize production facilities, and see if once lucrative foreign markets could be reopened to German exports. To be sure, there were divisions of opinion, but they pertained to the question of formal or informal empire only in an indirect way.

On the one hand, there were those who, like Rathenau, advocated a policy of compliance and fulfillment as a step toward Germany's reintegration into the world economy. They expected this strategy to accelerate the postwar economic reconstruction process, and mobilizing the country's industrial potential would in turn obviously also enhance her political and economic influence within Europe. On the other hand, there were entrepreneurs like Hugo Stinnes who opposed fulfillment and sought cooperation with Bolshevik Russia as a way of building up an anti-Western German position. However, the question of what should happen to the lands in-between had been complicated in the meantime by the disintegration of the Austro-Hungarian Empire and the emergence of a belt of smaller states among which Czechoslovakia, Poland, and Yugoslavia became allies of Germany's arch enemy France. Clearly, *Mitteleuropa* as a region of German predominance could at best be seen as a long-term project, unless one joined hands with those Ludendorffians on the radical Right whose visceral hatred, particularly of Poland, led them to think of another territorial change of the Central European map by armed force.

Moreover, if there was any lesson to be learned from the failure of Wilhelmine *Weltpolitik*, it was that Germany had taken on too much at a time.[31] Should another bid ever be made to establish her as a power "commensurate" with her industrial potential, it would have to be launched from a solid continental position.[32] A colonial empire might be built only afterward. Chances of creating a *Mittelafrika* were thought to be even more remote, except for the welter of small colonial pressure groups that never stopped agitating for overseas possessions. Above all, there were – as far as industry was concerned – the realities of the present which had a sobering effect on all speculations about a future German empire, whether formal or informal. Nor was it easy to say in the confusion of the postwar period who in industry had the upper hand politically, until the developments of the mid-1920s gave a boost to the gradualists who looked for cooperation with the West. The settlement of the thorny reparations question

---

30. G. D. Feldman, *Iron and Steel in the German Inflation* (Princeton, 1977).
31. See the statement by General W. Groener in: F. Fischer, *War*, i.
32. See also K. Hildebrand, *Foreign Policy*, 7ff.

through the Dawes Plan in 1924 and the appearance of American banks and industry helped the liberal-capitalists against the nationalist-conservatives in the business community.[33] They were also encouraged by the rise of Gustav Stresemann who, more than any other prominent politicians, came to embody Germany's Western orientation as well as its ambiguities.[34] A trained economist and before 1914 secretary general of the *Bund der Industriellen*, he had been an ardent annexationist during the war before becoming the leader of the then anti-Republican *Deutsche Volkspartei* (DVP) in 1919. But witnessing the shipwreck of German foreign and domestic policy that culminated in the Franco-Belgian occupation of the Ruhr and the collapse of the currency in 1923, Stresemann changed his mind and became an advocate of fulfillment. He was aware that industry was the country's main asset and remained a nationalist at heart, but he was smart enough to realize that German economic power could be projected most effectively not by proceeding alone, but by re-entering the world market. His position as Weimar's foreign minister and roving ambassador of German industry abroad was buttressed by the fact that the Ludendorffian formal imperialists had been pushed to the margins of the political spectrum. H.G. Schröter's article deals with how the chemical and electrical industries operated within this milieu. While foreign direct investments remained small, Germany's trading links were at least partially restored. At the same time it is significant that most of this trade was with immediate neighbors.

In general, their strategies were guided by a desire to regain pre-1914 export markets and, beyond this, by the quest for international cartels. Though advertised as spearheads of international economic cooperation, these cartels could not conceal the protectionist and defensive mentality that inspired them and the growing influence of the large German trusts that tended to promote them. It is also illuminating to see how international cartels pushed German business toward Scandinavia and Eastern Europe, and how some of the major

33. See, e.g. W. C. McNeil, *American Money and the Weimar Republic* (New York, 1986); K. H. Pohl, *Weimars Wirtschaft und die Außenpolitik der Republik, 1924-1926* (Düsseldorf, 1979); W. Link, *Die amerikanische Stabilisierungspolitik in Deutschland* (Düsseldorf, 1970); F. Costigliola, *Awkward Dominion* (Ithaca, 1984); B. Weisbrod, *Schwerindustrie in der Weimarer Republik* (Wuppertal, 1978); D. Abraham, *The Collapse of the Weimar Republic*, 2nd ed. (New York, 1986); S. Schuker, *American "Reparations" to Germany* (Princeton, 1988).

34. H. L. Bretton, *Stresemann and the Revision of Versailles* (Stanford, 1953); H. Gatzke, *Stresemann and the Rearmament of Germany* (Baltimore, 1954); H. A. Turner, *Stresemann and the Revision of Versailles* (Princeton, 1963); P. Krüger, *Die Außenpolitik der Republik von Weimar* (Darmstadt, 1985); M. Lee and W. Michalka, *German Foreign Policy, 1917-1933* (New York 1987).

electrical engineering companies and IG Farben succeeded in establishing an informal economic empire in Europe while professing openness towards the world market. With few exceptions, like Bosch, the advocacy of this kind of internationalism did not move beyond export drives and as a result failed to turn the corner towards a policy of foreign direct investments.

Meanwhile, the German steel industry was similarly busy trying to forge international cartels. They never enjoyed more than a precarious existence, partly because the more powerful German members tried to dominate them and partly because many non-German domestic producers liked to rely on their national governments for support against foreign competition. Cartels, it seems, were just not suitable as instruments to promote cooperation among equals.[35] Moreover, they furthered bloc-thinking and restrictive practices. It is hardly surprising that German industry in the Third Reich thought cartels were most suitable for becoming the vehicles of a far-reaching reorganization of European industry in Hitler's New Economic Order during World War II.

Still, the clout of the conservative-nationalist factions should not be underestimated even during the Stresemannian mid-1920s. If the power balances within industry had not yet put a brake on the policies of the more outward-looking industries, the onset of the Great Depression certainly stopped them in their tracks. Internationalization came to an end; the advocates of empire blocs raised their voices louder than before. If trade with the West was collapsing, where else could German industry turn? Once again the idea of *Mitteleuropa* began to sway more and more businessmen, who began to push for closer ties with those regions of Europe in which Germany had reestablished a strong position in previous years, especially in the East and Southeast. An early sign of things to come was the revival of the *Mitteleuropäische Wirtschaftstag* (MEWT) in 1927, devoted to research on "the economic and cultural conditions of the Central European states."[36] Supported by business, the Reich government propounded the idea of an Austro-German customs union in 1931, only to be frustrated in their endeavor by a vigorous French veto. Conceptions of economic bloc-building now made a strong comeback. The alternative of international cooperation and of the Open Door receded into the background. The new debate was merely about how closed and autarkic the *Großraum* should be in which German business expected to predominate. These developments were exacerbated by the eco-

---

35. See, e.g., C. A. Wurm (ed.), *Internationale Kartelle und Außenpolitik* (Wiesbaden, 1989).
36. R. Opitz (ed.), *Europastrategien*, 535ff.; D. Abraham, *Collapse*, 215ff.

nomic nationalism and protectionism of other countries, above all the United States. Consequently, Carl Duisberg, the head of the IG Farben chemicals trust and an erstwhile internationalist, argued in March 1931:

> Out of the small national economic space, the strong industrial states and the agrarian states looking for markets push towards greater international economic spaces .... This tendency was started by the United States ... [but] also in Europe this aim of the regional economic space seems to be gradually taking shape. For the southeast European states, the question of a market for their agricultural products is an existential question. They find their necessary markets for the most part in Germany. What could make more sense for these states than to look for an understanding with their strongest economic partner, i.e. Germany. Through this regional economic combination the European problem can be treated from the southeastern corner .... Only a uniform economic bloc from Bordeaux to Sofia is going to give Europe the spine which it needs to retain its importance in the world.[37]

RISE OF GROßRAUMWIRTSCHAFT

After this, what came to be debated among German businessmen and economists in the 1930s under the heading of *Großraumwirtschaft* assumed two already familiar guises. Overall there was now no question concerning the basic desirability and necessity of Germany building a *Mitteleuropa* empire. The question was merely how formal it should be, i.e. how directly German political and military power should be projected into the wider region, and how open this region should be toward the rest of the world. The point of no return was reached slowly, as the call for autarky became louder and louder. Not surprisingly, the Nazis and entrepreneurs close to them pursued the notion of formal empire in its most extreme, Ludendorffian form. To them, *Großraumwirtschaft* meant the formation of a closed, autarkic bloc and one that stretched beyond the German-speaking area into the Soviet Union up to the Urals. In their minds, the term was also synonymous with *Lebensraum* and all its racist and Pan-German connotations of resettlement and direct domination.

None of this proceeded without much debate both within the government and between the Nazi bureaucracy and Germany's industrial and financial elites that finally reached its culmination point at the height of the war in 1942.[38]

Much can be gained from reconstructing this debate. It tells us something about the shifting balance of political and economic

---
37. R. Opitz (ed.), *Europastrategien*, 581f.
38. See A. Dallin, *German Rule in Russia* (London, 1957); P. Hayes, *Industry*; J. Freymond, *Le IIIe Reich et la réorganisation économique de l'Europe* (Geneva, 1974); J.

forces, and it offers hints at what Europe would have looked like economically had the Third Reich and its allies won the war or at least achieved a temporary truce with Britain and the United States. In this case, the two Anglo-Saxon powers would have recognized Hitler's continental empire as a *fait accompli*, thus giving the *Führer* time to build his New (Economic) Order.

As to the old question of Germany's openness toward the outside world, the dogmatic autarkists remained in the minority for a long time during the 1930s. Those who spoke up for the creation of a bloc that was sealed off from the rest of the world economy were generally found on the agrarian wing of the Nazi Party. Big business by and large favored a more open arrangement that would allow at least some trade with other countries in the West. If Hitler had made up his mind on the basic question of the future shape of occupied Europe, the die might have been cast in favor of the one position or the other. But in this matter, as in others relating to future planning, he avoided a clear-cut decision, arguing that it was bound up with the larger issue of the entire relationship between politics and economics in the Third Reich to be settled after the war had been won. Leaving everything up in the air had the added advantage that there were no losers who would then have sabotaged the implementation of Hitler's final verdict, as happened with many other Nazi policy issues. This was also why Hitler tolerated the continuation of the old argument over *Mittelafrika*, which the colonial lobby had kept in the limelight throughout the 1930s and which led to the creation in 1940 of a colonial ministry charged with preparing administrators for later service in Africa.[39]

Certainly, Hitler, though at heart a formal imperialist, had a point when he thought it futile to talk about the Reich's economic relations with Europe and the rest of the world as long as its territorial conquests on the continent had not been secured. As he said in October 1941:[40]

> For me the object is to exploit the advantages of continental predominance. It is ridiculous to think of a world policy as long as one does not control the continent .... When we are masters of Europe, we have a

---

Gillingham, *Belgian Business in the Nazi New Order* (Ghent, 1977); R. E. Herzstein, *When Nazi Dreams Come True* (London, 1982); E. Jäckel, *Frankreich in Hitlers Europa* (Stuttgart, 1966); A. Milward, *The New Order and the French Economy* (Oxford, 1970); idem, *The Fascist Economy in Norway* (Oxford, 1972); D. Petzina, *Autarkiepolitik im Dritten Reich* (Stuttgart, 1968); W. D. Smith, *The Ideological Origins of Nazi Imperialism* (Oxford, 1986); E. Teichert, *Autarkie und Großraumwirtschaft in Deutschland* (Munich, 1984); L. Herbst, *Der totale Krieg und die Ordnung der Wirtschaft* (Stuttgart, 1982).
39. See W. W. Schmokel, *Dream of Empire* (New Haven, 1964); K. Hildebrand, *Vom Reich zum Weltreich* (Munich, 1969).
40. H. Trevor-Roper (ed.), *Hitler's Secret Conversations* (New York, 1953), 76.

dominant position in the world. A hundred and thirty million people in the Reich, ninety million in the Ukraine. Add to these the other states of the New Europe, and we'll be four hundred million compared with a hundred and thirty million Americans. [Four weeks earlier he had taken the view that] the struggle for predominance in the world will be decided in favor of Europe by the possession of the Russian space. Thus Europe will be an impregnable fortress, impregnable from all threat of blockade .... The essential thing, for the moment, is to conquer. After that, everything will simply be a question of organization.[41]

At the same time, things could not be compartmentalized and put on ice that easily. What undermined Hitler's delaying tactics was the "normative power of the facts" that the extremely violent forms of the Nazi conquest of Europe were creating.[42] These forms inevitably influenced the shape of the future New Order and gave a boost to the Ludendorffians who were waiting in the wings. They had long advocated direct rule. More generally, it was not part of the Nazi regime's self-image to project its power in velvet-gloves. The Social Darwinism that had pervaded the Third Reich at home during the 1930s became an export commodity. It seemed particularly suitable for Eastern Europe, where Nazi racism assumed the indigenous populations were too primitive to govern themselves. Not surprisingly, Heinrich Himmler began to make plans for the resettlement of German *Volksgenossen* in the Ukraine where they would live in neat towns surrounded by the Slav masses, who would be working as helots and whose living standards would be kept to a minimum. Meanwhile the mass murder of millions of Jews, Slavs, and Gypsies also began.[43]

Attitudes may have been different toward the populations of Western Europe insofar as they were seen as "Aryan cousins;" but the dynamics of the New Order racism in the East which unfolded from the first days of World War II in Poland as well as the persistent underground opposition that the occupying forces encountered in Western Europe moved German policies in the direction of formal

41. Ibid., 27f.
42. See, e.g., A. Dallin, *German Rule*; P. Hayes, *Ideology*; A. Milward, *New Order*; idem, *Fascist Economy*; M. Broszat, *Nationalsozialistische Polenpolitik* (Stuttgart, 1961); L. Kettenacker, *Nationalsozialistische Volkstumspolitik im Elsaß* (Stuttgart, 1973); K. Kwiet, *Reichskommissariat Niederlande* (Stuttgart, 1968); C. Madajczyk, *Die deutsche Besatzungspolitik in Polen* (Wiesbaden, 1967); E. Thomsen, *Deutsche Besatzungspolitik in Dänemark* (Düsseldorf, 1971); E. L. Homze, *Foreign Labor in Nazi Germany* (Princeton, 1967); U. Herbert, *Fremdarbeiter* (Berlin, 1985); W. Warmbrunn, *The Dutch under German Occupation* (Stanford, 1963).
43. See, e.g., R. Hilberg, *The Destruction of the European Jews* (London, 1961); L. Dawidowicz, *The War against the Jews* (Harmondsworth, 1976); G. Hirschfeld (ed.), *The Politics of Genocide* (London, 1986); C. Browning, *Fateful Years* (New York, 1986); R. D. Müller, *Hitlers Ostkrieg und die deutsche Siedlungspolitik* (Frankfurt, 1991).

empire. These larger visions of the New Order and their incipient implementation from October 1939 onwards, together with the political mentalities behind them, also affected the debate on the economic organization of the European *Großraum* that had continued throughout the 1930s. To begin with, the general ideological climate promoted in the business world the rise of individuals "whose dynamism degenerated into brutality and who could not be impressed by anything."[44] By the same token it pushed into the background those managers who believed that a softer touch in dealing with the industries of occupied Europe would yield better results in terms of company profits and of the general milieu in which future business would be conducted among the nations of the continent.

Peter Hayes's contribution examines how one of the country's biggest corporations, IG Farben, tried to maneuver in the minefield of reorganizing the European economy. While mindful of its traditional global interests, it kept an open mind about how autarkic the emergent German bloc should be. Still, the larger backdrop to IG Farben's strategy in those years remains important, and on this score the most contentious issue from the point of view of big business was from the 1930s onward: who would be in charge overall of reorganizing the European economy? Was this to be the task of private industry, assisted by its elaborate system of associations? Or would it be government agencies? When, after some theoretical discussion in the first years after the establishment of the Nazi dictatorship, this question became a tangible issue following the *Anschluß* of Austria in March 1938 and the destruction of Czechoslovakia a year later, matters were still largely left in the hands of individual entrepreneurs whose experts swarmed out either to take over Austrian and Czech companies or to acquire a stake in them and to offer cooperation. Yet from the start there were some state agencies whose leaders rejected this kind of "anarchic" capitalist penetration. One of them was Hermann Göring.

Just as he had set up the *Reichswerke* steel trust as a state-owned alternative to private industry in 1936,[45] he now began to push the government to assume a major role in the economic reorganization of occupied Europe after 1939. It is significant that Hitler once more avoided taking a stand and that not all ministries were behind Göring.[46] In other words, the business community had friends, espe-

---

44. L. Schwerin von Krosigk, *Die Grosse Zeit des Feuers,* vol. 3 (Tübingen, 1957/59), 560.
45. See, e.g., M. Riedel, *Eisen und Kohle für das Dritte Reich* (Göttingen, 1973); G. Mollin, *Montankonzerne und "Drittes Reich"* (Göttingen, 1988).
46. See, e.g., the documents in R. Opitz (ed.), *Europastrategien*; see also M. Popofsky, "The Quest for the Pax Germanica" (unpublished Brown honor thesis, 1990).

cially in Walter Funk's Economics Ministry, with State Secretary Gustav Schlotterer as the linchpin. There was also Carl Clodius in the Foreign Ministry who, himself an advocate of informal empire, warned not to "repeat the mistakes of Versailles" and postulated that coercion should not be part of securing "a somewhat more equitable distribution of the world's raw materials."[47] With Göring and his allies blocked by their rivals in the Nazi bureaucracy, industry had fairly free rein to move into occupied Western and Northern Europe in 1940.

The same patterns of behavior surfaced as in 1938-1939: Some managers knocked hard at the gates of French, Dutch, or Norwegian enterprises and behaved like colonial masters, flatly declaring that the firm in question had been taken over. Property rights and shareholdings were nullified with the stroke of a pen. But there were others who strenuously negotiated to work toward a partnership with non-German companies and who signed binding agreements that did not differ from those made with foreign firms in peacetime. In this situation it would be naive to assume that their Belgian, French, or Danish counterparts did not operate under perceived or real duress, even if they were pro-German collaborators.[48] However diplomatic and conciliatory their German visitors may have been, in the 1940s the reality of occupation and the daily display of German military power was hard to overlook. Clearly, the power relationship was unequal. It was lost on no one that the bloc that was emerging in continental Europe in the early 1940s would be geared to the interests of the Reich and that the Germans would call the shots.

However important it may be to differentiate between hardliners and moderates in German industry, it would be wrong to ignore that the tireless activities of men like Göring and Himmler had borne some fruit. As to the question of the role of the state, the balance began to shift in favor of increased interventionism and tighter control, including the economy. This in turn put pressure on private industry to offer more than an "anarchic" take-over program. There now started a debate in which the *Reichsgruppe Industrie*, industry's semi-public peak association, assumed a greater role with the encouragement of the Economics Ministry.[49] Schlotterer and others urged the *Reichsgruppe* to develop more concrete organizational proposals. When these were finally on paper, industry not surprisingly advanced as their ideal solution, the cartel model of capitalist organization that meanwhile – building on the Weimar experience – had

---

47. Quoted in: M. Popofsky, "The Quest," 114.
48. See, e.g., J. Gillingham, *Belgian Business*.
49. See the documents in R. Opitz (ed.), *Europastrategien*, passim; see also R. E. Herzstein, *When Nazi Dreams*; M. Popofsky, "The Quest," 109ff., also for the following.

been vastly expanded and refined as the basic organizing principle of business inside the Third Reich. This model was now to be introduced to the rest of occupied Europe. Its outward attractiveness was that cartels would have given formal equality to their members, whether foreign or German. In this sense the proposals did not smack of direct imperialism.

However, there is also the German experience of the international cartels of the interwar period. What had often contributed to the instability of those cooperative arrangements was that they had to operate in an environment of independent nation states with their own political dynamics and currency systems. It was at this level that the new Europe would differ from the old. In the conception of German business, there was no question about the Reichsmark being the leading currency. In this regard, as in respect of patents, commercial laws, and other aspects of intra-European economic relations, the entire legal framework would be redesigned to secure German predominance. Like the *Reichsgruppe* and other industrial associations, the German banking world was also busy drawing up its plans along these lines.

A major contribution to the debate on the economic organization of occupied Europe came from a number of experts attached to a variety of research institutes, where the belief that the world was evolving in terms of *Großraum* blocs was no less axiomatic than elsewhere in government and industry. Probably the most detailed proposal to organize Europe on the basis of cartels was produced by Arno Sölter, who in 1941 published his ideas in a very interesting book entitled *Großraumkartell*.[50] Apart from insisting on industrial self-management, the author invoked Funk and argued against the view that autarky and world economy were mutually exclusive. In this respect Sölter agreed with Professor Andreas Predöhl of the World Economics Institute at Kiel, where IG Farben's Max Ilgner also involved himself in his efforts to preserve the principle of occupied Europe's openness toward the rest of the world. Finally there was Werner Daitz who had long advocated the creation of a *Großraum* that stretched well beyond the borders of the Reich and insisted that this space must be German-dominated.[51] Daitz also made various contributions to the debate on the region's future economic organization. In his numerous writings and speeches he stressed the notion of New Order cooperation, albeit with a marked Germanocentric touch and later with an increasingly racist vocabulary. Daitz was also among those theorists to take a stand on the

50. A. Sölter, *Großraumkartell* (Dresden, 1941).
51. M. Popofsky, "The Quest," 107ff., also for the following.

question of how far the predominantly agricultural East and Southeast should be encouraged to develop their own industries.

Some of the big corporations with an interest in those regions had been favoring a degree of economic development, also as a way of expanding their own markets. Daitz similarly felt that the people of Eastern Europe needed Western technology and expertise, though apparently not beyond a level that would change their primary function as purveyors of raw materials and handicrafts. None of these proposals, whether they came from the *Reichsgruppe*, from Schlotterer, or from *Großraum* theoreticians in research institutes, held much attraction for the non-German nations of Hitler's New Europe. However, they were almost benign by comparison with those of the Ludendorffians, who had meanwhile sharpened their attacks on the "soft options" of 1940. More than ever before they aimed for formal empire, complete autarky, and the underdevelopment of the East through criminal exploitation. Herbert Backe, a blood-and-soil ideologue who came to play a leading role in the Nazi reorganization of agriculture in occupied Russia, was one of them. In 1942 he published a book *On the Self-Sufficiency in Foodstuffs in Europe* which bore the telling sub-title, *Great Space Economy or World Economy*.[52]

The agrarian wing in the Nazi movement and the SS with its resettlement plans were also united in the view that its members – like Göring, but unlike Schlotterer – were determined not to leave the organization of Europe to private industry and its cartellization program. They agitated for strong state powers, and the more the conquered territories in the East were given over in 1941-1942 to these forces as an experimental field for their racist New Order recipes, the more the balance of power tilted away from Schlotterer, the *Reichsgruppe*, and big business. While there was ultimately too little time for the New Economic Order in occupied Europe to solidify, Nazi economic policies certainly became more rigid. Reckless exploitation and Germanization slowly replaced the more indirect approaches of industrial cooperation of 1940. Purely biological visions began to overrun the proposals of the *Reichsgruppe* which, it might be argued, still contained some measure of rational calculation.

The setbacks on the Eastern front in 1941-1942, Germany's inability to defeat the Red Army, and other signs of an impending Nazi *Götterdämmerung* merely reinforced this trend. But the worsening of the military situation also prevented the emergence of a clear and irreversible economic policy vis-à-vis occupied Europe. Still, the preceding analysis should have made the contours of Hitler's New Economic

---

52. On Backe see A. Dallin, *German Rule*, 39f., 328ff.

Order sufficiently clear. By comparison with the Ludendorffians, large sections of industry continued to think in terms of indirect solutions. However, it also should have become evident how far these solutions had been moved from informal toward formal empire. Certainly it was not World War II, with its disruption of all international links and direct conquest of Western as well as Eastern Europe by the *Wehrmacht* that resulted in this particular resolution of the old German debate concerning the country's role on the European continent. The war was merely the vehicle to implement earlier Pan-German notions of *Lebensraum* and "ethnic cleansing." For the second time in this century the Ludendorffians, as at Brest-Litovsk, had gained the upper hand, pulling parts of the business community with them.

Yet, the euphoria of 1940-1941, which had spawned so many schemes for the economic organization of Europe as well as much conflict, soon turned into depression. By 1944, if not before, it was clear that Germany would lose the war. For the second time within a generation a resounding military defeat at the hands of the Allies destroyed the high hopes of empire that large sections of the business community had shared with the Nazis and the majority of the population. It is a reflection of the power of this dream that it did not die an immediate death in 1945. Rather it lived a postwar afterlife. It took German industry some time not only to appreciate the extent of the German defeat which, in the face of the crimes perpetrated during the war, was also a devastating moral catastrophe, but also to take in the total destruction of Germany's power position in Europe. The details of this phenomenon also await further investigation. Thus the diaries of Otto A. Friedrich, a prominent manager who had been Deputy Reich Plenipotentiary for Rubber in World War II, contain much revealing material about this question, as he ruminated upon a postwar German role as a peacemaker and bridge between East and West, between American capitalism and Soviet communism.[53] Eventually, even Friedrich came to accept that there was no such role for a defeated and discredited Germany. The more it became clear that Europe and Germany would be divided along the Iron Curtain into an American-dominated and a Soviet-dominated sphere, the more he agreed that Germany's place was within the western world's economic system that Washington was determined to establish after 1945.

The American design for a New World Order had emerged from the disasters of the 1930s and the period of economic nationalism

---

53. See V. R. Berghahn and P. J. Friedrich, *Otto A. Friedrich* (Frankfurt, 1993), 57ff.; see also L. Herbst, *Der totale Krieg*, 410ff.

and protectionism that followed the Great Crash of 1929.[54] It represented a stark contrast to the autarkic New Order that the Ludendorffians pursued in Germany at the same time, and it is worthwhile to compare the statements that came out of Berlin at the height of World War II in 1940-1941 with the messages to the international community drawn up by Washington and ultimately enshrined in the Atlantic Charter and the Preamble to the United Nations Charter. Indeed, from an economic perspective and leaving aside Hitler's intolerant racist ideology and the power-political dimensions of the world conflict, the war amounted to a gigantic struggle between two diametrically opposed views on how to organize the future world market: Closed Blocs vs. the Open Door. As one Nazi expert explained in 1940:

> And thus, in searching for the root cause of the quest for autarky, we encounter two opposing modes of thought: the world-economic, cosmopolitan and the national-economic view .... The notion of autarky hence finds its basic root in the distinction between national economy and world economy, or to be more precise: in the organizational principles which shape and regulate a national economy and its relations with other national economies.[55]

The defeat of Nazi Germany and Japan – which, at the same time as Hitler, tried to build a closed bloc of its own in the shape of the Greater East Asian Co-Prosperity Sphere[56] – meant that the idea of a liberal-capitalist, multilateral world trading system finally had a chance to assert itself.

GERMAN BIG BUSINESS AND POST-WAR EUROPE

With the benefit of hindsight, it may be said that West German industry, just like Japan's, fared well in the second half of the twentieth century under this system that was so different from what they had tried to construct in the years up to 1945. The paper by Reinhard Neebe deals with some of the aspects of how this was achieved largely by reverting to the strategies of the interwar period[57]: a concentration on

---

54. See, e.g., V. R. Berghahn, *The Americanization of West German Industry* (New York, 1987), 26ff.; R. M. Collins, *The Business Response to Keynes* (New York, 1981); R. D. Schulzinger, *The Wise Men of Foreign Affairs* (New York, 1984); M. Wala, *Winning the Peace* (Stuttgart, 1977); W. Minter, *Imperial Brain Trust* (New York, 1977).
55. Quoted in V. R. Berghahn, *The Americanization*, 28.
56. See J. Lebra, *Japan's Greater East Asia Sphere in World War II* (Oxford, 1975); R. H. Myers and M. R. Peattie (eds.), *The Japanese Colonial Empire* (Princeton, 1984).
57. See R. Neebe, *Überseemärkte und Exportstrategien in der westdeutschen Wirtschaft, 1945-1966* (Stuttgart, 1991).

exports aimed at traditional markets in Europe, including Eastern Europe, with little foreign direct investment. Ludwig Erhard, the Economics Minister of the Federal Republic saw trade as a precondition for a stable "social market-economy" that he was trying to build up in the 1950s. But West Germany's return to the world market was accompanied by much belly-aching because it required adjustments in the domestic organization of business and in deeply ingrained business mentalities. As Simon Reich's contribution demonstrates, there was considerable reluctance to forego the "fruits of fascism."[58] Protectionist arrangements continued, and the government – even one led by Erhard, the neo-liberal Economics Minister – was prepared to lend a hand when it came to favoring indigenous industries vis-à-vis foreign firms that had invested directly in the Federal Republic. The attitudes that come out in these policies harmonize well with the persistence of the cartel mentalities in industry and retailing. Here Erhard battled courageously to prevent the reemergence of cartels and syndicates, and eventually succeeded in getting a German anti-trust bill through the *Bundestag*.[59] But it took him until 1957 to achieve this. He was also skeptical of the creation of the European Coal and Steel Community and its later enlargement into the European Community, suspecting it would promote traditional thinking in terms of protectionist blocs and revive the old European cartels in a different guise. It was a suspicion that he, the free trader, never lost. It lingered at the time of the founding of the European Economic Community in 1958 and persists to this day, the Maastricht Treaty notwithstanding. Consequently, we should beware of painting too rosy a picture of the liberal 1950s.

At the same time and with Erhard's encouragement, West German industry exploited every opportunity to rebuild its pre-1930 markets. Once more Germany became one of the major exporting nations of the world, while proceeding cautiously with foreign investments.[60] It was only in the late 1950s that some companies began to venture into Western Europe and the United States to take stakes in local firms or to erect their own production facilities.

Memories of the past and of what had happened to direct investments after the two world wars no doubt acted as a brake in this respect. But even as the fear of World War III subsided, many West German entrepreneurs still continued to wonder if the American-inspired multilateral Western Open Door system would work. It is apparently this skepticism that led them to look East. As Mark

---

58. See S. Reich, *The Fruits of Fascism* (Ithaca, 1990).
59. See V. R. Berghahn, *The Americanization*, 155ff.
60. See, e.g., V. R. Berghahn and P. J. Friedrich, *Otto A. Friedrich*, 134ff.

Spaulding's article shows, *Osthandel*, though never important in terms of volume during the 1950s, nonetheless lived on as an idea. This trade was now more difficult, not only because Eastern Europe had its own memories of recent German formal empire-building, but also because of the Cold War and Western embargo policies. And yet trading links were never completely severed, not least it seems, because West German industry saw these regions as a fallback should the Western world economy for some reason not function as predicted or lapse into another 1930s-style crisis. The détente between the superpowers after the 1960s helped promote the expansion of trade with the East, while Western Europe became the main area of industrial involvement for the Federal Republic, most importantly through trade, but increasingly through direct investments and cooperation with companies in the European Community. The contributions by Margrit Köppen and Jeffrey Anderson provide good insights into recent debates on Germany's role and some of the strategic considerations underlying company decision-making in this field, including the much-vaunted *Standortfrage*.[61]

In light of German reunification and of recent upheavals in Eastern Europe, there has been a good deal of conjecturing about Germany's future economic role on the European continent. While there are few voices that conjure up a repetition of history and speak of another formal German empire, there is much talk of indirect domination by the country's manifestly powerful industrial system. Others are more sanguine and point to the inexorable multinationalization of European industry or even to the dangers of Japanese penetration.[62]

To give this debate a firmer statistical basis, several tables have been compiled at the end of this paper.[63] They demonstrate the weight of the German economy in both comparative and absolute terms even before reunification. The *Financial Times* chart of composite leading indicators for the major Western industrial nations puts the Federal Republic second in overall performance behind Japan during the 1980s (Table 1.1, p. 208).

61. See below pp. 159ff., 171ff. See also *Welt am Sonntag*, 27 February 1994, 41.
62. See P. Stakes (ed.), *The New Germany in the New Europe* (New York, 1992); R. Rhode, "Deutschland: Weltwirtschaftsmacht oder überforderter Euro-Hegomon?" HFSK-Report, No. 1 (February 1991); S. Young and J. Hamill, *Europe and the Multinationals* (Brookfield, Vt., 1992); C. Tugendthat, *The Multinationals* (Harmondsworth, 1971); D. van den Boelcke, "Multinational Companies and the European Community," in B. Nelson et al. (eds.), *The European Community in the 1990s* (Oxford, 1992), 106-23.
63. See below pp. 208ff.

Between 1986 and 1988, she moved into the first rank of exporting countries, only to be overtaken again by the United States by a slight margin thereafter. In 1991, Germany's share was 11.4 percent, compared to the United States's 12 percent (Table 1.3, p. 210). Two years later, Japan had almost caught up with Germany's second place. Up to 1970 only Britain's share of exports as a percentage of the Gross Domestic Product had been higher than that of the Federal Republic. By 1980 this ranking order had been reversed (Table 1.2, p. 209). In 1989 no less than 25 of the 100 largest companies in Europe were German, just one ahead of the British figure and six ahead of France (Table 1.4, p. 211). The remaining tables highlight above all three points:

1. Although German direct investments in other countries have increased with some 60 percent still going to the EU, the Federal Republic is still primarily an exporting nation, as it has been since the turn of the century. In this respect, the pattern differs from the behavior of Japanese industry, especially as far as the involvement with America's industrial system is concerned (Table 1.1, p. 208);
2. The European Union is by far the main trading area of the Federal Republic, both in terms of exports and imports.
3. The Germans are strongest in the export of engineering products, including automobiles, chemicals, and electrical equipment (Table 1.9, p. 216);

The impression that Germany is primarily a regional trading nation has been reinforced by the collapse of communism in Eastern Europe.[64] To begin with, the dissolution of the German Democratic Republic added the Saxon industrial basin, with traditional strengths in chemicals and engineering to the Federal Republic's economic potential (even if it will take some time for this potential to be realized).

Although trade with the former Soviet Union and with other east European countries experienced many ups and downs during the three decades before 1980, it always existed (Table 1.6, p. 213). Exports to the Soviet Union reached 11 billion marks in 1983 and, after another decline in 1986-1987 peaked at close to 12 billion marks in 1989. In the same year goods worth over 29 billion marks went to other East Bloc countries, compared with more than 46 billion to the United States and – confirming our earlier point – more than 352 billion to EU countries. Only Finland and Austria achieved a higher share than Germany's 3.8 percent.

64. See also W. Smyser, *The Economy of United Germany* (New York 1992), 194ff.

Now there is little doubt that Germany's involvement with Eastern Europe has gained new momentum since 1990. Partly because it feared the collapse of these countries, Bonn has sent millions of marks to support the material reconstruction effort and to help with the organizational transition toward capitalism. The current situation in the East remains too confused to say with any degree of certainty whether there will be a shift in German strategy away from trade toward direct investments.

In the case of the former German Democratic Republic, the first stages of economic reunification were marked by what has been called a West German *Blitzkrieg* on the underdeveloped consumer markets there.[65] German goods simply flooded former East Germany. Meanwhile it proved much more difficult to persuade West German companies to invest and establish and modernize production facilities in the five new Federal states.

The situation is even murkier with regard to Poland, Hungary, and the Czech Republic. Here a number of German companies have committed themselves directly, investing some 1.3 billion marks in former Czechoslovakia in 1991-1992 alone, while other countries, mainly France and the United States, injected no more than 600 million marks.[66] As of 31 December 1994, the German share in FDI in the Czech Republic was 36.2 percent, followed by the US at 21.2 percent, and France at 11.6 percent. Having bought up the Czech Skoda Works, Volkswagen eventually hopes to produce 450,000 cars there destined mainly for eastern markets. In Hungary, where foreign investments since the fall of communism reached some nine billion marks, Germany occupied the second place behind Austria. The Federal Republic also has tried to build up trading positions in these countries.[67] By 1992, Germany had emerged as Central Europe's largest trading partner, with a volume of some ten billion marks with Hungary and twice that amount with former Czechoslovakia and with Poland. In this respect they probably have the edge over other Western countries and Japan in terms of language and geographic proximity, even if one agrees with the verdict of Die Welt that, due to the changes in personnel and in the power structure in Eastern Europe, Germany found itself at the beginning again after the collapse of

---

65. G. Grass, "The West German Business Blitzkrieg," *Guardian Weekly*, November 11, 1990, 22.
66. *The Economist*, February 20-26, 1993, 94.
67. A. Inotai, "The Economic Impact of German Reunification on Central and Eastern Europe," AICGS Seminar Paper No. 1 (June 1992); Deutsche Bank (ed.), *Rebuilding Eastern Europe* (Frankfurt, 1991); *Financial Times*, 12 October, 1992; *Budapest Business Journal*, 15-21 July 1994; *Die Zeit*, 19 May 1995.

communism. Still, fears of German economic domination of the region are widespread, and many East Europeans would like to see more investments from other West European countries and from the United States as a counterweight to a perceived German danger.[68]

Yet, however powerful the statistical evidence and however much experts may agree that Germany is and in the long term will be the dominant economic power in both Western and Eastern Europe, the problems of evaluating how this power is going to be used are enormous. Accordingly, the spectrum of academic opinion ranges no less widely than that of the political and economic elites in all countries confronted with the "New German Question," with everybody asking themselves whether they face once more the "Old German Question."[69] German scholars, politicians, and entrepreneurs have tended to stress that, while Germany's position as an industrial power in Europe may be even stronger than it was in the first half of this century, attitudes and mentalities have undergone fundamental and irreversible changes. Certainly, they tell us, the ambitions of empire are no longer there.[70] This would appear to be perfectly credible as regards the question of formal empire. If Germany's elites have learned one historical lesson, it is that the repeated attempts to secure dominance through direct intervention ended in catastrophe and were, with hindsight, even unnecessary.[71] More patience and an earlier defeat of the Ludendorffians would, in the longer term, have resulted in a pre-eminence of the kind achieved after 1945 by peaceful means.

68. *Die Welt,* 10 October, 1992; *Wall Street Journal,* 19 December 1994, 1, 10.
69. R. Fritsch-Bournazel, *Europe.* Opinions have tended to vacillate, with fears strongest immediately after 1989. See. e.g., C. Krauthammer, "Return of the German Question," in *Time Magazine,* 25 September 1989. But there were also hopes. As Timothy Garton Ash put it: "If I have a fear for the next few years it is not that Germany will turn outward in any sort of bid for great power (economic) domination, but rather that it will turn inward, become obsessed with the problems flowing from unification, a little self-pitying, self-protective, and with a wall on its eastern frontier which its West European partners will only help to reinforce." He continued: "In short, the German eagle is unbound. The broken chains lie on the hillside. He has raised his wings a little and given a few friendly cries. Will he now spread his wings and rise up, this time to help, not to attack? Or will he rather ... sit sulkily on his perch, gobbling his ample food and disconcertingly scratching his breast with that great beak?" T. Garton Ash, "Germany Unbound," *New York Review of Books,* 22 November 1990, 15. For the view of a Germany absorbed by its own problems see also C. R. Whitney, "Europe Discovers the German Colossus Isn't So Big After All," *New York Times,* 21 April 1991, E3; K. MacGregor, "Weak behind the Mask," *Times Higher Education Supplement,* 12 February 1993, 40; J.T. Bergner, *The New Superpowers* (New York, 1991), 102; *Die Zeit,* 15 July 1994, 4.
70. See, e.g., A. Herrhausen, "Toward a Unified Germany," *New York Times,* 7 January 1990, F2; F. Froschmaier, "The Challenge Facing Germany and the Future of the European Union," Speech MS, September 1994, 5.

Does this mean that only the old divisions of opinion within Germany have disappeared and German entrepreneurs have all become informal empire-builders? There may be some who genuinely believe that despite the country's sheer industrial and financial weight, economic prosperity can be based on equality and peaceful trade. It is a view that has ancient roots in the economic liberalism of the 19th century and that we have encountered later on in the writings of Norman Angell and his supporters before 1914.[72] However, it may be more realistic to see a closer link between economic wealth and power differentials than the idealists have been prepared to concede. If wealth creates power, Germany's position as a regional economic force assumes special significance. Accordingly, there have been a number of recent cases when the Federal Republic, much to the alarm of her neighbors, began to throw her weight around. Thus the Federal Republic, "virtually alone in opposition for months, ... practically Germanized the community's Yugoslav policy overnight."[73] Some intriguing proposals have been made by leading bankers. During a trip to the Soviet Union in 1988, Friedrich Wilhelm Christians of Deutsche Bank was reported to have proposed to Eduard Shevardnadze that Kaliningrad, the former East Prussian Königsberg, "be transformed into a kind of free trade and settlement area, a major port linking the old Soviet republics with Scandinavia, Poland, and Western Europe."[74] He also founded a Königsberg Initiative. He went out of his way to emphasize that what he had in mind was not a "re-Germanization, but a Europeanization" of Kaliningrad as a center of "exchange for people, ideas, capital, and goods." But the ever suspicious French press immediately suspected more far-reaching ambitions, especially when it was suggested that the city might be attractive to Volga-German resettlers from farther East.[75] It was Boris Yeltsin who later put a damper on such plans when he asserted that Kaliningrad was Russian territory and would remain so in the future.[76]

While Christians' proposals may have been eccentric, and above all, quickly overtaken by events, recent policies of the Bundesbank have not only demonstrated the considerable clout of the deutsch-

71. W. Bührer and H. J. Schröder, "Germany's Economic Revival in the 1950s," in E. Di Nolfo (ed.), *Power in Europe*, vol. II (Berlin, 1992), 194f.
72. See above p. 6.
73. J. Joffe, "America in the Balcony as Europe Takes Center Stage," *New York Times*, 22 December 1991, E5; *Die Zeit*, 20 January 1995, 3.
74. J. Tagliabue, "A Would-Be Conqueror Is Now Russia's Booster," ibid., 15 February 1992.
75. E. Calabuig, "Quand les Allemands rétournent à Kaliningrad-Königsberg," *Le Monde Diplomatique*, August 1991.
76. *The Economist*, 3 August 1991.

mark, but also its use for purposes that put German interests over those of the Federal Republic's neighbors. Indeed, there is no question that the German Central Bank pursued its high interest strategy to the detriment of the rest of Europe and that its negative effects could be felt as far as Sweden, while the spokesman of Deutsche Bank, Hilmar Kopper, flatly denied the emergence of a "deutschmark nationalism."[77]

It is difficult to say if these developments are exceptions to the policy of self-restraint that has been observed so far or whether they are harbingers of a new pattern. In the latter case, the arguments of Konrad Seitz's bestselling study on the *Japanese-American Challenge* may have a meaning that goes beyond the book's publicly stated intentions. Criticizing the lack of an industrial strategy, Seitz has predicted the decline of Germany and the degradation of Europe to the status of a "technological colony" of Japan and the United States.[78] If this study was an appeal to develop a coordinated European technology policy, its implications, given Germany's position as a regional power, may well be to revive protectionist thinking and the traditional notion of bloc-formation. Despite official denials that "we have no interest in building fences," the possibility of a revival of earlier *Großraum* conceptions remains.

Now, it is true that some experts have argued that the path to a genuinely global economy will lead through a triad of co-prosperity spheres that they see emerging in North America, Europe, and the Far East.[79] The trouble with this scenario is that it looks too much like that of the early 1940s. The internal economic and political organization of these spheres is certainly different today from what it was then. Whatever global interdependencies that have been created already between the triad spheres through multinationalization, electronic communication, and global manufacturing systems pioneered in the auto industry, for Europe they only then would be too costly to break out of in 1930s fashion, if Germany ceased to be a regional European power and if her role as an exporting nation were complemented by policies of direct investment on a global scale that emulated the behavior of Japanese and American industry.

Accordingly, American firms bought 516 European companies worth $17.5 billion between 1988 and 1992 alone. Japanese companies made 204 acquisitions worth $12.5 billion during the same

---

77. Quoted in *Die Zeit*, 20 March 1992, 9; but see H. Schmidt, "Deutschland wird zum Störenfried," ibid., 18 December 1992, 3; idem, ibid., 6 October 1995, 1.
78. See G. Hofmann, "Ein Diplomat, der lieber zuspitzt," ibid., 21 February 1992, 2.
79. C. Tenbrock, "Block um Block," ibid., 26 August 1992, 10; ibid., 16 June 1995; *New York Times*, 15 January, IV, 1.
80. W. Smyser, *The Economy*, 201f; *Providence Journal Bulletin*, 13 January 1993, B6.

period.[80] No comparable investments have been made by German companies outside Europe.[81] The globalization of the world economy has been propelled from these two countries since the 1970s; they disregarded national frontiers, driving toward the transnationalization of the world economy. Germany has not been in the forefront of this development, regardless of BMW's and Daimler-Benz's recent decision to establish production facilities in the United States and even though some headway has been made with regard to the internationalization of top management personnel – another intriguing indicator that deserves closer sociological analysis. Instead, it has concentrated on Europe and now, given the capital needs of former communist Eastern Europe, it is easy to imagine how Germany's role as a regional power will be reinforced.[82] Seen in this light, German restraint and caution in international politics is not only reassuring to her neighbors, but represents another way of promoting interdependencies that it would be too costly to abandon in favor of a third attempt to create a German economic empire on the European continent.

81. D. Julius and S. E. Thomsen, "Foreign Direct Investment among the G-5," RIIA Discussion Paper No. 8 (London, 1988), 11; see also S. E. Thomsen, "The Growth of American, British and Japanese Direct Investment in the 1980s," RIIA Discussion Paper No. 2 (London, 1988).
82. J. Anderson and J. Goodman, "Mars or Minerva? A United Germany in a Post-Cold War Europe," Harvard Center for International Affairs Paper No. 91-8 (Cambridge, Mass., n.d.) See also the Epilogue in R.M. Spaulding, Jr. *Osthandel and Ostpolitik* (Oxford, 1996); H.G. Schröter, "The German Question, Europe, and the Market Strategies of Germany's Chemical and Electrical Industries, 1900-1992," in *Business History Review*, 67 (1993), 369-405; W. Wallace, "Deutschland als europäische Führungsmacht," in *International Politics,* May 1995, 23-28; W.D. Graf (ed.), *The Internationalization of the German Political Economy* (London, 1992).

Chapter 1

❖

EUROPE IN THE STRATEGIES OF GERMANY'S ELECTRICAL ENGINEERING AND CHEMICALS TRUSTS, 1919-1939

Harm G. Schröter

*U*ntil 1914 the chemical and electrical engineering industries of Germany concentrated their activities on Europe in both exports and foreign direct investments. On the whole, their business behavior was not marked by any special aggressiveness. While German firms devoted themselves to the peaceful penetration of foreign markets, trouble arose on the foreign policy front. Here the country posed as an "unsatiated" power. As Michael Stürmer put it recently, Wilhelmine Germany was "too small for European hegenomy and too large for the balance of power in Europe."[1]

After World War I no new political vision emerged to offer an alternative to the nation state. Even communism in its Soviet form soon adopted nationalism. With no alternative to turn to, Germany, by rebuilding its economic power, quickly succeeded in regaining its former political influence and soon also its military strength. As a result, the question of Germany's relationship with her neighbors remained unresolved during the interwar period. The purpose of

1. M. Stürmer, 'Deutschlands Rolle in Europa', *Frankfurter Allgemeine Zeitung*, 14 November 1991, 14.

this article is to examine the basis of German power, i.e., the economy, inasmuch as it was represented by the two most modern and expanding industries: electrical engineering and chemicals. What were their attitudes toward Europe, the traditional region of their activities? I will also contrast their business strategies with the foreign economic policies of the German government with the aim of identifying where the two diverged and where they overlapped. Finally, there is the question of which side, if at all, lagged behind the other and in which field.

It is possible to distinguish several phases of governmental foreign economic policy after World War I. During the early 1920s attention was focused on the Treaty of Versailles which had imposed heavy economic burdens on the country. Inflation and ultimately hyperinflation ruined the currency. In January 1923 the Ruhr area, the economic heart of Germany, was occupied by French and Belgian troops. In 1922, if not before, Berlin had officially begun to cooperate with Soviet Russia. While France was seen as the main opponent, the government pursued a more neutral course vis-à-vis the United States and Britain. In 1925 the Weimar Republic regained its sovereignty in matters of foreign economic policy and was able thenceforth to determine its own tariffs.

The second phase covers the second half of the 1920s, when France and Germany began to reconcile their differences and the Reich was admitted to the League of Nations. During this period the government was much more strongly oriented toward the West. In its trade policy it professed adherence to the principle of free trade, though tariffs were retained for agricultural produce, iron, steel, and various other products. The most-favored-nation clause became the basis for commercial treaties with other nations, and it did not permit preferential treatment of particular groups of states.

The third phase began with the catastrophe of the Great Slump of 1929, when the policy of the previous years was reversed. Like all other countries, Germany embarked upon a policy of "beggar-thy-neighbor." The most-favored-nation treaties were revoked and the government began to foster bilateralism. The results were the same everywhere: foreign trade suffered badly. At the same time, envy of Britain and France, who had large empires, and of the U.S., who had a vast internal market to fall back on, started to develop. It is against this background that the German government tried to create a cluster of countries bound together by a system of preferential trade treaties. This zone extended primarily toward the south and east, but also toward northern Europe. Most of these countries had primarily agrarian economies, and it was thought that commerce between them and industrial Germany offered good prospects for growth. When the Nazis came to power, German foreign economic policy was infused with notions of autarky and the stress was laid on countries that were within the range of German military power.

For the purposes of this essay, Europe therefore has a dual meaning. It is both seen as a market and a political sphere, and for two reasons. Interwar Europe was generally a political hot-house where issues quickly assumed shrill nationalistic overtones. This inevitably also politicized the activities of big business. Thus, the U.S. trusts like General Electric, Western Electric, or Du Pont were not only large employers with impressive technological capabilities; they also reflected national economic power. In Germany this was true of corporations like Siemens, AEG, or IG Farben. And this meant in turn that governmental decision-making became a matter of vital interest for certain divisions of these companies, and in some cases even a question of survival for the enterprise as a whole.[2]

Against the background of these general remarks, we can now turn to the year 1919 as our starting-point. During World War I, Germany had been cut off from its most important markets in Europe and the rest of the world. Most of its foreign direct investments, patents, and trade marks were seized as enemy property and subsequently sold to competitors. Meanwhile Lenin's Russia nationalized all German interests. Worse, the entire framework of doing business had undergone a profound change. Before World War I, international trade had been relatively free. The interwar period, by contrast, was characterized by a constant growth of trade barriers between nations, and insofar as they possessed formal or informal empires, these regions had to be added to the blocs of restricted access.

The War also dealt a major blow to the competitiveness of Germany's chemical and electrical engineering industries. The virtual monopoly which they had held in dyestuffs, for example, was broken. Siemens and AEG were dwarfed by General Electric and Westinghouse. To be sure, by European standards they were still very large and indeed the largest of their kind. IG Farben, created in 1925 largely from a merger of Badische Anilin- und Soda-Fabriken, Bayer, and Hoechst, the new corporation became the largest trust in Germany.[3] Compared with Du Pont's assets of 1929, those of IG Farben added up to no more than two thirds of the American company.[4] Nevertheless,

---

2. Government support of IG Farben during the Great Slump with regard to the production of nitrogen and oil from coal is a case in point.
3. It was surpassed a year later by Vereinigte Stahlwerke.
4. Calculated on the basis of A.D. Chandler, *Scale and Scope*, (Cambridge, Mass., 1990), Appendix A.2 and C.2.

"there was no operation of chemical industry which it could not undertake and no industrial combine in the world which it could not face or outface".[5] Overall, the situation of German firms after World War I was therefore one of financial weakness, on the one hand, and of organizational strength and technical potential, on the other.[6]

The subsequent analysis will look more closely at the attitude displayed toward Europe by such firms as Siemens & Halske, Siemens-Schuckert, Bosch, AEG operating in electrical engineering, and at such chemicals trusts as IG Farben, Wintershall, Burbach, and Oberkoks/Schering whose size and ranking may be gleened from Tables la and lb.

Table la: National Ranking of Major German Electrical Engineering Corporations in 1929.

Rank	Name	Assets (in $ mill.)
3	AEG	137.9
5	Siemens-Schuckert	100.2
7	Siemens & Halske	96.7
34	Bergmann	23.0
40	Bosch	19.8

Table lb: National Ranking of Major German Chemicals Corporations in 1923.

Rank	Name	Assets (in $ mill.)
2	IG Farben	497.6
6	Wintershall	98.1
11	Burbach	56.0
18	Oberkoks	32.4
31	Rutgers	24.0
47	Degussa	16.2
50	Schering	15.6

Source: Calculated from A. Chandler, *Scale and Scope,* Cambridge (Mass.) 1990, Appendix C.2.

In both branches concentration was even higher than is indicated by Tables la and lb. Thus Siemens-Schuckert was a wholly owned subsidiary of Siemens & Halske. Bergmann was taken over jointly by AEG and Siemens-Schuckert. Schering's stock was bought up by Oberkoks. Deutsche Solvay has been excluded from the set of enter-

---

5. W.J. Reader, *Imperial Chemical Industries,* Vol. I (London, 1975), 412.
6. See. W. Feldenkirchen, 'Big Business in Germany. Organizational Innovation at IG Farben, Vereinigte Stahlwerke, and Siemens', in *Business History Review,* 61 (1987), 417-51; A.D. Chandler, *Scale and Scope,* 538-49, 563-83.

prises to be examined here because it was a wholly owned subsidiary of the Belgian Solvay S.A.

By comparison with the U.S., German trusts were not strikingly large in size.[7] Thus Du Pont's assets amounted to $617.6 mill. in 1930, those of General Electric $493.9 mill. Still, German company sizes were considerable in a European context, where firms tended to be even smaller. Thus Imperial Chemical Industries (ICI), the largest British corporation in this field, had assets of $375.8 mill. General Electric of Britain a mere $70.5 mill.[8] Siemens and AEG were larger, however, than their American counterparts in respect of employees,[9] while their productivity was much lower.[10] The Germans were able to preserve their lead as regards know-how in organic chemistry, dyes, and pharmaceuticals. Their technologies in the field of high pressure processes for the production of nitrogenous fertilizers were sought after abroad. Later this also extended to the production of petroleum from coal and of synthetic rubber (Buna). IG Farben's cooperation with Standard Oil in the field of oil and with Goodyear in the field of rubber are but two examples. In 1938 Du Pont exchanged patents with IG Farben for synthetic fibres. However, during the 1930s, this technological lead was slowly being lost by Germany.[11]

By contrast, American industry was well ahead of Germany with regard to a number of products in electrotechnics and had also recovered much ground elsewhere. In the high tension sector, products were fast becoming more sophisticated, as safety standards were raised, power-grids were enlarged and electricity came to be used in many more places and for many more purposes. However, often it was more a problem of quantity than of quality. The low tension sector, on the other hand, saw plenty of change. Long-distance telecommunication and automatic exchanges arrived on the scene. Then came the radio. German firms assumed a leading role in these tech-

---

7. According to W. Feldenkirchen ('Zur Unternehmenspolitik des Hauses Siemens in der Zwischenkriegszeit', in *Zeitschrift für Unternehmensgeschichte*, 33 [1988], 22-57, 27) the German share of world exports in electrical goods was even larger than that of the U.S. throughout the interwar period.
8. A.D. Chandler, *Scale and Scope*, Appendix A.2 and B.2.
9. In 1938 Siemens had by far the largest number of people on its payroll – a total of 187,000, followed by AEG (85,000), GE (69,000), Philips (44,000), Westinghouse (42,000), Western Electric (30,000).
10. The rate of profits to turnover was much higher at GE and Westinghouse than at Siemens and AEG. Turnover per head was fluctuating around the 1,000 Reichsmark level between 1925 and 1938. See W. Feldenkirchen (note 7 above).
11. P.J. Morris, *The Development of Acetylene Chemistry and Synthetic Rubber by IG Farbenindustrie Aktiengesellschaft, 1926-1945*, MS (Oxford, 1982).

nologies in Europe, while relying on the basic research and the inventions that had been made in the U.S.[12]

Enterprises developed their strategies from visions which were then condensed into aims. Many of the visions of the companies discussed here were surprisingly similar, and it is possible to identify three groups, all of which comprised companies from both branches. Though they operated in different markets, all three pursued similar strategies.[13] But for German firms the additional problem was how to reconcile their visions with a much weaker profile. The alternative of adapting to less ambitious aims was never seriously considered. Although in the early 1920s the above-mentioned corporations remained confined to Germany, many of them nevertheless pictured themselves as becoming major players in the world economy again, and in this respect Europe was crucial for their future. It acted as a stepping-stone for Germany's re-entry into the world market at large. However, it should also be noted that the figure reflects averages, while the large companies in fact sent a higher percentage of exports overseas.

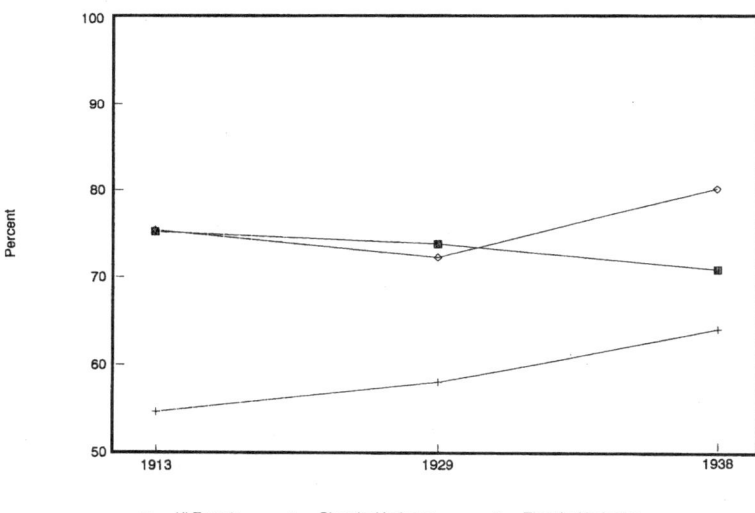

Figure 1: The Role of Exports to Europe for Germany's New Industries

One last factor must be mentioned here. While the percentage of German exports going to Europe declined overall, the trend for the chemical and electrical engineering branches was in the opposite

12. The basic types of switches (Strowger and Rotary) were invented in the US, and so was the coaxial cable.
13. W. Feldenkirchen (note 7 above), 23f.

direction. Chemicals in particular went into Europe on a much larger scale during the interwar period than before 1914. With markets in Western Europe still closed to German goods in the early postwar years, German electrical engineering firms started an export offensive which was greatly helped by the weakness of the German currency.[14] They also successfully targeted the neutral states of Europe, and in particular Scandinavia as well as Holland. Unlike the Eastern European nations, these states were prosperous enough to pay for these exports.[15] However, seen in a global context, the war and galloping inflation had weakened all the companies under consideration here – some like AEG or Rutgers more so, others like Siemens and the potash enterprises Wintershall and Burbach to a lesser degree. It is also important that many countries had built up an indigenous industry during the War as deliveries from the participants in that conflict were no longer forthcoming. This meant for the Germans that foreign market shares had to be regained. Siemens achieved a major breakthrough in this respect when it garnered the order for a large power generating plant on the Shannon River, a key installation for the electrification of Ireland. Although the company made but a small profit from the venture, it helped to rebuild its international reputation. At the same time it failed to regain its former position in other markets. Finland, for example, had meanwhile fostered its own electrical engineering industry, and what could not be manufactured in the country was supplied by ASEA, a Swedish corporation.

Although this had not been intended by the Allies, German reparations proved helpful to reestablishing the position of German industry in France, Italy, and Belgium, since deliveries were partly made in kind. This applied particularly to chemicals and electrical engineering, where former enemy countries which were generally not inclined to buy German manufactured goods, suddenly came to rely on German spare parts. The laying of a telephone cable from Paris to Bordeaux may serve as a case in point, demonstrating moreover that German technology, supplied as reparations, was superior to that of France.

German companies not only faced the problem of how to make a comeback, but also of how to secure their market positions in Europe. Before 1914 all the firms discussed in this article had had their own sales organizations both at home and abroad. These were also centers of technical advice, especially where the customer had to be introduced to technologically advanced machinery or where

14. See 'Dr. Felix Deutsch zum 70. Geburtstag', special issue of *AEG-Rundschau*, 16 May 1928, 36ff.; C.-L. Holtfrerich, *Die deutsche Inflation, 1914-1923*, (Berlin, 1980).
15. H. Schröter, *Aussenpolitik und Wirtschaftsinteresse* (Frankfurt, 1983), 328.

equipment, such as telephones, had been tailored to special requirements. As far as the Western Allies were concerned, Germany had to reconstruct such sales organizations from scratch after the War. This required foreign direct investments. However, German investments in foreign production facilities did not resume on a large scale. Here it was simply a lack of capital as well as the fear that they might suffer another expropriation.

Finally, there was the threat of foreign investment in Germany. During the postwar inflation, industry was particularly vulnerable to hostile takeover bids by companies holding hard currency. The German response was to close ranks and to cooperate even more closely than before. Concentration continued by exchange of shares, the creation of multiple-vote shares and other defensive measures.[16] A wave of mergers constituted another response, with the formation of IG Farben being the most striking case in point. National and international cartels helped to expand exports, and, like in most other European countries of the time, German industry developed close ties with the government in matters of foreign economic policy. Not surprisingly and in contrast to heavy industry and agriculture, the chemical and electrical engineering industries favored low tariffs. Their efforts in this direction ended in failure, but their support for most-favored-nation treaties was more successful. Overall, it may be said that the interwar period in Germany was the culmination of what Alfred Chandler has called cooperative managerial capitalism.[17]

As to electrical engineering, the prewar mix of competition and cooperation continued in the domestic market. The reconstruction of foreign markets proved more difficult after the War. Europe remained the main region for their exports (see Figure 1). The firms entered foreign markets not only as competitors of indigenous industries, but also sought understandings. It is interesting that corporations like Philips in Holland and ASEA in Sweden were not approached directly. The first step was to compete with them in their home markets to demonstrate that Germany had recovered her potential. The second step then was to try to come to agreements not with the indigenous European competitor, but with global ones. Thus in electrical engineering the major competitors were not European, but American companies, like Westinghouse and General

---

16. G. Feldman, 'Foreign Penetration of German Enterprises after the First World War: the Problem of Überfremdung', in A. Teichova et al., eds., *Historical Studies in International Corporate Business* (Cambridge, 1989), 87-110.
17. See W. Feldenkirchen, 'Concentration in German Industry, 1870-1939', in H. Pohl, ed., *The Concentration Process in the Entrepreneurial Economy since the Late 19th Century* (Stuttgart, 1988), 115-46.

Electric. No less important, on both sides of the Atlantic there existed a willingness to forge such understandings. General Electric openly pursued a policy of gaining a directing role in the electrical engineering industries around the world. Accordingly the trust signed an agreement with AEG in 1923. Westinghouse and Siemens followed suit a year later. General Electric and AEG proceeded to exchange patents and allocated markets, reviving a relationship that had first been established in 1903.

However, in respect of the allocation of markets, there occurred an interesting shift: the German firms failed to gain the major West European markets as a reserved area; only the less prosperous parts of Europe were left to them. In the case of the former agreement, Western Europe was to be accessible to both General Electrics and AEG, with Germany, Austria, Scandinavia, Czechoslovakia, Hungary and Holland given over to the German firm.[18] In the latter agreement, Siemens-Schuckert had the markets of Germany, Austria, Hungary, Estonia, Latvia and Lithuania handed to it – clearly an even less favorable deal than AEG's.[19] Still it was a sign of recognition and a relief that large American corporations should be signing deals with German industry at all. And bearing in mind General Electric's long-term strategy of building something like a global directorate of electrical engineering companies, the Americans actually helped AEG and Siemens to regain strength. Starved of investment, AEG handed a 15 per cent stake to General Electric which was raised to 25 per cent during the 1930s. Siemens, by contrast, avoided a direct American participation, but in 1930 General Electric gave the German firm a $14 mill. loan to be paid back after 999 (!) years. Although there was competition among the four companies, they also cooperated in strategic areas, and this cooperation in turn facilitated the expansion of the German firms, especially in Europe.[20]

Having worked out their relationship with their American competitors in this way, Siemens and AEG sought agreements with their counterparts in Europe. Here their position had meanwhile improved because they had begun to penetrate the home markets of these European companies and because their relationship with the mighty American trusts in this field had been newly defined by the above-mentioned agreements. As the other Europeans now had little hope of finding influential partners themselves, they were more

18. The U.S. and Canada were reserved for GE. See Siemens Museum, SAA4/Lf 793.
19. Like GE, Westinghouse was given the U.S. and Canada. See ibid.
20. See H. Schröter, 'A Typical Factor of German International Market Strategy. Agreements between the US and the German Electrotechnical Industries up to 1939', in A. Teichova et al., eds., *Multinational Enterprise*, 160-70.

willing to ease German competitive pressure by forging agreements with them. It is important to note that other European corporations were quite anxious to sign such accords and that this type of cooperative capitalism began to spread throughout Europe.[21] What differences and conflicts arose, were not over the idea of cartels and understandings as such, but over quotas and prices.[22] At the same time the formation of various cartels in the electrical engineering industry indicated that the German firms had lost their grip on the important French and British markets. As far as these firms were concerned, Europe had become divided into a Western half whose markets were accessible to all and the remaining regions of Europe in whose markets the Germans were still the leaders, but had lost their dominant position.[23]

It is in this context that Germany's electrical engineering industry came to give its strong support to Gustav Stresemann's foreign policy of cooperation and of reconciliation with France. At this point economics and politics went hand in hand. Thus when Stresemann negotiated the Locarno Treaty with his French counterpart Aristide Briand, the steel and electrical engineering industries of the two countries were working out their relationship. The breakthrough in politics was achieved when it became clear that the industrial accord had been reached.

From the perspective of AEG and Siemens the growth of indigenous industries in the European market gave rise to many problems. Thus ASEA in Sweden, Philips in Holland and Brown, Boveri & Cie in Switzerland, in which AEG had lost its stake, had gained a dominant position in their home markets of more than 30 per cent. Two factors tended to mitigate competition, though. To begin with, the range of competing products was relatively small. ASEA and Brown, Boveri & Cie. were mainly in the business of electric motors and transformers; Philips produced bulbs and later on radios. Secondly, they were bound by their membership in cartels with the Germans. ASEA joined such a cartel with AEG and Siemens in 1925. Philips was part of the Phoebus cartel signed a year earlier. Brown, Boveri and Cie.'s cooperations were often managed through its foreign direct investments in Germany. There were also many written and unwritten accords so that it is difficult to give a precise date. Still, the

---

21. F. Amatori et al., eds., *Global Enterprise*, forthcoming.
22. See E. Hexner, *International Cartels* (Chapel Hill, 1946); A. Plummer, *International Combines in Modern Industry* (London, 1938); H. Schröter, *Aussenpolitik*, 418ff.
23. For market domination we apply the criteria of the German Law on Competition: a *dominant* position exists if an enterprise has a market share of 33 per cent, or if up to three companies have a combined share of 50 per cent.

company's involvement with German competitors was no doubt closer than with other foreign companies.

The position of Germany's electrical engineering industry remained strong in Southeastern Europe, just as in Spain where even its foreign direct investments survived the War. Austria was used as a stepping stone to reestablish predominance with particular success. In 1937, Siemens had production facilities in Poland, Austria, Italy and Czechoslovakia. Meanwhile the company's network of technical bureaus for sales extended to remote places like Tirana, the capital of Albania.[24] Meanwhile AEG had succeeded in keeping its factory in Vienna and a power plant Romania. It also had a network of technical bureaus and a major trading firm in Yugoslavia. Before 1914, Siemens had owned Siemens Brothers in Britain in which the company regained a minority stake after the War.[25]

The telephone conflict of the interwar years represents a different chapter. At first all suppliers maintained an amicable relationship in their mutual export markets, while avoiding direct competition in each other's home markets. In 1922 the two largest companies in the field, Western Electric and Siemens & Halske negotiated an agreement which, though never signed, both tried to adhere to. However, this harmony came to an end when AT&T was forced to sell its foreign subsidiaries to ITT. The latter adopted a very aggressive strategy. It started a policy not only of selling equipment, but also of acquiring concessions for telephone services and of setting up service companies. ITT's competitors felt compelled to react. Siemens & Halske joined forces with Autelco of Chicago and Siemens Brothers of Britain. At the same time it tried to obtain telephone concessions as well. The struggle over markets took place in Europe and Latin America. Siemens prevailed in Italy, Greece, and Uruguay, but lost out in Romania and Argentina. In the end, after the parties were as exhausted by the fight as they were by the Depression, an agreement was negotiated by which Siemens & Halske obtained special rights in Central, Eastern, and Southeastern Europe.[26] Although the conflict raged in the midst of the Great Slump, as the trade policy of the German government began to turn its attention to the Southeast, there are no indications that this region became a preferential area for the

---

24. See the organizational scheme for Siemens in Southeast Europe in: H. Schröter, 'Siemens and Central and Southeast Europe between the two World Wars', in A. Teichova and P. Cottrell, eds., *International Business and Central Europe, 1918-1939* (Leicester, 1983), 173-92.
25. Amounting to 18 per cent. See ibid., 191.
26. V. Schröter, *Die deutsche Industrie auf dem Weltmarkt, 1929-1933*, (Frankfurt/Bern, 1984), 331-41.

company. Rather it seems that it pursued a global strategy causing it to fight no less hard for Argentina or Italy than for Romania.

Overall, between 70 and 80 per cent of Germany's exports in electrical engineering was taken by Europe and non-European markets were of correspondingly minor importance. In America, potentially the largest single market, AEG, Siemens & Halske, and Siemens-Schuckert maintained no more than a representation and did not engage in much selling. Indeed, the distribution networks set up by the companies provide a good gauge of the importance that they assigned to different parts of the world. In 1928, Siemens-Schuckert had some 65 Technical Bureaus as sales points in Germany. An additional 108 were located in the rest of Europe, as against 61 for the rest of the world.[27] No more than one or two Technical Bureaus were maintained for an entire country. China and the big states of Latin America were the exceptions to this rule. Siemens-Schuckert kept six to eight sales bureaus there, reflecting a concentration of sales activities. AEG presents a similar picture. Outside Germany, it registered some 25 local sales firms in Europe, but maintained no more than a total of 10 overseas.[28]

In the North, Osram became a subsidiary of AEG and Siemens,[29] manufacturing electric bulbs in each of the four Scandinavian states. In Italy Siemens invested in two indigenous companies.[30] All these foreign direct investments were not part of an offensive strategy, but must be seen as responses to competitors or resulted from government pressure. Because they had overcapacities in Germany, Siemens and AEG preferred to export rather than to invest abroad. If they could not uphold their market share in this way, they would make direct investments. But, significantly enough, their readiness to invest remained exclusively confined to Eastern, Northern, and Southeastern Europe. Clearly, Siemens and AEG felt more at home in those parts of Europe than elsewhere, except perhaps in Latin America where they had heavily invested before 1914.

Given that it became primarily a supplier of the auto industry, Bosch's strategy differed from that of Siemens and AEG. Since few

27. *Spezial-Archiv der Deutschen Wirtschaft*, Siemens-Schuckert-Werke, 1928.
28. Ibid., AEG, 1931.
29. GE also had a minority stake in it.
30. R. Giannetti, 'The Power Equipment Cartels', in T. Hara and A. Kudo, eds., *International Cartels in Business History* (Tokyo 1992), 190-209; P. Hertner, 'The German Electrotechnical Industry in the Italian Market before the Second World War', in G. Jones and H. Schröter, eds., *The Rise of Multinationals in Continental Europe* (Aldershot 1993), 155-72; idem, 'Vom Wandel einer Unternehmensstrategie. Die deutsche Elektroindustrie in Italien vor dem Ersten Weltkrieg und in der Zwischenkriegszeit', in H. Schröter and C. Wurm, eds., *Politik, Wirtschaft und internationale Beziehungen* (Mainz, 1991), 139-48.

of its products could be sold in the East, the company's main markets lay in the West. It is also for this reason that Bosch established itself in the U.S. market as early as 1921.[31] Later it also built up production facilities there and even managed to reacquire its pre-World War I company, merging all these ventures into the United American Bosch Corp. in 1930. Bosch began to produce in France in 1928 and in Britain three years later. Soon the company branched out into telecommunications (radio), household appliances (refrigerators) and power tools (drills), although its core business remained in the field of electrical equipment for automobiles. Bosch's strategy thus diverged from AEG and Siemens: it became only marginally involved in the cartel movement; its business concentrated on Western Europe and the U.S.; it made direct investments in former enemy countries. Bergmann meanwhile concentrated in the main on the domestic market. Subsidiaries that it had established in Austria, Sweden, and Holland confined themselves to sales activities. In the light of this and also because it was taken over by AEG and Siemens-Schuckert, the firm can safely be excluded from further consideration in our context.

The German home market became more and more important during the 1930s, especially that for military procurement. For the same reason small direct investments were also made in Czechoslovakia and Italy. As the governments of Europe tried to gain self-sufficiency in the field of military equipment, both Siemens & Halske and Siemens-Schuckert reluctantly enlarged their subsidiaries abroad, still preferring exports to foreign direct investments. Though cooperating with the Nazi government at home, neither Siemens nor AEG were prepared to abandon their external markets, and this occasionally led to frictions with the authorities. In 1940, when the Nazis saw themselves as the dominant power in Europe, they also asked the electrical engineering industry to put forward its ideas for the reconstruction of the Continent once the war had been won. Siemens responded very cautiously, claiming that it could not imagine "that we can suppress the economic freedom of sovereign states."[32] No doubt this position was much more realistic than the government's and it also differed markedly from that of other branches, including – as will be seen – the chemical industry.

All in all it can be said that the electrical engineering industry never regained its pre-1914 role in most of Europe. By 1928 it was again the largest *importer* in nearly all European states, with the

31. *75 Jahre Bosch* (Stuttgart 1961).
32. Siemens Museum, SAA 4/Lf 690, 31 October 1940.

exception of France; but imports represented only a fraction of the respective markets and indigenous producers had to be contended with.[33] However, it succeeded in carving out niches for itself in certain markets. Thus Siemens was exceptionally strong in medical technology. The company also gained a dominant market share in telecommunications through concessions, for example in Italy.[34] But in contrast to the years before 1914, there was little foreign direct investment, particularly in the West, and this proved to be a severe handicap in a situation where governments and many indigenous customers preferred to buy goods produced in their country. Nor did it help that German companies lacked the capital and that the German banks remained too weak to commit themselves.

The German chemical industry was able to preserve its influence in the markets of Europe to a much greater extent than electrical engineering. Basically it pursued the same aims as the latter, i.e. to regain its pre-war status, first in Europe and later on a global scale.[35] In doing so, it used similar strategies and applied the same means as the companies discussed so far, but did so with much greater success.[36] In this respect it certainly helped that, unlike the electrical engineering industry, chemicals relied in large measure on self-finance.

As may be seen from Table 1b, this branch was dominated by IG Farben.[37] Like its precursors, this giant corporation was reluctant to invest abroad after World War I. It concentrated on exports and shied away from foreign direct investments except to promote its distribution network. In contrast to what Gottfried Plumpe has maintained, this strategy and IG Farben's membership of cartels was not one of its own choosing.[38] A different strategy was adopted only with regard to the vast and competitive American market. Here IG Farben became convinced that without production in the U.S. it would prove impossible to recapture a substantial share of the market.[39] In Europe, by contrast, major foreign direct investments were made in

33. *Spezialarchiv der Deutschen Wirtschaft*, AEG, 1928, 8.
34. P. Hertner, 'How They Changed Their Strategy', in G. Jones and H. Schröter, eds., *The Rise of Multinationals*, 155-72.
35. G. Plumpe (*IG Farbenindustrie A.G. Wirtschaft, Technik und Politik, 1914-1945* [Berlin, 1990], 114-31) correctly stressed that IG Farben looked to the world market; but he underestimated that Europe, even for IG Farben, represented the bulk of business as well as a stepping stone for the world market.
36. Just as Bergmann had no strategy for Europe in the electrical engineering industry, so Rutgers had none in the chemical industry. Both companies concentrated on Germany.
37. The following is merely designed to complement the material presented in the contribution by Peter Hayes to this volume.
38. See G. Plumpe, *IG Farbenindustrie*, 115f.
39. The US represented the exception to this policy. See V. Schröter, 'Participation in

exchange for licenses and shares. This approach worked in the case of the Norwegian Norsk Hydro; but it failed in France where the government intervened.[40] In general it may be said that rather than investing abroad the trust encouraged international cartels as an alternative.[41] In fact, soon after its formation in 1925, it initiated negotiations to this end, while the German government promoted most-favored-nation commercial treaties.

By 1927, a first international dyestuffs cartel had been built. France was the initial partner, to be joined in 1929 by Switzerland and in 1932 by Britain. By 1939 nearly all dye-producing companies in the world had joined this cartel in one way or another. The members of this cartel allocated quotas and, in case these could not be fulfilled by domestic producers, other cartel members were to be given preference. IG Farben practically came to act as clearing house for deliveries and for the allocation of markets, with the exception of the Swiss companies none of which had difficulties fulfilling their quotas and selling their products.[42] As a result IG Farben was more or less in total control of Europe's dye markets, with the exception of Switzerland, France, and Britain. But in these latter countries, a smooth cooperation developed with indigenous cartels.[43]

The nitrogen cartel (CIA), which emerged from 1929 onwards, presents another example.[44] Its core was made up of the so-called DEN Group, named after its members, Germany, Britain, and Norway. It included ICI, Norsk Hydro (in which IG Farben had a 25 per cent stake) and the German Stickstoff-Syndikat (DSS) which was also dominated by IG Farben. Nearly all European firms were members of CIA which left national home markets to indigenous firms, while all exports, with the exception of those by British companies, were channeled through DSS. In the French case direction by DSS went so far that the distribution of the official French import quotas was

---

Market Control through Foreign Investment', in A. Teichova et al., eds., *Multinational Enterprise*, 171-84.
40. G. Plumpe, 'Ansätze zur Zusammenarbeit zwischen der deutschen und französischen Chemieindustrie vor und nach dem Zweiten Weltkrieg', in R. Cohen and M. Manfrass, eds., *Frankreich und Deutschland* (Munich, 1990), 224-33.
41. H. Schröter,'Risk and Control in Multinational Enterprise. German Businesses in Scandinavia, 1918-1939', in *Business History Review*, 62 (1988), 224-33.
42. IG Farben gave special help to the French firm of ETS Kuhlmann and to other smaller producers in Europe to sell their products. See H. Schröter, 'Cartels as a Form of Concentration in Industry', *German Yearbook on Business History*, 1988, 113-44.
43. G. Plumpe, *IG Farbenindustrie*, 197-200.
44. Convention Internationale de l'Azote. See R. Lachmann-Mosse, *Die Stickstoffindustrie und die internationale Kartellierung* (Zürich, 1940); H. Schröter, 'Privatwirtschaftliche Marktregulierung und staatliche Interessenpolitik', in H. Schröter and C. Wurm, eds., *Politik*, 117-37.

handed over in 1937 to be managed by the German syndicate. IG Farben dominated most European markets in nitrogen outside Britain and France. The CIA also maintained amicable relations with the American nitrogen industry. In the early 1930s, relations with the producers of Chilean saltpeter were very bad, but they improved over the following years.[45] Ultimately, Chile even joined the CIA. Like the dyestuffs cartel, the CIA tried to hamper the emergence of indigenous industries, and both ICI and IG Farben played a decisive role here, jointly succeeding in delaying or thwarting the opening of new production facilities in Europe.[46]

Once the world depression had struck, IG Farben tried to uphold Free Trade, but argued, perhaps somewhat incongruously, that it should be based on a Continental bloc – as Carl Duisberg put it – from "Bordeaux to Sofia", excluding Britain and the Soviet Union. In following this policy, the corporation supported all steps that could be interpreted as pointing in this direction, among them the plans for an Austro-German Customs Union in 1931 and for preferential trade treaties with the states of Southeastern Europe.[47] During the Nazi period, IG Farben tried to continue its foreign trade as much as possible, if necessary by means of privately negotiated compensation agreements, while collaborating with the regime at the same time.[48] The strategies of this firm thus diverged in some respects from official foreign economic policy.[49]

Wintershall and Burbach meanwhile found themselves in a very different situation. Both were connected with the potash industry, and next to nitrogen, potash was essential for the production of artificial fertilizer. The industry as a whole was cartelized in the Deutsches Kali-Syndikat (DKS) in which Winterhall held a 37.6 per cent production quota, while Burbach was given 16.8 per cent.[50] Before 1914 Germany had enjoyed a monopoly position for potash because it was the only country in which deposits had been found. The monopoly was broken when Alsace with its deposits was returned to France and when potash was discovered in other countries. Initially there was conflict between French and German producers until both joined a cartel. This international potash cartel became the only one to behave in economics textbook fashion in every respect. Thus it

---

45. The Chilean producers started to contribute to the fighting fund even before formally joining the cartel.
46. See Schröter (note 41 above).
47. C. Duisberg, *Abhandlungen, Vorträge und Reden aus den Jahren 1922-1933* (Berlin 1933). Duisberg was chairman of the IG Farben supervisory board at this time.
48. Such agreements were signed both with European states and with countries overseas.
49. See the contribution by P. Hayes in this volume.
50. H. Schröter, *Die internationale Kaliwirtschaft, 1918-1939* (Kassel, 1985), 16lf.

weathered the Great Slump between 1929 and 1932 without having to lower prices simply by reducing output. But prices came down sharply in 1933, when Spanish companies started to produce. The cartel also managed to attract into its orbit all major producers, either as members or as partners, American and Soviet firms not excluded.[51] Its German and French core members jointly directed the exports of all other members. Europe remained the main area for potash sales, and changes in German foreign policy had little impact on the activities of this international cartel.

During the German inflation of 1923, the Oberschlesische Kokswerke & Chemische Fabrik auf Aktien A.G., Oberkoks for short, had bought up Schering. Oberkoks was a large enterprise which was mainly engaged in the coking business. But it had also acquired several chemical firms from which it tried to forge a single chemicals trust based on coal as feedstock. The plan failed because all the companies that were acquired, while specialized in fine chemicals, had no large throughput. Consequently, there was no need or advantage for them to hold large amounts of coal. Along came Schering, a renowned pharmaceutical enterprise. In 1928 Oberkoks/Schering made a direct investment in Austria which became the site for several products. All other investments made around the world were in sales outlets. Unlike IG Farben, Oberkoks/Schering did not concentrate its activities in Europe, though all its production facilities, with one exception, were in Germany. Exports overseas were at least as important as those to Europe. The history of the hormone cartel underlines this which had been formed by the three leading companies in the field, i.e. Oberkoks/Schering, Ciba of Switzerland, and Organon of Holland. However, unlike many other cartels, this one did not divide up its markets geographically, thereby offering preferential zones to its members.[52]

Finally, there is the story of the Deutsche Gold- und Silber-Scheideanstalt (Degussa) which is in many ways similar to that of Oberkoks/Schering.[53] The firm was engaged in the production of non-ferrous metals and some other specialities. In 1930/31 it merged with two other chemical companies. It made one foreign direct investment in Austria. Other investments were only to establish sales

---

51. At the start of the Franco-German cartel, the French side was allocated 30 per cent of all exports; the German side received 70 per cent. With other countries soon joining, production quotas for 1935-39 were as follows (in per cent): Germany – 53.4; France – 22.9; Spain – 11.1; Soviet Russia – 9.5; Poland – 3.1. The onset of World War II stopped American companies from participating in the export cartel.
52. M. Tausk, *Organon de geschiedenis von een bijzondere Nederlandse onderneming* (Nijmegen, 1978), 132ff.
53. Degussa, ed., *Aller Anfang ist schwer* (Frankfurt 1973).

offices abroad. Degussa's exports went to all countries of the world, and it had no special strategy for Europe.

What are the conclusions to be drawn from the experience of the electrical engineering and chemical industries? In both branches, as we have seen, there were a number of enterprises whose strategic focus was explicitly on Europe, while they also pursued global aims. It is no coincidence that these companies were AEG, IG Farben, Siemens & Halske, and Siemens-Schuckert, the largest in their respective branches. Their size was a precondition of their particular strategy. In their eyes, Europe was the most important part of the world market, and most of their exports hence went to this region. However, Europe represented for them also a stepping stone to the world market. The same picture emerges when we consider the geographical distribution of foreign direct investments, in particular for production facilities rather than for sales organizations. In 1930, in the case of the chemical industry, some 67 out of 85 such units were in Europe and another 11 in the U.S.[54] In short, Europe was their main area of operation.

Another group of enterprises, again comprising both branches, embarked upon a policy that was oriented towards the world market. Among them were more highly specialized enterprises like Bosch, Wintershall, Burbach, Degussa, and Oberkoks/Schering. Their products were difficult to obtain elsewhere in the quality and quantities that they were able to offer. This group also secured its markets with the help of cartels, but it is difficult to discern Europe as an area of concentration. The third group of larger companies in electrical engineering and chemicals consisted of Bergmann and Rutgers. Facing giants like AEG or IG Fraben, both firms felt neither big nor specialized enough to pursue an independent strategy beyond Germany's borders. Ultimately, it was therefore only the largest enterprises of German big business – and they were large even in comparison with their American competitors – which felt confident enough to aim for both Europe and the world market and to use the former as the launching pad for their activities overseas.

Compared with the two decades before World War I, German foreign direct investments were small during the two decades after 1918. International cartellization became a proxy for investments abroad. Cartel agreements guaranteed a certain share of the home market to indigenous producers. Meanwhile and for the same reason their exports remained severely restricted. Their expansion was thus

---

54. H. Schröter, 'Die Auslandsinvestitionen der deutschen chemischen Industrie, 1870-1930', in *Zeitschrift für Unternehmensgeschichte*, 1 (1990), 1-22, Table 1.

blocked, because whatever was left of the total was distributed by a German-led international cartel. Moreover, what was not produced for the home market was to be handed over to the cartel for delivery abroad. In these circumstances many smaller firms refrained from costly R & D, a decision which would have endangered their survival in the long run.

Differences between the two branches concerning their path of growth and success were relatively minor; but the objectives that they had set for themselves beforehand were not fulfilled to the same degree. On the whole, the chemical industry fared better than eletrical engineering. Through its combination of exports, foreign direct investments, and international cartels, IG Farben managed to establish something like an informal economic empire in Southern, Eastern, and Northern Europe in the early 1930s. Winterhall and Burbach, on the other hand, did not have a Eurocentric strategy. Electrical engineering may have had a preference for certain European countries, but it never gained enough influence to build an informal empire comparable to IG Farben's. Worse, it lost the technological and financial edge it had enjoyed before 1914, while the chemical industry largely succeeded in carrying it across to the interwar period.

Finally, as far as these industries were concerned, Germany indeed proved "too small for European hegemony and too large for the balance of power in Europe".[55] However, IG Farben and the potash companies were at least strong enough in their fields of activity to achieve economic hegemony over large parts of Europe. Siemens and AEG, by contrast, lost the preeminent position that they had held before 1914. The other firms reviewed here were much smaller, both in absolute and in relative terms. They never gained a strong position in Europe; nor did they long for one.

What remains an open question is to what extent the European strategies of the enterprises examined here counteracted or reinforced Nazi policies and how far they were directed by the Hitler regime. One of the aims of Nazi foreign policy was to construct a German-dominated economic sphere, a *Grossraumwirtschaft*. No less important, notions of a preferential zone in Europe as a German alternative to the British Empire, the French Empire or the vast domestic market of the U.S. existed even before 1933. What was new were the means by which the Nazis pursued their political aims.[56] When Hitler came to power, IG Farben had already founded in a number of its fields of

---

55. See note 1 above.
56. Since the publication of Peter Hayes's *Industry and Ideology* (New York, 1987) it has been generally accepted that the involvement of the chemical and electrical engineering industries in war crimes and in the implementation of *Grossraumwirtschaft*

activity which the Nazis were then merely dreaming of: a preferential zone in Europe that was respected by competitors and friends alike. Although IG Farben had a stake in it, *Grossraumwirtschaft* was most vigorously promoted by state- and SS-owned enterprises.[57] Later the German war economy harnessed all the economic resources of occupied Europe to the military effort; but not even the Nazis thought this war economy to be identical with the proposed *Grossraumwirtschaft* to be established in Europe after a victorious war. Still, the Nazis succeeded in using the dynamic power of big business as a tool for their expansionist ambitions. No less significantly, the corporations did not feel violated, but were eager to take advantage of the territories conquered by the Wehrmacht.

---

though undisputed and tangible – has not been as extensive as Marxist authors had assumed. Plumpe (*IG Farbenindustrie*, 2lff., 546ff). also gave several examples showing that Marxist authors had actually changed the meaning of quotations.

57. P. Hayes, *Industry*, 217f.; idem, 'Zur umstrittenen Geschichte der IG Farbenindustrie A.G.', in *Geschichte und Gesellschaft*, 18 (1992), 405-17; J. Ludwig, *Boykott, Enteignung, Mord. Die 'Entjudung' der deutschen Wirtschaft* (Hamburg, 1989); G. Ranki, *Unternehmen Margarethe. Die deutsche Besetzung Ungarns* (Vienna, 1984). In countries, such as Denmark, the Netherlands, and Norway, where there was little activity of Nazi enterprises, preparations for Grossraumwirtschaft were also minimal. See H. Schröter, 'Bürokratie zwischen Organisation und Chaos. Deutsche Besatzungsverwaltungen und Grossraumwirtschaftsplanung in Norwegen und Dänemark, 1940-1945', in T. Pirker and C. Schulten, eds., *Das organisierte Chaos. Zur Besatzungspolitik des NS-Staates* (Munich, 1993).

Chapter 2

❖

THE EUROPEAN STRATEGIES OF IG FARBEN, 1925-45

Peter Hayes

*L*ike the nation in which it was based, the IG Farben corporation spent the decades prior to the end of World War II largely reacting to the results of World War I. And, though it did so with greater success than the Weimar Republic and with less willfull aggressiveness than the Third Reich, it ended – as Germany did – diminished, damaged, and divided.

To understand Farben's reactions and their results, one must begin by comparing the combine's commercial and technical position when it was founded in 1925 with the aggregate situation of its predecessors in 1913. Broadly and somewhat contradictorily put, sales and assets were up, but prospects were down. By virtue of accumulated know-how and plant, Farben still enjoyed a technological and physical lead over its burgeoning foreign rivals. The German concern, therefore, continued to earn handsome proceeds, even abroad, from its flagship products, dyes and nitrogen. But by all accounts its competitors were catching up, its share of international trade in chemicals was falling, its chief markets were shifting from industrial countries to less politically and economically reliable underdeveloped ones, and its dependence on domestic purchasers was rising. Moreover, the enterprise's capacity to reverse these trends was restricted by its losses of subsidiaries, trademarks, patents, and even skilled personnel to competitors between 1914 and 1924, as well as by the spread of protectionism.[1] Since this situation largely brought IG Farben into being in 1925, it is not surprising that the concern rapidly elaborated a strategy to deal with it. Neither is it altogether startling that the resulting program bore the stamp of experience rather than imagination.

What were the main elements of Farben's European strategy? First, the combine continued to assign top priority to earnings from exports. To expand them amidst adverse conditions, IG streamlined its overseas sales operations; engaged in aggressive advertising and promotion; placed greater emphasis on high quality, high priced specialty products (so that rising returns would offset declining sales volumes of more easily imitated goods); and undertook a constant quest for new markets. The export drive was initially aimed at Russia, China, and British India, until Stalinist industrialization, Japanese expansionism, and the Ottawa System erased most of Farben's gains. Thereafter, the concern turned increasingly toward the Latin, Baltic, and Balkan states.[2]

Second, when foreign markets appeared indefensible or ruinous price warfare threatened, Farben tried "to save what is saveable" through cartel and license agreements. Prototypical of such deals was the Gallus Vertrag, by which from 1919 to 1924 Farben conceded the loss of its patents and production processes in France and provided the new native producers with valuable know-how in return for a share of their profits on dyes output. The pacts between Standard Oil and Farben in 1927-30 constituted another example, these delimiting patent and production rights and sales regions for

1. For the appropriate statistics and fuller depictions of IG Farben's founding situation, see Peter Hayes, *Industry and Ideology: IG Farben in the Nazi Era* (New York, 1987), 7-18, 32-47, and Gottfried Plumpe, *Die I.G. Farbenindustrie AG: Wirtschaft, Technik und Politik 1904-1945* (Berlin, 1990), 96-144, 176-99. While essential as a source of statistical data on the history of IG Farben, the latter book must be used cautiously in other respects; see Peter Hayes, "Zur umstrittenen Geschichte der IG Farben," in *Geschichte und Gesellschaft*, 18 (September 1992), 403-14

2. On the rationalization of sales operations, see Verena Schröter, "The IG Farbenindustrie AG in Central and South-East Europe, 1926-38," in A. Teichova and P. Cottrell (eds.), *International Business and Central Europe, 1918-1939* (New York, 1983), 144; on the development of Farben's foreign trade, G. Plumpe, *IG Farbenindustrie AG*, 114-19, 451-56, 560-84. One should not overstate, however, Farben's interest or success in southeast Europe. During the 1930s, though the region purchased an increasing share of IG's exports, the actual value of this trade did not rise; while IG provided a growing share of the region's chemical imports, these fell as a share of the region's chemical consumption. In short, neither the firm nor the region became dependent on the other in this period; see P. Hayes, *Industry and Ideology*, 297-98.

applications of IG's hydrogenation process. Above all, there were the Four-Party Agreement governing dyes output and sales, the CIA Agreement, which did the same for nitrogen, and the international conventions concerning light metals and explosives. All of these creations of the late 1920s slowed the rates of decline in IG's shares of world consumption, though their success in other respects varied.[3]

Third, when nothing else remained, IG reluctantly began manufacturing in a foreign country. Reticence in this regard had long characterized the German organics makers, whose operating subsidiaries prior to 1914 were concentrated in France and Russia, the two countries most protective of their own producers and least protective of outsiders' patents. Similarly, only the extent of American protectionism explained the establishment of the Agfa-Ansco facility in America before World War I and its expansion in the 1920s, as well as IG's determination during that decade to regain as many as possible of its other former American holdings.[4] As befits a course of last resort, however, Farben's overseas production was relatively infrequent and relatively unprofitable. Only 70 of IG's 726 branches, agencies, and participations outside of Germany in 1939 were manufacturing operations, and most of them merely finished and repackaged goods for local markets.[5] In relation to total earnings in the years 1930-43, proceeds from foreign operations fell even more rapidly than did exports, indicating that overseas production generally could not compensate, at least in the aggregate, for the effects of protectionism and competition.[6]

While engaged in these three essentially defensive marketing strategies, IG recognized that real growth depended on the success of a fourth, productive one. The concern devoted enormous outlays to research and development of new products. These, the combine's leaders hoped, would replicate either (a) the organic chemical industry's initial experiences with dyes and nitrogen, which had superseded scarce natural substances and sold in bulk at home and

---

3. See P. Hayes, *Industry and Ideology*, 32-36, supplemented by Harm G. Schröter, "Cartels as a Form of Concentration in Industry: The Example of the International Dyestuffs Cartel from 1927 to 1939," *German Yearbook on Business History* (1988), 113-44 (also in *Vierteljahresschrift für Sozial- und Wirtschaftsgeschichte*, 74 [1987], 479-513), and "Privatwirtschaftliche Marktregulierung und staatliche Interessenpolitik: Das internationale Stickstoffkartell 1929-1939," in Harm G. Schröter and Clemens A. Wurm (eds.), *Politik, Wirtschaft und Internationale Beziehungen* (Mainz, 1987), 117-37.
4. See G. Plumpe, *I.G. Farbenindustrie AG*, 57-63, 120-29.
5. H. Schröter, "IG Farbenindustrie AG in Central and South-East Europe," in Teichova and Cottrell (eds.), *International Business and Central Europe 1918-1939*, 139.
6. See G. Plumpe, *I.G. Farbenindustrie AG*, 434, 453, 547, 561-69, and esp. 663-64 for the relevant statistics.

abroad, or (b) the branch's later experience with sophisticated dyes, which had proved superior to competing substances in specialized applications even at high prices. Vision (a) led Farben into its massive investment in synthetic fuel during the mid-1920s; vision (b) was the initial inspiration for the firm's venture into synthetic rubber at the same time. But, gradually during the 1930s, rubber replaced fuel-from-coal as the new mass product that would reap monopoly profits in the early stages or, at the very least, highly rewarding license fees, so its development became governed by vision (a) as well.[7]

The defects and virtues of this mix of strategies became apparent during the Depression. On the one hand, Farben would not have had to fund part of its dividend payments out of reserves rather than proceeds in 1931-32 had the fourth line of strategy not propelled the firm into two successive and vast rounds of overinvestment in nitrogen and fuel, on both of which the combine lost millions. On the other hand, there would have been no dividends at all had Farben's exports of dyes and pharmaceuticals not held up better than German exports as a whole or than the enterprise's domestic sales. This was the result of excellent marketing, qualitative superiority, and the wave of cartellization, which both sustained prices and spread the consequences of the downturn over many producers.[8]

In this context, the inauguration of the Third Reich brought, not a fundamental corporate reorientation, but only a shift in emphasis, one that initially seemed ordained more by prevailing world economic conditions than new national policies. Faced with stagnant levels of international trade, hence unable ever to regain the export returns of 1927-28, Farben felt compelled to concentrate ever more heavily on the domestic and increasingly state-defined market.[9] Thus began the transformation of the concern's sales from 70 percent on traditional consumer oriented products (dyes, pharmaceuticals, photographic supplies, and fertilizers) and 30 percent on all others in 1933 to the reverse ratio ten years later.[10] To be sure, the firm's profits on products fostered by the Nazi programs of autarky and armaments were held to 5 percent of investments in contracts with the government. Under the prevailing international circumstances and

---

7. See Peter Hayes, "Carl Bosch and Carl Krauch: Chemistry and the Political Economy of Germany, 1925-1945," in *Journal of Economic History*, 47 (1987) 35-65.
8. See P. Hayes, *Industry and Ideology*, 42-43; and G. Plumpe, *I.G. Farbenindustrie AG*, 433-50.
9. On the beginnings of this shift, see Anton Reithinger's report of 1934, discussed in P. Hayes, *Industry and Ideology*, 128-31.
10. P. Hayes, *Industry and Ideology*, 326-27. See also G. Plumpe, *I.G. Farbenindustrie AG*, 550, 592, on the shifts in Farben's profits and investments, and 296-338, on PVC fibers and plastics.

domestic regulations, however, there were few other ways to earn even that much. Besides, non-investment of funds as the state desired meant that they would remain idle and be taxed away, whereas investment as the state directed at least allowed IG to retain them in the forms of plants, equipment, and acquired know-how.

Thus, Farben went along with Nazi economic policy, hoping to ride rearmament and autarky like post horses to the point where familiar and new competitive products could take advantage of an upturn in international trade.[11] Meanwhile, within Germany the firm contented itself with: (a) making sure new factories were at least sited on economic, cost related grounds rather than military ones, (b) avoiding excessive haste in the development of synthetic rubber, the combine's principal hope, (c) reducing Farben's exposure in fields with poor long-term prospects, notably synthetic fuel, where IG held its output constant from 1934 until the war and encouraged the emergence of other manufacturers, and (d) protecting its fundamental monopoly in the lucrative but under-utilized sphere of dyes production.

The horse, however, rapidly became the rider. By 1938 the steady militarization of Farben's production had brought on a liquidity crisis and undermined research and development for commercially promising plastics and synthetic fibers. At least in part, IG's long-term prospects were being sacrificed to short-term pressures, as was generally the result of the Nazi practice of "strip-mining the economy."[12] Moreover, the first successes of Nazi expansionism, namely the acquisitions of Austria and the Sudetenland, transformed formerly foreign cartel partners into potential domestic competitors. Farben's determination to head off this danger drew the concern into the first of the corporate takeovers that gave it a reputation for rapacity.[13]

Still, as long as peace prevailed, the enterprise clung to its external strategies. Continuing to market aggressively in some quarters, especially given the Reich's shortage of foreign exchange, IG also loyally upheld cartel agreements in others for the sake of market stability, even when this meant sacrificing sales to assertive foreign producers. Meanwhile, the concern expanded its foreign manufacturing operations where necessary, starting or adding to twelve overseas productive units between 1936-39; entering joint production arrangements with firms in the U.S., Latin America, and England; and even authorizing the founding of new factories in France.[14] Finally, the search for

11. As background to the remarks in this and the following paragraph, see P. Hayes, *Industry and Ideology*, 69-212.
12. For the quotation, see Joachim Fest, *Hitler* (New York, 1975), 538.
13. See P. Hayes, *Industry and Ideology*, 219-43.
14. See ibid., 159-60, 199, 210, and 286.

new markets went on, now under the heading of Max Ilgner's and Georg von Schnitzler's call for "intervention in the industrialization of the world." This initiative reflected a significant difference of opinion, even if only one of degree rather than kind, with Nazi economic priorities. Though neo-mercantilist in conception, like Nazi visions of the Greater German Economic Sphere *(Großraum)*, Ilgner's and Schnitzler's proposals called for the transfer of some German capital from projects serving arms and autarky to overseas investments that would stimulate demand for German goods.[15]

In other words, even before Hitler launched World War II, the tension between the demands of IG's short-range, regime-oriented and long-term, international-centered strategies had become unmistakeable to the firm's leaders. That they never freed themselves from their dilemma under wartime conditions and while dealing with an often hostile and poorly coordinated bureaucracy is understandable. That their efforts to serve two masters made them complicitous in the crimes of the Third Reich gives the history of their decisions in 1940-45 tragic importance.

The principal elements of IG's fatefully pragmatic attempt to reconcile traditional considerations and new realities developed in the course of 1940. Cut off from overseas markets worth hundreds of millions of marks and faced, regardless of the war's outcome, with dubious prospects for their recovery, IG's leaders imparted a more ambitious and aggressive twist to their European strategy. Their "peace planning" or New Order proposals outlined a program to rationalize continental chemicals production in such a way as to both offset the concern's immediate losses and best position it in postwar competition. Specifically, the concern sought the Reich's assistance in monopolizing future European exports of key products, depriving smaller rivals in continental markets of their tariff and legal protections, and subordinating the surviving major producers in lucrative fields. While output and competition were thus being reduced in overbuilt sectors, especially dyes and medicinal preparations, Farben intended to focus rigorously on preserving its position in the technically and commercially promising ones, such as liquid gases, light metals, and synthetic rubber, where the Nazi regime was pressing for ever greater manufacturing capacity. These updated defensive considerations led to IG's most exploitative initiatives in occupied Europe: its campaign to acquire control of the French organic chemicals industry; its plant takeovers in Poland, Alsace-Lorraine, and the Soviet Union; and its construction of large manu-

---

15. See ibid., 160-61, 196, and 300-02.

facturing complexes in Norway and at Auschwitz.[16] On the few other occasions when the concern sought to acquire or build new plants, it acted on the basis of the old desire to circumvent trade barriers, now in the form of the imbalanced clearing accounts with Balkan states that impeded further purchases of German goods.[17]

Two points need to be made about Farben's pursuit of this European strategy during World War II, though neither does nor can relieve the concern of responsibility for the ghastly consequences. First, the firm's attempt to serve both the present and the future was clearer in conception than practice. Coordinated planning proved difficult in an environment where the members of the Vorstand received little information about their colleagues' activities; even the highest ranking managers could only guess at the extent of IG's production for the Wehrmacht, and the threat of arrest could be invoked to make the case for economically unsound decisions.[18] As before the war, therefore, R&D expenditures continued to drop as a percent of sales, and further commercially promising new lines of development were either abandoned or slighted.[19] The firm partially succeeded in grouping operations of only military value under its Luranil and Anorgana subsidiaries, and went so far in 1944 as to contemplate a complete split into two enterprises, rather like the one accomplished by Wasag.[20] But the fact that nothing came of this scheme fittingly symbolizes the way in which the pressures of war often overwhelmed strategic considerations.

Second, IG's revised European strategy was essentially reactive, a result less of independently formulated corporate objectives than of trying to set and stick to them within the context created by the Nazi state. This is especially apparent with regard to the genesis of the worst of Farben's criminal involvements during the Third Reich: the employment of forced and slave labor. Caught between the Reich's appetites for soldiers and output, at least one member of IG's managing board made clear in 1940 that he preferred to fill out his workforce with German women rather than imported and increasingly involuntary foreigners.[21] But, once the regime rejected this course, the same executive not only complied with the decision, but also labored to defend IG against an alternative means of reducing the need for foreign labor at his plants, namely the transfer of some pro-

16. See ibid., 244-97, and, on Auschwitz, the discussion below.
17. See ibid., 297-316.
18. See ibid., 24, 185, 306.
19. See G. Plumpe, *I.G. Farbenindustrie AG*, 609-10, and note 10 above.
20. G. Plumpe, *I.G. Farbenindustrie*, 668; P. Hayes, *Industry and Ideology*, 333, 369.
21. See P. Hayes, *Industry and Ideology*, 342-44.

duction of profitable goods like film and aspirin to factories in occupied Europe. In consequence, within the context of the regime's decisions, a commercially oriented, long-range strategic interest in the protection of markets and know-how became an incentive to take part in an increasingly exploitative labor policy that the firm initially had opposed.[22]

Both of these points are relevant to understanding the history of IG Farben's synthetic rubber (buna) program and its infamous climax near the village of Auschwitz. They help explain why the concern's decade-long effort to confine the volume of production to predictable needs, to control the siting of plants, and to design them with an eye to long-term profitability degenerated into a rear guard action, in which the price of partial success was ever deeper involvement in murder.

Since the late 1930s, when the Nazi regime began arguing for building a synthetic rubber plant in Silesia, IG had dragged its feet, favoring both a slower pace of expansion and more cost efficient locations.[23] Consequently, Germany's second and third buna factories were constructed near the Rhine, and in 1940, following the defeat of France, Farben persuaded the Reich to let it cease preliminary work on a new installation near Breslau. With the failure of the air offensive against Great Britain, however, Berlin reverted to the idea of a large plant "in the East," out of the reach of British bombers. The concern complied, lest a refusal prompt the state to proceed on its own and thus to break IG's monopoly on synthetic rubber, as it had done with regard to other key military supplies, notably magnesium and poison gas.[24] After a first-choice site near Gogolin became unavailable, Farben settled on a plain east of the village of Auschwitz, where the water table, transportation connections, and raw material supplies appeared advantageous.

In all probability, the proximity of the concentration camp on the other side of the village was not a factor in the choice of the Auschwitz site. Though the surviving documents dating from or referring to the period prior to the selection envision various sources of labor, they say *nothing* of relying on inmates. Nor is there any reason to regard this silence as startling or suspicious. When the decision was made, the use of such workers by private industry was still virtually unprecedented. Furthermore, IG was not in a hurry to build the

---

22. See P. Hayes, "La stratégie industrielle de l'IG Farben en France, 1940-44," forthcoming in *Histoire, Economies, Sociétés*.
23. For a fuller statement of the argument and evidence concerning IG-Auschwitz summarized here, see P. Hayes, *Industry and Ideology*, 347-68.
24. See ibid., 137, 139.

plant, hence not particularly desperate to find a workforce. Its own current production was equal to existing demand and highly profitable, and it had made preliminary offers to erect buna plants in southern France and Italy as part of joint ventures with allied firms. Thus, even before the vast American development program of 1941-43 assured that Farben would have to reckon with vastly increased postwar competition in synthetic rubber, the concern calculated that the new plant would prove rewarding only if it met the latest standards of efficiency. That argued for carefully planned, patient, and expert construction, as well as for intricate integration of the manufacturing process with that of other products in order to reduce costs.[25] Having but reluctantly accepted the idea of another buna plant, then made sure that its capacity would be only half of that originally slated for the Rattwitz site, IG intended to proceed deliberately and with an eye to long-term returns.

Neither can one contend that Farben compacted with mass murder at the moment it chose to locate at Auschwitz. In February 1941, when the die was cast, the regime's decision to massacre the Jews was still months away, the first experimental gassings more than half a year off, the initial rail shipments of doomed Jews almost exactly one year in the future.

Yet IG's plans drew it unprotestingly into terrible complicity with both slave labor and annihilation. While the Reich's determination to hasten construction of the plants led it to press inmates on the firm as construction workers, the resulting prospect of earning profits on them provided Heinrich Himmler with a new reason to expand the camp. Thereafter, Farben's complex of factories, known as Monowitz, became the scene of a tug-of-war between the regime's insistence on speed and the concern's desire to assure future competitiveness. Determined not to provoke the Reich's intervention by seeming laggard but indifferent to the fate of the inmate workforce, IG took some 30,000 camp prisoners between 1941 and 1944, 90 percent of whom died there or in the gas chambers when they could no longer work, yet only one installation was ever completed. No buna had been produced on the site by the time IG's managers evacuated it in January 1945.

At Auschwitz and at earlier moments of strategic choice, Farben could have acted otherwise. As even the most recent and sympa-

---

25. For a highly speculative and tendentious appreciation of this point, see Karl Heinz Roth, "I.G. Auschwitz. Normalität oder Anomalie eines kapitalistischen Entwicklungssprungs?" in *"Deutsche Wirtschaft": Zwangsarbeit von KZ-Häftlingen für Industrie und Behörden*, ed. Hamburger Stiftung für Förderung von Wissenschaft und Kultur (Hamburg, 1991), 79-95 (also published under the same title in *1999*, 4 (1989), 11-28.

thetic study of IG has conceded, the concern could have avoided or desisted from its nitrogen and fuel construction projects of the late 1920s without collapsing.[26] Neither the firm nor the Reich had to follow the trade policies of the 1930s or the labor policies of the war years.[27] Like Germany, IG Farben generally rejected alternatives for two reasons: doing so seemed more convenient or expedient in the short run, and it accorded with an antinomian sense of victimization that stilled doubts. Both the nation and the firm could claim that externalities structured the choices. Of course, each exaggerated the situation when doing so.

It is nonetheless essential to note that one source of both the Nazi regime and Farben's behavior was Germany's post-World War I economic situation. Thus, alongside the moral message of IG's road to Auschwitz lies an economic lesson about the circumstances that helped put the firm on that road. In other words, in the economic context of the 1990s, it is worth recalling that, among other things, the history of IG Farben's European strategies stands as a warning against the consequences of rising protectionism, for it demonstrates the extremes to which such a trend, in conjunction with other, explosive national resentments, can drive states and firms that must rely on foreign trade for their prosperity.

26. See G. Plumpe, *I.G. Farbenindustrie*, 232, 284-85, 295, 435-36, 466.
27. See P. Hayes, *Industry and Ideology*, 130-31, 342-44.

Chapter 3

❖

FASCISM AND THE STRUCTURE OF GERMAN CAPITALISM
The Case of the Automobile Industry

Simon Reich

The study of German history can be characterized as having two related tendencies, one understandable, the other perhaps not as obvious. The first tendency is to focus on the causes of the downfall of democracy and the advent of fascism. The domestic and global consequences of the "Nazi seizure of power" and the salutary lessons implicit for all liberal democracies makes this endeavor both credible and legitimate. The second tendency in the study of German history, evident in the work of a variety of notable historians, is to adopt an approach that employs a "grand sweep" of history, attributing causation to events in Germany that are traced back over decades, if not centuries.[1] The prime example of this is the linking of the form of German unification to the onset of fascism. Thus, the historians' debate over continuity and

---

1. For some of the major works that provide examples of this tendency see Fritz Fischer, *The War of Illusions* (New York, 1975) and his *Germany's Aims in the First World War* (New York, 1967); John A. Moses, *The Politics of Illusion: The Fischer Controversy in German Historiography* (New York, 1975); Hans-Ulrich Wehler, *The German Empire 1871-1918* (Dover, NH, 1985); Alexander Gerschenkron, *Economic Backwardness in Historical Perspective* (Cambridge, Mass., 1962). For examples of works that debate the appropriateness of the "grand sweep" approach see Richard J.

change in studies of Wilhelmine and fascist Germany has focused on the issues of where responsibility lay for the outbreak of World War I and the preconditions for the rise of fascism – and whether the two issues are related. A bitter argument has raged over whether these developments were the inevitable outcome of the internal politics of Wilhelmine society or were simply the state's response to external factors beyond domestic influence.[2] This discourse, in turn, has given rise to a further debate over the issue of whether, and to what degree, periods of German history can be analytically insulated so that the events of one period can be used to explain developments in another, or if the patterns of German history are too interwoven as to make the attribution of causation of events from one discrete period to another a justifiable and meaningful exercise.

One interesting, if aberrant and baffling, product of the conjunction of these two tendencies is the complete neglect of the question of the consequences of fascism. It is assumed that German history, particularly in the area of economic policy, is either divisible into discrete periods (thus unlinking the Third Reich from the Bonn Republic) or that epochs of German history are linked, but that postwar German capitalism finds its historical origins in Wilhelmine Germany, and emphatically not in the Third Reich.

This chapter contests the tendency of the "grand sweep" approach to systematically ignore the possibility that the structure of capitalism in the Bonn Republic has any link to the Third Reich. I do not offer a generalized argument here, but by focusing on data concerning the auto industry, try to demonstrate that, at least in that sector, the relationship between the state and individual firms was formative in dictating the structure of the market and the fortune of firms in the first two decades of the Bonn Republic. Using illustrative data drawn from a comparative, more detailed study, I argue that historians, economists, and political scientists have overlooked a possibly very important component in explaining the pattern of German postwar economic development in ignoring the links between the structure of capitalism in the Third Reich and the Bonn Republic.[3]

Evans (ed.), *Society and Politics in Wilhelmine Germany* (New York, 1978); Wolfgang Mommsen, "Domestic Factors in German Foreign Policy before 1914," *Central European History*, VI, 1973, 3-43; Volker Berghahn, *Germany and the Approach of War in 1914* (New York, 1973); and both Geoff Eley's, *From Unification to Nazism*, particularly 4, 7-8, 11-13, and his *Reshaping the German Right: Radical Nationalism and Political Change after Bismarck* (New Haven, 1980).

2. See particularly Fischer, *The War of Illusions* and his *Germany's Aims in the First World War*; Moses, *The Politics of Illusion*; Wehler, *The German Empire*; Eley, *Reshaping the German Right*.

3. The argument and date for this paper is directly drawn from my book, *The Fruits*

I therefore suggest that the patterns of continuity in German economic development do not transcend the fascist period but, on the contrary, include the fascist period. State economic policy in that period has made a significant contribution to the postwar pattern of German capitalism – at least in the limited realm of the German auto industry. Indeed, the innovations of the German fascist state revolutionized the state's attitude about economic policy and how it conceived of the scope and domain of its power. That state legitimated the notion of conscious discrimination, acting prejudicially against foreign direct investors and those domestic firms that refused to cooperate with the state authorities. The result was the formation of a core of firms that cooperated with the state and each other – and isolated peripheral firms. Furthermore, I argue, these changes were sustained during the Allied Occupation and survived into the Bonn Republic, being reflected in the Bonn government's behavior in the auto sector. The automobile industry's structure can therefore only be explained through the study of the fascist period. Those historians who study twentieth century German capitalism, I thus argue, cannot consign the fascist period wholesale to a residual category where events were unrelated to later developments. Ultimately, any research agenda engaged in the study of postwar German development, either economic or social, should consider the question of the influence of reforms in the fascist period, instead of assuming that none exist.

THE AUTOMOBILE INDUSTRY'S IMPORTANCE

Why choose the auto industry for this study? In his book, *Finance Capital*, Rudolf Hilferding offers a conception of "organized capitalism," with its traditional corporatist structure, that seems highly relevant to older industrial sectors where the firms were more firmly rooted, such as the chemical, electronics, optical, or coal industries.[4]

---

of Fascism: Postwar Prosperity in Historical Perspective (Ithaca, 1990). Inevitably, as a summary, this chapter lacks the theoretical depth and empirical detail of the larger work. The book mainly uses primary data in examining four very detailed case studies about the relations between individual auto firms and the state in Britain and Germany, as well as comparative chapters that examine the state's treatment of all the major auto producers in Britain, France, Germany, Italy, and Japan, with reflections on developments in the United States.

4. Rudolf Hilferding, *Finance Capital: A Study of the Latest Phase of Capitalist Development* (London, 1981). For assessments of this issue see Fritz Fischer, *Germany's Aims*, 14-16; Peter Hayes, *Industry and Ideology: IG Farben in the Nazi Era* (New York, 1987), 2-46; and John Gillingham, *Industry and Politics in the Third Reich: Ruhr Coal, Hitler and Europe* (London, 1985), 5-38.

But, interestingly, the younger, smaller, less innovative, and U.S.-dominated German auto industry, which was to become the bulwark of Germany's postwar economy, certainly differs from this organizational pattern. It did not initially develop until the Weimar period, and did not significantly expand until the Nazi period.[5]

Certainly the critical feature distinct to the auto industry was the presence of foreign firms with extensive domestic manufacturing facilities. Ford formed its own subsidiary, starting local production in 1926, and General Motors purchased Opel, a subsidiary, in 1929. These subsidiaries constituted two of the larger and more dynamic firms producing in Germany, and their presence created an impenetrable barrier to the formation of a cartel for the auto industry. Their size, technological advantages, great resources (which reduced their concern about the effects of the product cycle), and their ideological preference for entrepreneurial free-enterprise distinguished them from their domestic counterparts. Thus the auto sector did not follow the classic pattern of German industrial development. To consider the traditional explanation of "organized capitalism" as responsible for the auto industry's postwar prosperity therefore seems inappropriate.

The answer to the question of why concentrate on the automobile sector if its pattern of development is not typical of German industry lies in the fact that, unlike the pre-1933 period, the domestic automotive industry between the late 1940s and the 1960s constituted the new Federal Republic's elite economic sector, largely due to its growth under the Third Reich.[6] Between 1933 and 1939 alone, German motor truck output grew by 263 percent, car output by 74 percent, and motorcycle output by 176 percent, to become the industry that generated the second largest sales income behind coal mining.[7] The Adenauer and Erhard governments considered the economic

---

5. See Richard J. Overy, *The Nazi Economic Recovery, 1932-1938* (London, 1982). For a description of the relative, technically underdeveloped state of domestic German automobile firms before 1933 see Anita Kugler, "Von der Werkstatt zum Fliessband: Etappen der frühen Automobilproduktion in Deutschland," *Geschichte und Gesellschaft*, 13 (1987), 304-339.
6. For an indication of the transformation and the significance of the auto sector to the general economy between the Weimar Republic and the Third Reich see Overy, *The Nazi Economic Recovery*, 36, 49; and the same author's "Cars, Roads and Economic Recovery in Germany, 1932-8," *Economic History Review*, 2nd Series, XXVIII, (1975), 467-83. For a discussion concerning the postwar strategic importance of the auto industry to the German economy see Glen Yago, *The Decline of Transit*, (New York, 1984).
7. United States Strategic Bombing Survey (USSBS), Munitions Division Report, "German Motor Vehicles Industry," 3 November 1945, 3, and Maurice Olley, "The Motor Car Industry in Germany During the Period 1939-1945," British Intelligence Objectives Sub-committee (BIOS) Report 21, Imperial War Museum, 7.

welfare of the domestically owned auto firms to be critically important because of their leverage as major employers; they were two of Germany's most profitable firms, among its largest exporters, and the highest earners of foreign currency.[8] In aggregate, the auto industry was clearly the dominant postwar German sector, explaining the rationale for its selection for examination in this chapter.

THE POLICIES OF THE FASCIST STATE

In the opening decades of the twentieth century the German state treated all auto firms in an egalitarian manner, to the benefit of the American firms that dominated production in Germany. But there was a sharp change in the 1930s and 1940s, when the fascist state developed a new aggressive ideology. It created a number of new instruments that invoked coercive measures, such as the creation of certificates of origin, new rationalization requirements, and skewed allocation procedures for the distribution of labor, resources, and government contracts in a period where production was exclusively for the public sector. These measures not only consciously, systematically, and directly discriminated against foreign firms, but also made a comparable distinction among domestic firms, fragmenting the unity of domestic producers. This change had a lasting effect on the structure of capitalism in the auto sector, segmenting the relationship between capital, labor, and the state, and influencing the distribution of benefits and prospects for prosperity in the Third Reich and Bonn Republic.[9]

In formal terms, the fascist state distinguished between a favored core of firms and a periphery of firms that were, at best, neglected or, at worst, driven out of business. The general characteristics of core and peripheral firms are identified in Table 3.1.

Both public sector firms created by the state and private sector firms coopted by the state and integrated into the state's decision-making apparatus were favored because they shared a common interest with the state. These firms wanted to maximize profits. The state primarily wanted these firms to remain competitive in order to earn foreign currency and maintain technological development.[10] As

---

8. For indicative figures on VW's and Daimler-Benz's profits, sales, export, investment, and employment figures see, for example, *The Wall Street Journal*, 5 July, 6 and 20 August 1956, and 10 October 1962.
9. This effect on the distribution of benefits and prospects for prosperity is not assessed in any detail in this chapter. It is assessed extensively, however, in S. Reich, *The Fruits of Fascism*.
10. See James Womack and Daniel Jones, "The Competitive Significance of Govern-

Table 3.1: The Characteristics of the Core and Periphery of the Automobile Industry

	Core	Periphery
Mass Production	VW NSU-Audi 'Child of the State'	Ford Opel 'Multinational Firm'
Specialist	Daimler BMW Porsche MAN 'Coopted Partner'	Borgward 'Paternal Industrialist'

a result of this mutual interest, the two cooperated in significant ways, benefiting from advantages denied to other firms, such as the sharing of technical information. Core members were protected by the state in the sense that they were less subject to the vagaries of the marketplace than peripheral firms – their risk, for example, being underwritten in periods of short-term cash-flow crises both before and after 1945.[11]

Symmetrically, peripheral firms consisted first, of foreign direct investors whose very presence, by virtue of their ownership, was antithetical to fascism's nationalist ideology; and second, of a group of paternal industrialists whose owners' insistent belief in the pre-eminence of private sector autonomy drove them continually to resist integration into the state's apparatus. In contrast to core firms, peripheral auto firms were subject to the harsh rigors of the marketplace and were not supported in times of crises, some even going bankrupt.[12] Peripheral firms, having a difficult time finding indigenous funding for long-term research and development, generally did not receive government research grants, which therefore limited their economic prospects. Among peripheral firms, only the multinational corporate producers, whose home base lay elsewhere, generally succeeded in securing extensive financing – through their parent companies. In general peripheral firms more closely assimilated a distant, aloof relationship with the state while core firms benefited from a more intimate relationship that provided them with the basis for a competitive advantage.[13] But, more importantly, this dis-

---

ment Technology Policy in the Auto Sector," research paper published by "The Future of the Automobile" program, 1-10.
11. Examples of short term aid include the Federal government's activities to aid VW during the mid-1970s as discussed in Wolfgang Streeck, *Industrial Relations in West Germany: The Case of Auto Industry* (New York, 1984).
12. For example, see the discussion of Borgward below pp. 88ff.
13. One implication of this analysis is that much of the contemporary literature on

criminatory ideology and the institutions it spawned survived the downfall of fascism and dominated the policies of the allied powers and the early democratic governments, with an equally dramatic effect on these firms in the postwar period.

THE HISTORICAL DEVELOPMENT OF THE GERMAN AUTO INDUSTRY

Between the 1930s and the 1960s there were six major producers in Germany: Bavarian Motor Works (BMW), Borgward, Daimler-Benz, Ford, Opel, and Volkswagen (VW)-Auto Union-NSU. These firms reflected contrasting forms of ownership, technological production processes, and most importantly, relations with the German state. The most notable firm in relation to the Nazi state was, of course, VW because it was Hitler's favored project, the focus of attention among both bureaucrats and auto industrialists for most of the 1930s. It retained this status as the largest industrial concern, being the symbol of the "German model" in the Federal Republic in the 1950s.[14] Hitler initially discussed the concept of mass-producing a car for sale under RM1,000 in 1934.[15] He first tried to turn responsibility for its development over to private manufacturers,[16] but this scheme failed because only Opel, a despised American firm, could possibly fulfill Hitler's demand that 100,000 cars be produced annually by 1940 for a price approaching the stipulated target.[17] Furthermore, none of the

---

Germany has characterized the system of industrial relations as corporatist. See, for example W. Streeck, *Industrial Relations in West Germany*. This may be accurately characterized as a consensual, cooperative, and intimate attitudinal and institutional relationship when describing that between core firms and the German state. But, in extending the generalization, the same characterization is often inaccurately attributed to peripheral firms whose relationship with the state has been strained, and whose inclusion in the tripartite process has generally been at the insistence of the state for coercive, repressive purposes.

14. For figures see Woratz, "Betr.: Besprechungsunterlagen für das Zusammentreffen der Automobilindustrie mit dem Herrn Minister", B102/5196, Bundesarchiv.
15. See "Niederschrift über die Besichtigung der von Herrn Dr. Porsche gebauten 2 Probewagen am 24.2.1936 im Ausstellungsraum der Daimler-Benz AG, Berlin," taken from the archive of the Hamburger Stiftung für Sozialgeschichte des 20.Jahrhunderts.
16. See BMW AG, "RDA/Besprechung über das Problem 'Volkswagen' um 28.5.34," Hamburger Stiftung Archive.
17. See Vortrag, "Beiratssitzung Deutsche Bank," 28 October 1938, File 16, Volkswagen Popp, VW Project, Bochum. For the figures on Opel production see BMW AG, "RDA/Besprechung über das Problem 'Volkswagen' um 28.5.34," Hamburger Stiftung Archive. See letter, F. Popp to Dr. E.G. von Stauß, 11 June 1937 in File 16 VW Popp, ibid. On the issue of the exclusion of U.S. firms see letter from

other firms had any financial incentive for supporting the scheme's success because the successful development of such a cheap car would have a salutary effect on their own sales.[18]

By 1937 the failure of the private initiative led to a state-sponsored scheme that resulted in the construction of the world's largest and best-capitalized auto plant at Wolfsburg, financed and supervised by the Deutsche Arbeitsfront (DAF).[19] This scheme was advocated and supported by Franz Popp of BMW and Wilhelm Kissel of Daimler-Benz, whose fortunes were to become inextricably intertwined with those of VW.[20] The government's partisanship toward the project was reflected in the structure of investment financing, tax relief, method of sales, and financing of construction.

The following year the first foundation stone was laid for what was to become the world's largest auto production plant, built on 770

F. Popp to W. Kissel, Archiv der Daimler-Benz AG., Best. Kissel VII/5, in Hamburger Stiftung Archive.

18. For an example see letter from Kissel to Director Ernst Hagemeier, Leiter der Wirtschaftsgruppe Fahrzeugindustrie, Berlin-Charlottenburg, 21 January 1937, Daimler-Benz file in Daimler-Benz Archive entitled VW Kissel, DB Archive, Fremdfirmen Inland 35 VW, in Hamburger Stiftung Archive.

19. Armed with the funds that the DAF had confiscated from the German labor unions and wealthy cooperative societies, Robert Ley created a financial empire based on two holding companies, the Vermögensverwaltung der Deutschen Arbeitsfront GmbH (VV) and the Treuhandgesellschaft für Wirtschaftliche Unternehmungen mbH (TWU). Between them they owned 97 companies with a total capital of RM500 million, a former cooperative society comprised of some 50 factories, 137 job supply centers, a chain of retail shops (that had a turnover of RM770 million in 1943), building societies valued at over RM100 million, and the Bank der Deutschen Arbeit with a capital in excess of RM50 million. The membership of the DAF was theoretically voluntary for German workers, but proved to be conscriptive in practice. Over 15 million German workers therefore each contributed five marks a month to the funds of the DAF, providing a constant cash flow from 1933 onward of approximately RM 75 million per month. Among prospective German owners, in the private or public sector, the DAF was uniquely placed to finance and implement the development of the VW project. Taken from the Foreign Office report entitled "The Heritage of the DAF" in file FO 371/46829, Public Records Office (henceforth referred to as the PRO), London, England.

20. The most supportive piece of evidence for Popp's claim to have been the original proponent of this scheme is in a letter written by Popp to Jacob Werlin, a personal friend of Hitler, member of the Aufsichtsrat of Daimler-Benz, who was later to become a member of VW's preparatory board. In Popp's letter to Werlin he claimed that he had previously written to Kurt Frey, Reichstreuhänder der Arbeit, with his idea. Frey had then informed Robert Ley, leader of the DAF, and Heinrich Simon (who was Leiter der Zentralstelle für die Finanzwirtschaft and later to become the Vorsitzender of the VW plant) and they approved of his proposal. See letter from Popp to Werlin, 29 July 1936, Archiv des Dokumentationszentrums der Staatlichen Archivverwaltung der DDR, DK713, supplied by the Hamburger Stiftung.

acres and designed to annually produce 150,000 VW's, at an initial cost of RM215 million (to which another RM644 million investment in plant and machinery was added between 1939 and 1945). Although there was no extensive auto production there before 1939, the plant contained the largest press shop in Europe, 2,700 of the finest specialized machine tools, and the right to use the best raw materials and labor available.[21]

Once the war started, however, the lack of available raw materials precluded any mass production of civilian goods and the plant lay idle until late 1940, when it was seized for military production.[22] But subsequent jeep and arms production after 1941 was, in fact, accompanied by the production of 51,224 sedans. This proved to be the test model that was to become the famous postwar "Beetle."[23] Indeed, as the war progressed, a greater emphasis was placed on civilian, not military production, thus reducing conversion problems in 1945.[24]

The plant thus continued to grow dynamically and prosper until 1944, fed by an abundance of government contracts, subsidies and machinery confiscated from both occupied territories and Jews in Germany.[25] VW's labor force grew by over 600 percent, from 2,732 to 17,365, between 1939 and 1944 in the context of a tightening labor market, partially as the result of the use of slave labor, foreign work-

---

21. "Es begann 1934: Die Geschichte des Volkswagenwerks" – a short history of the VW plant drawn from the personal archival material collected by Ian Turner. All references to data received from Turner will henceforth be denoted by the term "Turner Personal Files." All these prewar figures come from the USSBS 88, 7; wartime investment figures from Chief Custodian, "Preliminary Report: VW Chief Custodian's Report 1946," FO 942/197, PRO.
22. "The German Automobile Industry," BIOS Report 768, BIOS B, Box 20, Imperial War Museum (IWM), 11. See also "Volkswagen Chief Custodian's Report 1946."
23. "Es begann 1934;" see also "Investigation into the Design and Performance of the Volkswagen or German People's Car," BIOS Final Report 998, Item 19, Imperial War Museum, 1-2; see also "Subject: The Volkswagenwerk Complex in Control Under Law 52," 3, FO 371/65114, PRO; "Subject – Wolfsburg Motor Works," FO 1046/193, PRO, and Memo from Property Control Branch, Finance Division to Chief, Finance Division: "The Volkswagen Complex in Control Under Law 52," 7, MinSupp 14/397, PRO. For full details concerning arms production figures see USSBS 88, 4-5.
24. "Volkswagen Chief Custodian's Report 1946."
25. The most publicized example of the former being the confiscation of 300 machines from Peugeot's French plant. See BIOS Report 768, or Hirst, "The Volkswagenwerk under the British Trusteeship," from Turner Personal Files, p. 168. The most publicized example of the latter was the "forced purchase" of the Luckenwalder Feintuch-Fabrik near Berlin. See "The Volkswagen Complex in Control Under Law 52," MinSupp 14/397, PRO.

ers, and prisoners-of-war.[26] It is therefore not surprising that VW, after its massive initial losses, made operating profits during the war.[27]

Of course, these developments would have been of little significance had Allied strategic bombing proved effective. But three Allied aerial attacks against the strategically vulnerable Wolfsburg plant resulted in no heavy damage, signaling a breakdown in intelligence.[28] The use of dispersal sites, and a well-executed plan in which VW's management deliberately collapsed the roof in non-essential parts of the plant to give the aerial appearance of damage, kept damage to a minimum. Only 9.8 percent of the machine tools were destroyed, although 55 employees died and 174 were wounded.[29]

At the end of the war factory officials tried to implement the Third Reich's "scorched earth" policy, and to destroy the factory and its power station. But Wolfsburg's mayor, recognizing both the plant's manufacturing potential and the importance of the adjacent power station for the area, called out the local militia to protect both until the U.S. troops arrived.[30]

By 1945 VW was thus primed for peace, and production resumed.[31] Contrary to a popular myth, British authorities fully recognized the

---

26. See USSBS Report 88, 8 and I. Hirst, "The Volkswagenwerk under the British Trusteeship," 168. For details on the numbers of these workers and their treatment see Klaus-Jörg Siegfried, *Rüstungsproduktion und Zwangsarbeit im Volkswagenwerk 1939-1945: Eine Dokumentation*, (Frankfurt/New York, 1986). For an evaluation of the book see "Porsche und die Geheimsache Kirschkern: Historiker erforschen NS-Zwangsarbeit im Volkswagenwerk," in *Der Spiegel*, 13 April 1987. For the comparable debate on the role of Daimler-Benz see Hans Pohl, Stephanie Habeth and Beate Brüninghaus, *Die Daimler-Benz AG in den Jahren 1933 bis 1945* (Stuttgart, 1986); Karl Heinz Roth, "Der Weg zum guten Stern des 'Dritten Reichs': Schlaglichter aus der Geschichte der Daimler-Benz AG und ihrer Vorläufer (1890-1945)" in: *Das Daimler-Benz Buch: Ein Rüstungskonzern im Tausendjährigen Reich*, (Nördlingen, 1986), 28-40; and Hans Mommsen's comments on both of these books in *Der Spiegel*, 13 April 1987. See also Bernard P. Bellon, *Mercedes in Peace and War: German Automobile Workers, 1903-1945* (New York, 1990).
27. See "Volkswagenwerk GmbH," VW Financial Reports File, Turner Personal Files.
28. See USSBS Report, Munitions Division, "German Motor Vehicles Industry Report," 3 November 1945, 15.
29. See CIOS Report XXXII-122, Imperial War Museum; Nelson, *Small Wonder: The Amazing Story of Volkswagen* (Boston, 1965) 95; Hirst, "The Volkswagenwerk under the British Trusteeship," 168; USSBS Report 88, 11.
30. Ian Turner, "British Occupation Policy and Its Effects on the Town of Wolfsburg and the Volkswagenwerk, 1945-1949" (PhD. thesis, University of Manchester Institute of Science and Technology, 1984), 68.
31. For the details of the debate concerning the VW plant see "Extracts from the Thirteenth meeting of the NACMII," 20 April 1948, AVIA 49/65, PRO; Letter from Sir Percy Mills, CCG, to Mark Turner, Control Office for Germany and Austria, 22 May 1946, BOT 211/92, PRO; H.A.R. Binney, "Minute Sheet," 12 September 1946, BOT 211/92, PRO. "The Zoning of Commerce and Industry Group,"

plant's potential. But after an extensive debate, in a victory for the British Treasury, the view prevailed that the revenues VW would generate – contributing to the alleviation of Germany's massive balance-of-trade problems – were more important than issues concerning future competitiveness or present reparations payments.[32]

The renewal of production began with the placement of an order in August 1945 for 21,200 vehicles by the Control Council for German (CCG) for use by Allied military personnel.[33] To facilitate this process, plant and machinery were repaired by British military engineers, who also retrieved production materials from the dispersal sites.[34] VW production for the Allied forces was designated as mandatory; their raw material requirements thus took priority over those of other auto producers, and they received their allocation of resources directly from the Industrial Division of Property control rather than through the new trade association, the Produktionsausschuss der Automobilindustrie (PADA), which determined the allocation of resources for all other firms. VW was therefore unique in that it had a predetermined, relatively plentiful raw material quota over which the rest of the resource-starved producers had no access.[35] The British military thus did everything they could to stimulate production, rather than suppress it; enforcing a policy that gave VW advantages over the rest of the industry in terms of access to resources, a consumer market, and a guaranteed rate of profit.[36] Despite the change in political regime, therefore, VW maintained an exclusive political relationship with the governing authorities, giving the company an excellent springboard upon which to revive its fortunes.

The settling of the issue of whether to sustain VW raised another issue, that of VW's ownership and control. While the property of the

---

Bipartite Control Office, BOAR Frankfurt, 15 April 1948, FO 1046/193, PRO; I. Turner, "British Occupation Policy," 154.

32. See, as examples, "The German Automobile Industry: Visit from 10 February to 3 April 1946," 11, BIOS Report 768, BIOS B, Box 20, IWM; FIAT report 300, BIOS B, Box 7, IWM; Minutes from "The NACMII, Thirteenth Meeting," 20 April 1948, Avia 49/65, XC/A59211; Letter from John Schuy to G.M. Jennings (HM Treasury), 17 October 1946, BT 211/92, PRO; Letter from John Selwyn (BOT) to Colonel Rowell (COFGA), 17 November 1946, BT 211/92, PRO, outlining the Board of Trade's position on this issue and "Notes on an Informal Meeting held 11 October 1946 on the subject of production and possible export of the Volkswagen Car," BOT 211/92, PRO; and letter, R.H. Bright (MinSupp) to Derek Wood (BOT), 3 September 1946, BOT 211/92, PRO.
33. I. Turner, "British Occupation Policy," 182.
34. "Subject: The VW Complex in Control Under Law 52," 3 and Hirst, "The Volkswagenwerk under the British Trusteeship," 168.
35. The PADA briefly replaced the RDA before the Verband der Deutschen Automobilindustrie (VDA) was formed.
36. I. Turner, "British Occupation Policy," 189.

now defunct DAF had been confiscated and used for reparations payments, the decision not to dismantle the plant left the question of who owned it unresolved.[37] After exhaustively examining countervailing claims from labor unions, unpaid creditors, the local state government, and the federal government, the CCG officials felt that only the federal government could be entrusted with adjudicating the company's fate.[38] When the first federal government was formed in September 1949, authority over the plant was therefore formally transferred to it in an act that Ian Turner describes as a "masterpiece of equivocation" with control ambiguous, ownership undecided, and an unspecified decision-making apparatus.[39] The foundations provided by the Nazis, coupled with the advantages extended to VW by the Allies, meant that no company was better placed to profit from any postwar surge in demand.

Was this tendency maintained by the new democratic German government, and if so, how? Evidence here can only be indicative rather than exhaustive, but I would suggest it was sustained primarily through the breadth and scope of state intervention in pricing policy; the nature of VW's restrictive practices in terms of its research and development agreements with the state and other core firms; and the unique nature of VW's industrial relations agreements with the labor unions.

Economics Minister Ludwig Erhard saw one of his major tasks as being the systematic, revolutionary dislocation of the FRG's economy and state structure from its fascist past.[40] He favored the immediate privatization of VW but it was over a decade before the ownership issue was settled through an agreement sharing ownership between the federal government and state government of Lower Saxony.[41] The most prominent and persistent opponents to Erhard's plans for privatization and his liberal economic principles in general, despite their membership of the same political party, the CDU, were located in the Finance Ministry.[42] They preferred to sustain a closer relationship between state and economy, one in which

37. "Subject: The VW Complex in Control Under Law 52," 11.
38. On the issue of ownership see VW Senior Control Officer (Dir. Kemmler), "Minutes of the Eleventh Board of Control Meeting of the VWW GmbH and DAF Properties," 6 December 1946, FO 371/76723 (VWW), PRO; CCG Memo, Meeting with Erhard, 8 October 1949, B115/3377, Bundesarchiv; Turner, "British Occupation Policy," 660-661; H.A. Goff, "Subject – Wolfburg Motor Works," Letter from Mechanical Engineering Industry Branch, Minden, to the Chief, Industry Division, "The Volkswagenwerk Complex and Control Council Directive 50," 11, FO 371/65114, PRO.
39. I. Turner, "British Occupation Policy," 664.
40. See, for example, *Hamburger Abendblatt*, 10 June 1958.
41. *The Times* of London, 8 January 1955.
42. See "Betr., Plenarsitzung des Deutschen Bundestages", 10/11 January 1957, B102/5196, Bundesarchiv.

the state controlled strategic economic levers through a variety of mechanisms, including the ownership and control of major industrial concerns and the building of consultative forums designed to enhance collaboration betwen state and societal actors.[43] The leading Ministry officials, all members of the CSU, were willing to make use of any appropriate instruments provided by the Nazis, although not consciously conceiving of them as such.[44] This view was compatible with the more forceful ideological position of the Christian Social Union (CSU), led by Franz Josef Strauss, who opposed Erhard's neo-liberal position. Strauss supported the proposition that the state should play a decisive interventionist role in molding industrial adjustment in the conservative "dirigiste" tradition.[45]

The Finance Ministry triumvirate of Fritz Schäffer, Alfred Hartmann, and Heinz Maria Oeftering (who was also the chairman of the supervisory board of VW), thus took a variety of positions systematically designed to stall the privatization process, and their strategy proved effective in strangling any real debate until 1955. Thereafter they emphasized economic impediments to privatization, claiming that VW was not yet ready for market competition; that the privatization scheme would need to be improved prior to implementation; and that the unresolved legal dispute would have to be conclusively settled.[46] They considered VW to be a key instrument of state policy and a symbol of the FRG's prosperity, a view supported by the firm's Director-General Heinrich Nordhoff.[47]

The most pointed and influential opposition to Erhard's plan came from the highly respected Finance Minister Schäffer. Initially passive,

---

43. Interestingly, this dominant perspective in the Finance Ministry proved most compatible with the views of both the SPD and union leadership who despite their differences on a variety of social and economic issues, shared the same views on the importance of state ownership and control of strategic economic instruments as a means of instituting both macro and micro-level policies. See, for example, *The Times*, 7 May 1962.
44. See, for example, *Hamburger Abendblatt*, 10 June 1958.
45. See Aline Kuntz, "Conservatives in Crisis: The Bavarian Christian Social Union and the Ideology of Antimodernism" (PhD thesis, Cornell University, 1987), 198-201. Kuntz argues that the CSU has always subsumed the role of the market to broader social goals and has shown little concern for individual rights in the face of state power. Rather, the CSU has emphasized the role of the state as a decisive political and economic actor in maintaining political stability and protecting domestic industry.
46. See *Die Welt*, 12 January 1957; *Industriekurier* (Düsseldorf), 3 May 1957; "Zur Frage des Eigentums am Komplex VWW," 9-11 in Bestand I-395 031-1, Adenauerstiftung, Bonn.
47. See, for example, letter from R.J. Jackling, Office of Economic Advisor, U.K. High Commission in Germany to Burns, Board of Trade, 20 November 1953, MinSupp 14/397, PRO. See also the report of Nordhoff's speech against privatization in the *Hamburger Echo*, 18 May 1957.

Schäffer slowly took a more public position on the issue, decrying the firm's sale to anyone, but particularly to foreigners, thus creating a rift between the Finance Ministry and Erhard's Economics Ministry.[48] Erhard responded by pushing the issue of privatization at the CDU congress in the spring of 1957, and he won.[49] Erhard then portrayed the general election in the following fall as a referendum over his policies, rather than those of the government, in seeking to bolster further his standing within the party. The ploy worked, as the CDU/CSU coalition won the election in a landslide and returned a third Adenauer cabinet to power. The victory was seen as a triumph for Erhard and a defeat for Schäffer.[50] It certainly signaled a new phase in the privatization issue that was finally resolved with the implementation of a scheme in 1961. Yet on reflection, according to Brumlog and Jürgens, VW's eventual privatization should not mislead us into believing that the federal government was any less influential in the company's subsequent affairs, their power being reflected in the position of federal official on the company's supervisory board.[51]

The issue of ownership was, however, only one dimension of the state's involvement with VW in the 1950s. Perhaps of greater concern in understanding that it was treated as an instrument of state policy was the nature of its relationship with the various ministries and the representatives of domestic capital and labor. VW continued to benefit from special labor contracts in this period, as it did from a series of exclusive research and development agreements with both other core automobile companies and the federal government.[52] These agreements were often designed to forestall foreign takeovers, examples being the attempted purchase of BMW by GEC in 1960, NSU by FIAT in 1968, and subsequently Daimler-Benz by Iranian investors in the 1975, when this informal consensus was formalized by legislation explicitly designed to ensure the protection of these companies from foreign takeover.[53] Furthermore, VW's lucrative

48. See *Handelsblatt*, 23 February 1955, and *Manchester Guardian*, 27 June 1957.
49. *Financial Times*, 15 May 1957.
50. *The Economist*, 5 October 1957.
51. For a discussion of the federal government's influence on the company's decision-making process see A. Thimm, "Decision-making at Volkswagen, 1972-1975," *Columbia Journal of World Business*, Spring, 1976.
52. On labor contracts, see Eva Brumlop and Ulrich Jürgens, "Rationalization and Industrial Relations in the West German Auto Industry: The Case of Volkswagen," Das Internationale Institut vergleichender Gesellschaftsforschung, Papers/ DP 83-216, Berlin, September 1983, 7. For an example concerning R&D, the Federal government offered to provide VW with a grant of DM 500 million to help pay for research and development. *Hamburger Abendblatt*, July 1960.
53. *New York Times*, 21 February 1960; 3 June 1960; 22 February 1968; 15 January 1975; 16 January 1975.

monopoly on a popular market segment was protected by a government that also encouraged core German firms to combine forces. The momentum toward mergers involving VW, NSU, Auto-Union, and Daimler-Benz was tempered only by the legal barriers preventing the merger of Daimler-Benz and VW.[54]

The story of VW is one that transcends the shift from fascism to democracy. But its public ownership means that it is a unique example in this context, only one component of the story about the formation and maintenance of the core formed in the Third Reich and sustained in the Bonn Republic, and might not alone vindicate an argument about the auto industry. But, I suggest, whether part of the core or the periphery, all other auto firms can be characterized as sustaining their relationship to the state despite the transition to liberal democracy. The following discussion attempts to justify this claim.

The starkest contrast to the favorable treatment of VW is that of Opel, which dominated the German automobile industry in the prewar period. In an insulated internal market protected by tariffs and quotas, Opel repeatedly accounted for over 50 percent of car sales.[55] With the exception of Ford, the remainder of the German auto industry was divided between a number of small German producers, such as Wanderer, Horch, Audi, and Zchopauer (all eventually merged to form Auto-Union in 1932), which were trying to institute mass production principles, and specialist producers, such as Daimler-Benz and BMW, which were struggling to survive as they sought both to create market niches and attract lucrative government armaments contracts.

Opel sustained its market dominance despite the onset of the depression in the early 1930s. The new Nazi regime's recognition of Opel's significance was reflected in its initially tolerant treatment of the company. Its market strength meant that Opel could dictate the terms of standardization as the Nazis sought a pragmatic means of rapidly rationalizing the automobile industry.[56] Opel offered the cheapest German car available on the market, selling about 150,000 of their cheaper units per annum (those ranging in price from

---

54. See, for instance, *Frankfurter Allgemeine*, 26 October 1964.
55. See "Organizational and Management Basic Data Book: Ford of Germany," Cologne, Germany, Fordwerke AG, 1951-1952, AR-75-63-430:93, Ford Industrial Files. In the late 1920s Ford and General Motors occupied positions in the German market that were opposite those they each held in the English market, where Ford was a more significant force as a producer and General Motors' subsidiary was of relatively minor importance.
56. See E.J. Palumbo, "Germany 1948: Economic and Political Review. Survey of German Vehicle Industry," Appendix, Exhibit B, 15 April 1948, AR-75-63-430:86, Ford Industrial Archives, 4-12.

RM1,450 to RM1,650), and therefore seemed the most likely firm to achieve Hitler's goal of producing a car for RM1,000.[57]

By 1935 Opel was the major governmental supplier, commanding over 42 percent of the domestic market share, and, despite government ordered price cuts, the company earned net profits in excess of RM35 million.[58] Prohibitive legislation stipulated that profits from lucrative government contracts were to be reinvested at their German plants. Designed to achieve capacity growth, this legislation ensured that Opel could not send its surplus capital abroad.[59]

In contrast, Ford had always been considered dispensable to the Nazi government plans and had suffered extensively from state discrimination, initially being barred from involvement in the VW project – and thereby from access to all government resources. Then Ford was excluded from all government contracts, which constituted the overwhelming percentage of domestic production, when all their production was prohibited by virtue of not being accorded a certificate of German origin.[60] Opel, unlike Ford, experienced no problems being thus certified, despite the paradox that far more of Ford's shares were German-owned than were Opel's.[61] Subsidized by state aid, Opel was willing to undertake relatively risky and unrewarding ventures to maintain cordial relations with the authorities, such as an agreement in 1938 to export cars to Great Britain at below German prices in order to secure valuable foreign currency.[62] Accordingly, Opel was then responsible for over 50 percent of car and 24 percent of commercial vehicle exports.[63]

Yet this cordial relationship between Opel and Nazi officials was dependent upon a coincidence of interests. Opel's involvement in the VW project was initially considered to be pivotal to its success, but once Daimler-Benz and BMW executives managed to convince

---

57. See ibid., 39.
58. See "The Importance of German Passenger Cars and Truck Factories, 1935," Accession 38, Box 33, Edison Institute, and letter Diestel to Sorensen, 2 March 1936, Accession 38, Box 33, ibid.
59. Allan Nevins and Frank E. Hill, *Ford: Decline and Rebirth, 1933-1962* (New York, 1962), 99.
60. For an extensive discussion of Ford's relationship with the German state over four decades see S. Reich, *The Fruits of Fascism*, 107-146.
61. See letter by Albert to Reichsverband der Automobilindustrie, 13 January 1936, Accession 38, Box 28, Edison Institute; and Mira Wilkins and Frank E. Hill, *American Business Abroad: Ford on Six Continents* (Detroit, 1964), 270.
62. *Business Week*, 25 June 1938.
63. Ministry of Economic Warfare, "German Motor Industry: A Summary," from 745015RG 165, Regional File, 1933-44, Germany 4330, Box 1255, 14 October 1940, BICO 451.I, Office of Military Government of the U.S. (OMGUS), Imperial War Museum, 11.

state officials that the project should be implemented by the public sector rather than a private sector consortium, Opel lost its influence and the firm was ostracized by competitors and treated with increasing hostility by the Nazis.[64] Nevertheless, Opel's management persevered in trying to maintain a cordial relationship with the Nazi government, and was therefore eager to fulfill government orders.[65] But by 1935 the relationship started to disintegrate when Opel quarreled with a government demand that it build its new plant at Brandenburg, located east of the Elbe, for fear that it would lose the plant in the event of war. Opel's management considered this site strategically vulnerable, being geographically isolated from large resource centers and Opel's other plants. Furthermore, there were few geographical barriers to thwart an invasion from the east. The Nazi authorities nevertheless insisted that the plant be built in Brandenburg at Opel's expense, consistent with the implementation of Germany's *Lebensraum* policy.[66]

Relations between firm and state worsened when Opel could no longer supply military trucks at the government's rapidly increasing rate of demand. It broke into open hostility when Opel failed to fulfill a government contract for 10,000 half-track vehicles. Ford, the longtime victim of the Nazi state's open hostility, was then offered the chance to restart production, and subsequently successfully completed Opel's contract.[67] Ford, the firm traditionally unfavorably compared to Opel, therefore had, at last, proved the more "cooperative" of the two – a most damning indictment in the eyes of the Nazi authorities.[68] Opel's two largest plants, at Rüsselheim and Branden-

64. Letter Franz Popp to Wilhelm Kissel, Archiv der Daimler-Benz AG, Bestand Kissel VII/5, in Hamburger Stiftung Archive. And see the letter written by Albert Pietzsch, Präsident der Industrie-und Handelskammer, München, Leiter der Reichswirtschaftskammer to Generaldirektor Popp of BMW, 2 June 1937. A second source for this evidence is the comment attributed to the influential Jacob Werlin to Hitler that in the case of a national works it would be better if firms with an American orientation were excluded from the process in "Besprechung am 21.7.1936 im RDA in der Volkswagen-Angelegenheit", Hamburger Stiftung Archive. A third source is a letter written by Werlin to Popp on 31 May 1937 with the same theme to be found in File 16, Volkswagen Popp, Archive of the VW Project, Bochum.
65. Wilkins and F.E. Hill, *American Business Abroad*, 283.
66. Opel's fears were realized a decade later with the destruction of the plant and the loss of its contents to the invading Soviet forces. See USSBS, Munitions Division, "German Motor Vehicle Industry Report," 3 November 1945, 6; OMGUS 451, Box 326, Military Field Branch, National Archives and Records Administration, Washington, DC.
67. See "Report of the German Company" prepared by the Office of Lord Perry in "Historical Data" (A), CF, ID, Germany Wartime, Wilkins Personal Files.
68. Note that S. Reich, *The Fruits of Fascism*, includes an entire case study chapter

burg, were subsequently seized by the state and integrated into the German war economy under the new management of Nordhoff, the same man who subsequently became the first postwar managing director of VW.[69]

Although the treatment accorded to Opel by the state in the opening years of the Third Reich thus differed drastically from that accorded Ford, it converged over time because both were foreign direct investors. At both firms the indigenous management was eventually replaced by political cadres, the hierarchical "leadership principle" was instituted, and both were reclassified as foreign property, making them subject to discriminatory measures. Neither were compensated by the Nazi authorities for war damages incurred, and at Opel, unlike at Ford, the war damages were extensive as its major plants were destroyed.[70] Opel thus encountered numerous problems getting their production restarted after the war, giving VW a crucial advantage in those early years.[71] When Opel's production did recommence, the Allied government insisted that it concentrate exclusively on unsubsidized, loss-generating foreign sales, denying Opel the crucial capital needed for reinvestment in a period of surplus demand.[72] The ravages of war and Nazi and Allied policies therefore combined to leave Opel floundering in comparison to its chief rival – a situation that grew worse over time. The company that held between 40 percent and 52 percent of the German market in the immediate prewar period fell to 19 percent in the late 1940s (compared to VW's then share of 25 percent) and bottomed-out at 17 percent in 1952.[73] When the Allied and embryonic Bonn governments refused to provide Opel with any comparable financial support to that accorded to VW, General Motors then provided the funding to begin the process of its reconstruction.[74] The vacuum created by Opel's lost output, however, had been filled by VW, and Opel never again approached its prewar market share – even trailing behind the formerly much smaller Ford in the 1950s.[75]

Even this superficial description of events at Opel between 1933 and the late 1950s is indicative of the firm's precipitous decline.

---

devoted to examining the evolution of Ford's relationship with the German state in the four decades originating in the 1920s.
69. D. Wilkins and F.E. Hill, *American Business Abroad*, 331.
70. Ibid., 345; and E.J. Palumbo, "Germany 1948," Ford Industrial Archives, 12.
71. D. Wilkins and F.E. Hill, *American Business Abroad*, 346.
72. G.S. Hibberson and A.T. Platt, "Fordwerke AG Cologne Audit Report, August 1949," AR-83-69-891:4, Ford Industrial Archives, 55.
73. "Organizational and Management Book."
74. D. Wilkins and F.E. Hill, *American Business Abroad*, 391.
75. E. Nevins and F.E. Hill, *Ford: Decline and Rebirth*, 402.

Opel's relationship with the state in the Third Reich was contingent upon sustaining a mutuality of interest that inevitably ended. Opel's inability to expand its capacity at the exponential rate demanded by the Nazis precipitated its shift from the core to the periphery and, with it, the onset of discriminatory state policies that marked the beginning of its swift and steep economic decline.

Daimler-Benz represents an interesting contrast to Opel. Far from its success of the last two decades, Daimler-Benz struggled in the aftermath of World War I and was reliant on the financial assistance of the Deutsche Bank throughout the 1920s and early 1930s.[76] The bank's chair, Emil Georg von Stauß, considered Daimler-Benz's capacity for military production critical to the eventual rejuvenation of Germany's armaments industry. Daimler-Benz's management even approached government officials in the 1920s with the suggestion that the government defy the terms of the Versailles Treaty and recommence armaments production, but the idea was rejected.[77]

Daimler-Benz's senior management, led by Wilhelm Kissel, actively supported the NSDAP in the early 1930s.[78] With the Nazi accession, Daimler-Benz became influential in formulating state policy, as epitomized by their formentation of the idea that Ford and Opel be excluded from involvement in the VW project.[79] The company became an able and willing military producer, providing Daimler-Benz with a lucrative source of revenue in the Third Reich when the Bank der Deutschen Luftfahrt subsidized the mass production of Messerschmidt engines.[80] Max Kruk and Gerold Lingnau's (company-sponsored) clinical treatment of the history of Daimler-Benz emphasizes that the company was subjected to state coercion and therefore an unwilling partner to the state's demands.[81]

76. For a discussion of the fiscal relationship between Daimler-Benz and the Deutsche Bank see H. Pohl et al., *Die Daimler-Benz AG in den Jahren 1933 bis 1945*. For a discussion of the political implications of this relationship see K. H. Roth, "Der Weg zum guten Stern des 'Dritten Reichs'," 28-40.
77. The Daimler-Benz officials explained that the economic health of their company was the dominant motivating factor. See letter from Kissel to von Schleicher, 1925, Hamburger Stiftung Archive.
78. For an extensive discussion of this contentious point see K.H. Roth, "Der Weg zum guten Stern," 71-103.
79. See for example the exchange of letters between Popp of BMW and Kissel, Archiv der Daimler-Benz AG., Bestand Kissel VII/5, in Hamburger Stiftung Archive.
80. For details concerning Daimler-Benz's military aero-engines see OMGUS, Decartelization Branch, Economic Division, "The Automotive Industry of Germany," 31 December 1946, Box 479/775092, Automotive Industry Folder, Military Field Branch, National Archives and Records Administration, Washington DC, 3.
81. Max Kruk and Gerold Lingnau, *100 Jahre Daimler-Benz: Das Unternehmen* (Mainz, 1986), 133-159.

Yet their own figures demonstrate the lucrative nature of government contracts, which peaked in 1943, and alternative sources suggest that the company may have been more willing partners than Kruk and Lingnau concede.[82] Kruk and Lingnau explain the record growth in the size of the labor force to meet this heightened demand by focusing on the employment of female workers as replacements.[83] Both Bernard Bellon's and Jörg Mettke's examination of state-firm cooperation on the use of slave labor in armaments production at Daimler-Benz plants provide, however, rather more unsympathetic, contentious views.[84] Both offer substantial historical data to corroborate the claim that Daimler-Benz was keen to use slave labor (Jews and foreign workers), explaining the apparent anomaly that the firm's employment figures reached record levels while increasing numbers of Germans were being conscripted for military service.

Another detailed, systematic study of Daimler-Benz is that by Karl Heinz Roth.[85] Roth's study includes hundreds of pages on indictments leveled against Daimler-Benz on the use of slave labor, which he suggests may have amounted to as many as 50,000 people – ten times as many as the company's sponsored historical study on this subject by Pohl, Habeth, and Brüninghaus concedes.[86] Specific data concerning the behavior of company officials towards slave laborers at "operation goldfish," Daimler-Benz's largest dispersal site, certainly provides incriminating evidence, including their recommendation to Nazi officials toward the end of the war that workers should be killed when no longer needed.[87]

Specific claims made by Mettke and Roth in particular, such as those concerning the cooperative relationship between Daimler-Benz's management and officials at concentration camps like Buchenwald, have met with conspicuous silence by German company officials. The evidence suggests that Daimler-Benz fostered a close working relationship with the state, reflected in their influence on the treatment of other firms, their willingness to pursue state goals in the armaments industry, and their treatment of foreign labor.

---

82. Ibid., 324.
83. For the figures on growth in employment see ibid. For the claim that so many replacements were women see, for example, ibid., 155.
84. See B.P. Bellon, *Mercedes in Peace and War;* Jörg R. Mettke, "Die Herren nahmen nur die Kräftigsten" in *Der Spiegel,* 7 April 1986, 79-104.
85. K.H. Roth, "Der Weg zum guten Stern."
86. H. Pohl et al., *Die Daimler-Benz AG.*
87. See Rainer Fröbe, "Wie bei den alten Ägyptern: Die Belegung des Daimler-Benz-Flugmotorenwerks Genshagen nach Obrigheim am Neckar 1944/1945," in K.H. Roth (ed.), *Das Daimler-Benz Buch,* 452-53 and Mettke, "Die Herren nahmen nur die Kräftigsten."

Claims that company policy was pursued as a result of state coercion therefore appear unfounded, given the extensive nature of contrary evidence drawn from company documents.

By the end of the war, Daimler-Benz had not been as fortunate as VW, having had much of its property destroyed by strategic bombing.[88] It received a further blow when its owner, Friedrich Flick, was arrested and convicted as a war criminal in 1947 for having been a member of Hitler's elite – as the owner of the huge Flick armaments combine, of which Daimler-Benz was just one component. Flick was found guilty of being responsible for plundering large sections of the industrial wealth of eastern European and domestic Jewry, backed by the Nazi state; of then destroying that property when the regime's downfall became inevitable; and of enthusiastically using slave labor in his plants.[89] His combine was seized under Allied law and dismantled, while Flick himself was stripped of all his property and sentenced to seven years imprisonment. The new Bonn government, however, soon rehabilitated Flick. The War Crimes Court's sentence was flagrantly ignored; he served only three years in prison, being released in 1950, and the government returned much of Flick's former property to him, including his dominant 39 percent holding in Daimler-Benz.[90]

With his renewed position and wealth, Flick and his managing-director, Fritz Könecke, sought to rebuild Daimler-Benz, based primarily on production at the large Stuttgart plant. The firm manufactured its traditional luxury sedans primarily for export. As a core firm, Daimler-Benz's management had privileged access to state officials, reflected in the fact that, apart from VW, Daimler-Benz officials appear to have been the only auto firm executives who had regular, formalized contact with government officials to discuss the formulation and adjustment of company policies – making accusations of a collusive relationship more plausible.[91] Similarly, Daimler-Benz officials shared an intimate relationship with the leaders of the CDU, who were the dominant partners in the governing coalition.[92] En-

---

88. See reports on the destruction of Sindelfingen and Gaggenau in "Report on the Visit to Daimler-Benz AG at Stuttgart-Untertürkheim" 28, BIOS Final Report 35, BIOS B, Box 1. For the details demonstrating that the idea that VW rose like a "phoenix from the ashes" was not true see S. Reich, *The Fruits of Fascism*, 147-201.
89. See Klaus Drobisch, "Flick und die Nazis" in *Zeitschrift für Geschichtswissenschaft*, 14 (1966), Heft 3, 380-397; and *The New York Times*, 12 April 1958.
90. See *The New York Times*, 15 January 1975.
91. The minutes of these meetings are extensive and the formal records are distributed throughout several locations in the Bundesarchiv, Koblenz. For just one example see Pollak, "Besuch des Herrn Dr. Könecke beim Herrn Minister," 28 May 1957, B102/5196, Bundesarchiv.
92. Aline Kuntz, "Conservatives in Crisis," 198ff.

couraged by the new German government, the firm entered into a variety of patent, research, marketing, and sales agreements with other core manufacturers in order to protect themselves and their partners from competitive American subsidiaries. What followed was a systematic attempt to tie core German firms together in a network of agreements and mergers that guaranteed their corporate independence from foreign economic interests and their economic supremacy over multinational subsidiaries at home. Daimler-Benz and VW proved to be the two pivotal firms in pursuing this strategy, supported by both government officials and major German banks.

This process of integrating the network of core German producers began with Daimler-Benz's merger with the ailing firm of Auto-Union in 1958. This move was justified on the grounds that the enlarged company would be better prepared for the heightened competition stimulated by the formation of the EC, even though Daimler-Benz was a niche producer with no direct competitor in this expanded market.[93] Unfortunately for Daimler-Benz, this merger was followed by the media's exposure of members of the company's management, including Könecke, bribing high-ranking government officials in exchange for government assistance in generating foreign orders. Even Adenauer's personal secretary, Hans Kilb, was indicted, suggesting that the firm had both formal and informal privileged channels of access to the government.[94]

In the year following these revelations about Daimler-Benz it became evident that BMW, characterized by incompetent management and capital shortages, faced impending bankruptcy and the threat of liquidation or a foreign takeover. BMW's directors thus turned to Daimler-Benz in hope of a merger, proposing a deal whereby a planned reduction in their basic capital – by writing off the company's losses at the expense of the shareholders – would allow Daimler-Benz to buy the new cheaper company with the assistance of the three major banks by forming an ownership consortium.[95] Daimler-Benz responded with a lower counter-offer, which BMW rejected, and domestic ownership appeared threatened when the General Electric Comapny (GEC) of Britain then made a takeover offer for BMW.[96] Daimler-Benz could not match GEC's offer, but the CSU Bavarian state government temporarily purchased the company, justifying their action "out of local pride and concern for the company's 15,000 employees," although there was

93. *The New York Times*, 12 April 1958.
94. Ibid., 15 November 1958.
95. Ibid., 10 November 1959.
96. Ibid., 12 December 1959.

no evidence to indicate that a GEC purchase would threaten local employment.[97] The Bavarian state government then orchestrated the subsequent purchase of BMW by the Augsburg-Nuremberg Machine Company (MAN), which made an identical offer to GEC's. Patriotic reasons tipped the balance in MAN's favor, with the CSU's Bavarian leader and federal government defence minister, Franz Josef Strauss, exercising his influence as the chief negotiator with BMW on behalf of MAN.[98] This purchase marked the start of BMW's rehabilitation.

Details about the state's treatment of BMW, as opposed to that accorded Borgward, reveal much about the relative treatment accorded to core and peripheral firms in this period. Historically, BMW's pre-fascist development shares many parallels with that of Daimler-Benz. BMW was considered a specialist producer (of luxury sedans and motor bikes) and like Daimler-Benz, it suffered from the terms of the Versailles Treaty, which forbade armaments production in Germany. Like Daimler-Benz, BMW was financially supported by von Stauß and the Deutsche Bank in the 1920s because it, too, was considered a crucial component of the "South German auto bloc" that had to be sustained in order to guarantee the capacity for future military production. Like Daimler-Benz, BMW's officials also proved to be influential with government officials in the formulation of the terms of the VW project; BMW's managing director Popp repeatedly claimed credit for both the exclusion of the American subsidiaries from the project and as the originator of the idea that the project's control should be shifted from a private consortium to the public sector through the DAF's assumption of ownership.[99] BMW was an influential and supportive arms producer during the 1930s and 1940s, and its plants were seized at the end of the war when they fell under American control. The plants and their contents were

---

97. Ibid., 21 February 1960.
98. Ibid., 3 June 1960. Note that Strauss repeatedly expressed dissatisfaction with Erhard's neo-liberal economic policies. Strauss explicitly favored an activist state policy designed to mold industrial adjustment – a view that found support among factions of the CDU. Strauss criticized, for example, the Federal government's lack of decisive action in assisting the steel and coal industry during periods of crises and, supported by the CSU, argued for an enlarged state role during the recession of the 1960s.
99. See letter Franz Popp to Wilhelm Kissel, Archiv der Daimler-Benz AG, Bestand Kissel VII/5; or the letter sent by Popp to the Reichsverband der Deutschen Automobilindustrie suggesting that the RDA should oppose Ford's involvement, 8 May 1934, both from the Hamburger Stiftung Archive. The strongest supporting evidence for Popp's claim to have originated the idea of the DAF's ownership is found in a letter from Popp to Werlin, 29 July 1936, Archiv des Dokumentationzentrums der Staatlichen Archivverwaltung der DDR, DK 713.

returned to BMW's owners (who renewed civilian production), however, because the firm was under private, not public ownership.

As already suggested, unlike the success stories generally associated with the *Wirtschaftswunder* (Economic Miracle), the first fifteen years of BMW's postwar development proved disastrous. A Daimler-Benz study of BMW suggested that the basis of BMW's problems lay in a combination of incompetent management decisions and a poor product line. After the 1961 rescue (when BMW held less than two percent of the market), the company's fortunes began to reverse, and by 1967 its share of the domestic market had doubled. That year, while the German auto industry experienced its first recession in the postwar period, BMW proved to be highly profitable. This success provided the basis for expansion, and BMW purchased Glas GmbH in order to extend its range of products, helped by both the federal government and the Bavarian state government, the latter providing DM50 million to finance BMW supported by both IG Metall and the Banks.[100] At a time when widespread accusations were made against German auto producers of inflating their prices, inefficient management, and a lack of foresight, BMW took a major step in securing a prosperous future by acquiring new capabilities that expanded its operations into new market niches.[101]

The contrasting example concerns Borgward, a Bremen-based company that shared some important attributes with both BMW and Daimler-Benz as a low-volume, specialist producer. Founded in 1905, the firm consisted of three production plants under the personal ownership of Carl Borgward. Borgward had grown from a components producer to an auto manufacturer who specialized in the production of high quality (if not high-priced) sedans and commercial vehicles, noted for its innovative designs reflected in models such as the "Isabella".[102] Borgward was generally described as a benevolent autocrat – reminiscent of the *'Herr im Haus'* syndrome – and a loner who maintained tight control and had only a limited amount of contact with other producers.

Borgward was the largest automobile producer in the industrial town of Bremen, employing approximately 8,000 people at the start

---

100. *The Times*, 5 October 1967. Note that in 1967 the company awarded shareholders a 12 percent dividend as registration of new BMW cars in Germany rose by 27 percent. Worker productivity rose, as did the number of new dealerships rose, as did export turnover which increased by DM30 million
101. Article from *Hannoversche Presse* quoted in a bound volume of *The German Tribune*, 1966, 12.
102. Borgward's creativity is indicated by the fact that he produced 50 models in 40 years – an engineering accomplishment but a sign of economic ineptitude on his part. *The Times*, 7 February 1961.

of the war. During the war the firm produced over 9,000 heavy goods vehicles and 16,000 armored cars and LKWs.[103] Furthermore, Borgward employed one of the highest percentages of foreign laborers, forced laborers, and prisoners-of-war of any auto producer in Germany, peaking at an aggregate total of 65 percent.[104] Borgward therefore appears to have been one of the pillars of the state armaments program during the Third Reich – and the company's subsequent liquidation provides evidence that appears anomalous to my claims.[105] Yet, characteristic of such conservatives, the owner disdained involvement with the Nazi state and maintained only a peripheral role in the peak associations.

Towards the end of the war, Borgward's plants were largely destroyed by strategic bombing, necessitating complete recapitalization.[106] By 1961 it was the fifth largest German automobile company, commanding about five percent of the market (sales of about 100,000 cars per year) and employing 20,000 people, 23 percent of the city of Bremen's total labor force.[107] Yet its incapacity to either fully establish itself in an insulated market niche or to become a mass producer left Borgward in a precarious position.[108] Under these circumstances it was inevitable that Borgward would run into financial problems. What was surprising was the rapidity with which these problems embroiled the firm. In the space of a few months in 1961 the firm went from financial stability to bankruptcy, with debts of $27.5 million, as the same industry-wide cyclical market downturn that had afflicted BMW caught Borgward in a cash-flow crisis. Like BMW, Borgward then faced the imminent threat of liquidation. Yet, it should be recalled that Borgward then commanded over twice as large a market share as BMW and, unlike BMW, had excellent production facilities – and therefore seemed better placed to prosper. Borgward's main flaw, according to analysts, was its poor management – one easily rectified under new ownership. As was the case with BMW, Borgward could have been purchased and restructured; unlike BMW it already had technically sound products and could, therefore, presumably be restored to profitability sooner.

103. See Ministry of Economic Warfare, "German Motor Industry," 28.
104. See Ulrich Kubisch and Volker Janssen, *Borgward – Ein Blick zurück auf das Wirtschaftswunder: Werksalltag und ein Automythos* (Berlin, 1984), 30-31.
105. Ibid., 27. Note that, unlike other industrialists who used a lower percentage of forced laborers, Borgward was not imprisoned for their use at his plant because the Allies considered their use by Borgward was involuntary and their treatment acceptable.
106. *The New York Times*, 29 July 1961.
107. *The Times*, 14 June 1960 and 31 January 1961.
108. U. Kubisch and V. Janssen, *Borgward*, 114.

Borgward himself, however, historically shared a different relationship with the banks, federal government, and other auto producers than the owners of BMW, and his personal appeal to them for help was made in vain. His failure to sell the company intact to another private producer led to its purchase by the state of Bremen, just as the Bavarian state government had done with BMW. Borgward was removed from control. The state restructured the company at a cost of $15 million in public funds, but intended to relinquish ownership of it as soon as possible by either selling it to new owners or returning control to the former owner if he could find the necessary capital.[109] But none of the industry's members, nor the banks or the federal government, were willing to assist Borgward in regaining control of his company. The Bremen state government then unsuccessfully appealed to bankers, industrialists, and politicians to purchase the company from them because, as the smallest German state, Bremen did not have the resources to sustain its financing of the company. Without an alternative, they then had to let it lapse into liquidation. Attempts to revive Borgward by an association of customers, dealers, and employees failed, and it was declared bankrupt. Some plants were sold off to save jobs, but thousands of workers were left unemployed, and local debts to over 150 creditors amounted to over DM200 million – creating a devastating ripple effect throughout the whole local economy.[110]

If one examines the Borgward case in isolation, the decision of bankers, industrialists, and the federal government seems reasonable when adjudged in purely economic terms. Borgward was a mismanaged company with outstanding debts and an ill-defined position in the industry's market structure. It had a quality product, but a small market share and a limited potential for growth. In social terms, because of the resulting employment problems, the demise of Borgward could be treated simply as an example of the failings of the *Soziale Marktwirtschaft* or an illustration of the preeminence of liberal principles.[111] Yet, when considered in comparative terms, this response is unable effectively to explain why the federal government went to such great lengths to save BMW – not only from liquidation, but from foreign ownership – and ignored Borgward, a company in much better economic condition where, conversely, the

---

109. *The Times*, 18 February 1961. See also *The New York Times*, 29 July 1961.
110. *The Times*, 31 July 1961. For a full discussion of the nature of the company's decline see U. Kubisch and V. Janssen, *Borgward*, especially 112-125.
111. For a discussion of these conflicting interpretations see Wilhelm Eberwein and Jochen Tholen, "Der Borgward-Konkurs im Jahre 1961" in *Arbeitsmarkt Bremen* (Bremen: Kooperation Universität, Arbeitskammer), 10.

local effects of the firm's closure were much more dramatic. But an explanation emphasizing the significance of core and peripheral membership does explain this anomaly.

Borgward had served the German state as an armaments producer, but its owner, an authoritarian conservative, had refused to be integrated into the Nazi state apparatus, therefore remaining on the political periphery during the Third Reich. Like many conservatives, Borgward endured the Nazis once they seized power but did not support them. His cooperation did not hide his contempt for the Nazis, and, as a result, he was tolerated by, but never integrated into, the decision-making structure of the Third Reich. Borgward therefore never shared, as part of the network of industrialists, bankers, and government officials, the pattern of relations that formed the safety net for core producers. Edwin Hartrich develops this theme in the wider context of his discussion of the postwar German banking community's lack of support for maverick entrepreneurial capitalists.[112]

The federal government's considered neglect thus led to the downfall of Borgward, despite the efforts of the state government of Bremen and evidence of the company's continued financial viability.[113] BMW was in a worse economic situation with inferior products, a smaller market share, and its less-pressing employment problems. But it had an advantage over Borgward in one crucial respect: BMW had traditionally been part of the core of the German auto industry from its formative period in the early days of the Third Reich, and it had cultivated and sustained a close relationship with politicians, bureaucrats, bankers, and industrialists, which it had maintained in the postwar period. When in need, BMW could rely on this network while Borgward could not.

In the 1960s the process of integration of core firms accelerated. After Daimler-Benz failed to purchase BMW, its management tried to increase the company's foreign sales and secure the firm's domestic market share through network agreements, both abroad and at home. Temporary agreements with Curtis-Wright to build jet engines and Studebaker to market Mercedes cars in the U.S. were complemented by a strategy designed to deny American firms a market share at home, where Daimler-Benz sold a controlling interest of

112. Edwin Hartrich, *The Fourth and Richest Reich* (New York, 1980), 206-213.
113. An additional factor in the Borgward case may have been that the Bremen state government was composed of an SPD majority and the Federal government, led by Erhard, was composed of members of the CDU. The CDU leadership may have hoped that the demise of Borgward in Bremen, the smallest state in the FRG, would increase the local unpopularity of the SPD and therefore provide the CDU with political advantage in the next state elections. This is only conjecture without substantial empirical support.

Auto-Union to VW in 1963 (giving VW and Daimler-Benz a formal link).[114] The German government then encouraged VW to assume full ownership of Auto-Union two years later.[115] To maintain this active cooperation between Daimler-Benz and VW, however, the government suggested that they pool patents and cooperate on basic R&D.[116] As Daimler-Benz's and VW's relationship grew stronger, it stimulated discussion concerning a possible merger between the two companies, but the terms of the law that privatized VW in 1961 did not permit private institutions or organizations to hold stock in the firm, which imposed an impenetrable barrier to any merger. The two companies did, however, create a joint-stock company to fund the coordination of their R&D and safety projects in April 1966.[117] The terms of the agreement made provisions for the joint company to buy parts together, to manufacture parts for both companies in either firm's respective foreign plants, and to sell products through either firm's dealer agencies.[118] Nordhoff left no doubt as to parties' motivation behind the agreement, pointedly suggesting that this agreement "was designed to counter the 'overpowering economic weight' of the big American car manufacturers."[119] It gave VW, Auto-Union, and Daimler-Benz the chance to compete head on against the American subsidiaries in separate market segments without substantial indigenous competition. The pattern of integrating Auto-Union into the prosperous German core by merger was replicated by VW's purchase of NSU, designed to prevent Fiat or Honda from buying it and acquiring the revolutionary Wankel engine technology. VW subsequently merged its NSU subsidiary with Auto-Union to form Audi-NSU. A further set of agreements between VW and Porsche, and the merger of BMW and Glas, only served further to tighten the close relationship among core firms.[120]

The preceding description thus allows us to categorize auto producers in Germany in accordance with the distinction made earlier between core and peripheral firms, as reflected in Table 3.2.

---

114. See *The New York Times*, 30 December 1964.
115. George Heaton, "Government Structural Policies and the Automobile Industry," a paper presented at the Hakone Prince conference in Japan under the auspices of "The Future of the Automobile" Program, 16-20 May 1982, 10.
116. James Womack and Daniel Jones, "The Competitive Significance of Government Technology Policy in the Auto Sector," a research paper published by the "Future of the Automobile" Program, 8.
117. *The Wall Street Journal*, 11 and 25 April 1966.
118. Ibid., 30 June 1966.
119. *The New York Times*, 30 June 1966.
120. Ibid., 23 August 1966 and 10 January 1967.

Table 3.2: The Firms in the Core and Periphery of the German Automobile Industry Corporate – State Relations

	Core	Periphery
Membership Characteristics	Public Firms Coopted Partners	Multinationals Paternal Industrialists
Labor Relations	Formal Legalistic	Informal Market Oriented
Relationship to State	Cordial Cooperative	Aloof Constrained
Relationship to State Goals	Shared Interest	Diverse but Generally Conflictual
Prospects for Prosperity	Extensive	Limited

Conclusion

Analysts have often described the structure of Germany's postwar economy as corporatist. They suggest that the origins of this structure can be traced back to the emergent structure of German capitalism in the late nineteenth century. There is, however, a significant difference between the generalized claim that the structure of the relationship between the state, society, and the economy is corporatist, and one that an economy is segmented within or between sectors, e.g., that one component of a sector tangibly benefits from a discriminatory structure that replicates aspects of corporatism, while the other component replicates a liberal economy whose members suffer from tangible discrimination by the state, by other components of capital, and by labor. I argue that the latter characterization is more representative of the relationship between the state and the economy in the case of the German auto industry.

Therefore, this chapter concludes by suggesting that the fascist legacy for the structure of postwar German capitalism was evident in two respects. In general terms, it introduced the concept of the discriminatory state, one that was prejudiced in its treatment of firms, creating and sustaining rival operating conditions contingent upon historical, non-economic factors. Fascism thus divided capital. More specifically, for those then favored by the state, the legacy included a series of cumulative fiscal advantages that created, in its strongest form, the basis for economic prosperity in the postwar period, or, in its weakest form, a safety net.

This argument may not be sustainable in an examination of other German sectors, although a comparable argument appears feasible for the textile industry.[121] But even if it is not applicable in general, the fact that it appears relevant to the biggest and most important sector in the first two decades of the Bonn Republic suggests that it is significant in understanding the dynamics of postwar German capitalism.

---

121. See Werner Hagemann, "Zur Entwicklung der Bekleidungsindustrie," in Ernst Melzer (ed.), *Die Bekleidungsindustrie* (Darmstadt, 1955), 1-15.

Chapter 4

❖

GERMAN BIG BUSINESS AND THE RETURN TO THE WORLD MARKET AFTER WORLD WAR II*

Reinhard Neebe

At the end of World War II, the German economy found itself in an unprecedentedly bleak situation. Industrial production in 1946 amounted to just 23 percent of the 1939 level. Twenty percent of all commercial buildings and productive capital, 40 percent of all transport capacity, and 25 percent of all residential property had been destroyed in the war. The situation was aggravated further by the near total collapse of passenger and freight transport in the area of the former German Reich. The industrial and commercial supremacy in Europe that Germany had enjoyed for half a century seemed to have been lost irretrievably through World War II.[1]

After the unconditional surrender, the Allied military government assumed absolute political power, including the authority to control the German economy. Under these circumstances, German foreign

---

* For the translation of this paper from the German, I thank John Larew.
1. See Gerd Hardach, *Deutschland in der Weltwirtschaft 1870-1970* (Frankfurt/New York, 1977), 54; Werner Abelshauser, *Wirtschaft in Westdeutschland 1945-1948. Rekonstruktion und Wachstumsbedingungen in der amerikanischen und britischen Zone* (Stuttgart, 1975).

trade after 1945 could develop only within the guidelines laid down by the respective occupying powers. In the eastern zone, the Soviets built up the structures of a centrally planned economy, while the economic reconstruction in the western zones proceeded mainly according to the wishes of the United States.

As the dominant world power after World War II, the United States considered the creation of a new liberal world economy a central political goal. The collapse of the world economy in the Great Depression and the fragmentation of the international monetary system into several competing monetary blocs in the period before World War II[2] led to a new system of international economic cooperation. Under the leadership of Secretary of State Cordell Hull, the United States had already begun in the mid-1930s to lay the groundwork for a reconstruction of a liberal, multilateral trading regime by compelling its trading partners in bilateral treaties to accept the "most favored nation" principle. This principle formed the basis of the General Agreement on Tariffs and Trade (GATT) organization, which was founded in 1947 in Geneva to promote trade liberalization through multilateral agreements to reduce tariffs and non-tariff barriers. The recasting of the international payments system in the Bretton Woods agreement of 1944, which provided for freely convertible currencies at fixed exchange rates with the dollar as the international reserve currency, acted as guarantor of stable economic growth under American hegemony until the end of the 1960s.

In the American vision, Europe was to play a key role in shaping this New World Order; the liberalization of trade and a reduction of protectionist barriers among the European nations were considered indispensable preconditions for economic prosperity. With the beginning of the Cold War, the proclamation of the Truman doctrine, and the setting forth of the Marshall Plan of 1947, Western Europe became the cornerstone of the American policy of containment, which sought to use economic means, among others, to halt the advance of communism. The subsequent development of commerce and trade was determined to a large degree by the East-West conflict and the formation of a new bipolar world system between the United States and the Soviet Union.[3]

From the German point of view, the significance of reintegration into the world economy for a successful reconstruction of Germany and Europe was evident from the very beginning. The preamble to

---

2. Charles P. Kindleberger, *The World in Depression, 1929-1939* (Berkeley, 1973); see also note 32.
3. See note 32.

the export-import control plan of March 1946 for the *Länderregierungen* (regional governments) of the US zone stated:

> The reintegration of German foreign trade is of inestimable importance for the maintenance and employment of overpopulated Germany in its present form and economic structure ... .German foreign trade is an important component of the European economy, which cannot develop without it in the way necessary for all the people of the world. But German foreign trade can only prosper and serve its vital function if it is freed in greater measure from the restrictions which have so far been thought necessary ... .The merchants of the world have to resume their old business connections if the catastrophe of the war is to be overcome ... .For the entire foreign trade, initiative of private enterprise has to be employed on as large a scale as possible. There can be no involvement of state import and export organizations.[4]

Nevertheless, it took a long time before regular German foreign trade could start again. At the beginning of 1947 in the British-American zone, the Joint Export Import Agency (JEIA) was founded and granted a monopoly on foreign trade; it remained responsible for all foreign trade agreements until 1949. All export deals needed the special permission of the JEIA, and most importantly, they all had to be settled with dollar payments. This so-called "dollar clause," contained in a directive of the Allied Control Council of 20 September 1945, decreed that only dollars could be accepted as payment for German exports. In the American view, this policy would forestall autarkic tendencies in German foreign trade and compel the reintegration of Germany into a trade system based on convertible currencies and the international division of labor.[5]

Although the JEIA order No. 1 of 8 April 1947 allowed for the first time direct agreements between German export managers and foreign customers, there was no foreign trade in the ordinary sense of the word before the currency reform in 1948. The first trade treaty after World War II was signed in February 1947 between the JEIA and Belgium. Until the middle of 1947, there were so-called counterpart agreements with the Benelux countries, France, Italy, Austria, Switzerland, and Czechoslovakia. In 1948, twenty more trade agreements were signed, though they were accompanied by no considerable sales.[6] The main reason for this was the previously mentioned

4. Ludwig Erhard, *Deutschlands Rückkehr zum Weltmarkt,* (Düsseldorf, 1953), 52ff; see also Friedrich Jerchow, *Deutschland in der Weltwirtschaft 1944-1947. Alliierte Deutschland- und Reparationspolitik und die Anfänge der westdeutschen Außenwirtschaft* (Düsseldorf, 1978), 376-77.
5. For a more complete discussion of the importance of the dollar clause, see Christoph Buchheim, *Die Wiedereingliederung Westdeutschlands in die Weltwirtschaft 1945-1958* (München, 1990), 1ff.
6. Erhard, *Deutschlands Rückkehr zum Weltmarkt,* 71ff., 87.

dollar clause, which, in complete contradiction to its original purpose, encouraged the barter of goods. The Allies ordered above all the export of raw materials, while the export of finished goods remained remarkably low. Of $145 million in exports from the British zone, only 1 percent represented finished goods. As late as 1947, raw materials accounted for 67 percent of exports, compared to 11 percent for finished goods. Thus, in the first years after 1945, the traditional structure of German foreign trade as it existed before the war had been stood on its head.[7]

Setting the Stage

Although a wealth of important research already exists on the systemic conditions surrounding Germany's return to the world market, studies that analyze how the leading actors in the German economy in 1945 behaved and what strategies they developed are still lacking.[8] Consequently, this paper attempts to reconstruct the essential political and economic conditions and decisions that, from the point of view of German businessmen, enabled the return to the world market and shaped the expansion of German foreign trade at the end of the 1940s and in the 1950s.

This analysis is based on the example of Ferrostaal AG and its long-time president Dietrich Wilhelm von Menges.[9] Hermann Reusch, who had taken over as chairman of the board of the Gutehoffnungshütte (GHH) group in 1945, appointed von Menges in January 1947 to be member of the executive board of Ferrostaal in Essen. One year later, von Menges was made president of Ferrostaal, which he remained until 1966. Succeeding Reusch, von Menges took over as chief executive of the GHH group, which he developed from 1966 to 1975 into the largest European mechanical engineering concern. Dietrich von Menges is among the prominent big business personalities in the Federal Republic. During the reconstruction years after 1945, until

---

7. Werner Abelshauser, *Wirtschaftsgeschichte der Bundesrepublik Deutschland 1945-1980* (Frankfurt, 1983), 30-31; L. Erhard, *Deutschlands Rückkehr zum Weltmarkt*, 72-73.
8. See Werner Link, *Deutsche und amerikanische Gewerkschaften und Geschäftsleute 1945-1975. Eine Studie über transnationale Beziehungen* (Düsseldorf, 1978); Volker Berghahn, *Unternehmer und Politik in der Bundesrepublik* (Frankfurt, 1985).
9. Ferdinand Simoneit, "Dietrich Wilhelm von Menges," in: *Die neuen Bosse. So wird man Generaldirektor* (Frankfurt/Hamburg, 1966), 132-144; Dietrich Wilhelm von Menges, *Unternehmensentscheide. Ein Leben für die Wirtschaft* (Düsseldorf/Wien, 1976); Reinhard Neebe, *Überseemärkte und Exportstrategien in der westdeutschen Wirtschaft 1945 bis 1966. Aus den Reiseberichten von Dietrich Wilhelm von Menges* (Stuttgart, 1991) [hereafter cited as *Überseemärkte*].

his retirement as president of GHH, he distinctively molded the foreign economic strategies of West German export companies.

Ferrostaal AG in Essen functioned as the trade organization of the GHH group in Oberhausen (now MAN Munich), one of the most important German and European firms in the iron and steel industry, especially in mechanical engineering. The GHH group comprised, among others, Maschinenfabrik Augsburg-Nürnberg (MAN); Deutsche Werft AG Hamburg; Schloemann AG Düsseldorf; Maschinenfabrik Eßlingen AG; as well as Hackethal Draht- und Kabelwerke in Hanover. Success in foreign markets was vitally important for the GHH-group, just as it was for other firms with a similar structure. The iron and steel industries traditionally have been among Germany's most important export industries, with an export share sometimes in excess of 50 percent. Current figures confirm this: in 1989, the proportion of iron and steel production sold abroad amounted to 74.4 percent; for mechanical engineering, the figure was 63 percent (compared to 65 percent for chemical products, 55 percent for vehicles and 48 percent for electrical goods).[10]

At the center of this analysis is the question of how German export firms (for example, Ferrostaal AG) tried to take advantage of increasingly broader economic and political opportunities to sell their wares abroad. Which general patterns were significant? On which markets did they set their sights? Which products did they sell and which general strategies did they formulate? And finally, what essential problems and barriers to return to the world market did the firms face – and what did they undertake to overcome them?

It is undeniable that West Germany benefited from generally favorable conditions for its return to the world market. The new economic order that was installed on the basis of multilateralism and liberalization after World War II by the United States provided a framework in which German industry, which was traditionally export oriented, could grow and thrive. Inside Germany, the fundamental decision for the model of the "social market economy" was an essential condition for the long-term success in foreign markets. But even within this framework, a broad range of alternatives remained, and the course actually taken – especially seen in the light of the sharp controversies over economic policy during the Federal Republic's first decade – was only one of many possible paths.

Moreover, politicians and businessmen in the first years of the Federal Republic did not take it for granted that reintegration into the

---

10. Bundesverband der deutschen Industrie (BDI), ed., *GATT-Uruguay-Runde* (Köln, 1992), 3.

world market would proceed quickly or without major complications. The historic experience of the generation that rebuilt the political and economic system of West Germany after World War II had been indelibly marked by the Great Depression of 1929 to 1933 and the disorder of the world economy in the era between the two wars.

As von Menges correctly pointed out, there was in the first years of the postwar period no talk of an "economic miracle;" that "misleading misnomer" first appeared on everyone's lips much later. "We saw," said von Menges, "only the efforts and risks connected with the decisions which had to be made, and we were convinced that this was just the beginning."[11] The return to the world market after 1945 was no economic abstraction. To the leading actors in economy and politics at that time, it comprised specific foreign markets and the various problems, possibilities, and risks associated with them. Seen against the background of the Cold War, the global conflict between the United States and the Soviet Union, and especially the division of Germany and Europe, it is obvious that the reconstruction of West Germany's foreign economic relations looked much more difficult then than it does at first glance today.

RETURN TO THE WORLD MARKET

The rapid expansion of German foreign trade in the early fifties is greatly attributable to the activities of German firms during the Allied "export ban" between 1945 and 1948, which they used to make long-term strategic preparations for an export offensive. The specific details of this process can be seen in the example of the Ferrostaal AG's corporate strategy in the first few years after 1945.

The foreign trade of Ferrostaal until 1945 was divided into three branches: first, the rolled steel business, which concentrated primarily on the Netherlands, Scandinavia, Italy, and the Balkan states, but also on South America; second, the machine business (MAN, Schloemann, etc.), which was largely connected to the iron trade; and third, the business in complete systems and plants, which concentrated on South America, the Balkan states, and the Near East.[12]

Exports represented the bulk of Ferrostaal AG's pre-war business, but it was the domestic market that played the leading role in the first years following the capitulation. The steel business was most impor-

---

11. D. von Menges, *Unternehmensentscheide*, 95.
12. Statement by von Menges at the sixth meeting of the Allied Control Committee at GHH Oberhausen, 17 February 1948, Dietrich Wilhelm von Menges-Archiv, Essen, vol. 109, (hereafter cited as DvMA).

tant during this period, but there was also good sales potential in manufactured goods. Machines, motors, and mining equipment intended for export, the delivery of which had been stopped by the end of the war, could be substituted for those removed from factories for reparations and the restoration of bombed out plant equipment. This domestic trade enabled Ferrostaal AG to maintain its corps of experienced export salesmen throughout a period in which possibilities for export business did not yet exist.[13] Ferrostaal's export staff could first be used for actual export business when it became possible to fulfill orders that had been interrupted by the war ("precapitulation orders"). From this point on, the company could develop its export business systematically from its humble beginnings based on the domestic market.

A first chance at the recovery of foreign markets was offered by neighboring European lands, especially Holland. Because currency exchange was still tightly restricted, only barter transactions could be negotiated. As early as 1946, Ferrostaal made its first breakthrough in this kind of export business.

The Essen trade firm succeeded in securing for a Ruhr-area consortium an agreement with Holland to process 105,000 tons of rolled-steel products.[14] The Netherlands had taken the initiative on the deal at the end of August 1946 through Thomas Hartelust, the leading manager of Ferrostaal N.V. in the Hague.[15] Under the terms of the agreement, the Netherlands would provide the raw materials (ores and fuel) and would receive in the end a corresponding share of finished rolled goods.

In contrast to this success, the interest on the part of Holland, Denmark, and Italy in expanding their deliveries of surplus foodstuffs to Germany, while simultaneously increasing their imports of German finished goods, ran up against the obstacle of the dollar clause. Nevertheless, the first significant breach in the international isolation of German industry had appeared, and this most primitive form of exchange was to have far-reaching consequences.

In the European market, Sweden presented further possibilities for reciprocal deals, as it could provide the iron ore needed by the Ruhr iron and steel industry and was interested in sheet metal for its shipbuilding industry. Even the overseas business was already up and running again at this point. As von Menges attested in February 1948: "Most of all in South American countries we have encountered

---

13. Ibid., 7.
14. Ibid., 9. For the particulars, see D. von Menges, *Unternehmensentscheide*, 52ff.
15. Memo by von Menges, "DM-Eröffnungsbilanz," 25 October 1988, 2 (in possession of this author).

great interest among the customers. More agreements could be reached within the bounds of the prevailing JEIA regulations."[16]

Re-establishment of pre-war business relationships with German companies was widely sought in South America, where demand was primarily for machines and spare parts.[17] By the beginning of 1948, the JEIA granted the South-America specialist at Ferrostaal AG, Werner Schulz, permission to travel to Latin America "in order to study the current possibilities for expansion of export business in this area."[18] In June 1948, Schulz could report hopefully from Buenos Aires: "The people are of course very nice to me; they see in my visit a sure way to resume commercial relationships with Germany."[19] Schulz immediately began to put back in motion the foreign apparatus of Ferrostaal AG in South America, and brought back from his trip an order from the Chilean national railroad for the delivery of rack-railway locomotives.[20] Von Menges traveled in November 1948 for two weeks to Sweden and Denmark, and in May 1949 to Italy to take part in business negotiations.[21]

The revival of business in Eastern and Southeastern Europe proved to be more difficult than in South America. Most of all in Romania there was an active interest in the resumption of precapitulation orders, the fulfillment of which had been prevented by the advance of the Red Army. As most of Eastern Europe remained under German domination long after West European and trans-Atlantic trade had been cut off by the Allies, the interruption of the export trade in the Eastern market was the shortest of all. But when it was a question of the resumption of deliveries that had been interrupted by the end of the war, the JEIA, in keeping with the Foreign Trade Directive of 20 September 1945, responded negatively.[22] These restrictions actu-

16. Statement by von Menges at the sixth meeting of the Allied Control Committee at GHH Oberhausen, 17 February 1948, DvMA vol. 109, 8-9.
17. Concerning the relative importance of Latin America in the foreign economic relations of Germany, Great Britain, and the United States until 1945, see Stanley Hilton, "Lateinamerika und Westeuropa: die politischen Beziehungen bis zum Ende des Zweiten Weltkrieges," in: Wolf Grabendorff and Riordan Roett (eds.), *Lateinamerika-Westeuropa-Vereinigte Staaten: Ein atlantisches Dreieck?* (Baden-Baden, 1985).
18. Statement by von Menges at the sixth meeting of the Allied Control Committee at GHH Oberhausen, 17 February 1948, DvMA vol. 109, 8-9.
19. Schulz to Mrs. Schulz, 27 June 1948 (Information by von Menges to this author, August 15, 1989). A detailed account of Schulz's trip to South America is not contained in the files.
20. von Menges, *Unternehmensentscheide*, 81-82.
21. Application for Temporary Travel Document, 20 August 1949, DvMA vol. 138. Accounts of and documents for these trips could not be found.
22. Statement by von Menges at the sixth meeting of the Allied Control Committee at GHH Oberhausen, 17 February 1948, DvMA vol. 109, 13.

ally had little to do with the later instrumentalization of Western foreign trade in the form of economic warfare against the Soviet Union and its satellite states. For instance, the JEIA granted permission to Ferrostaal AG to ship more than 10,000 dump trucks to Bulgaria.[23] Similarly, it is interesting to note that Czechoslovakia in 1946 ranked fourth among nations importing goods from the US zone, representing 9.1 percent of the zone's exports.[24]

Measured by the volume of goods traded, the agreements up until 1947 through 1948 were not all that important. "The important thing," declared von Menges in 1948, "is that connections are being restored and experiences gathered."[25] Thus, one can speak only in a very limited sense of a fundamental "rebirth" of trade dealings after 1945. Rather, it was more a case of companies returning – as Allied restrictions were gradually lifted – to old, familiar markets and establishing relationships that the war had interrupted.[26] Like other firms, Ferrostaal AG looked to develop its new foreign business in the countries where it had previously had a strong presence. Von Menges remarked appropriately in early 1948, "There hasn't been any shifting around yet. We have for the most part simply reestablished our old pre-war dealings."[27] In this regard, the utility of old personal contacts and of the existing "good will" that German firms enjoyed abroad were of critical importance in the beginning phase of German foreign trade after 1945.

The currency reform of 20 June 1948 marked the end of the period distinguished by provisional, reciprocal barter trade. The basic decision underlying the currency reform – the decision to abolish the command economy and establish the social market economy – can hardly be overestimated in its middle- and long-term importance.[28] For companies, the currency reform meant at last the necessary clarification about how assets and debts from the wartime were to be judged on the balance sheet, so that they could see what was left over

23. Ibid., 12.
24. See F. Jerchow, *Deutschland in der Weltwirtschaft*, 341, 344, 422.
25. Statement by von Menges at the sixth meeting of the Allied Control Committee at GHH Oberhausen, 17 February 1948, DvMA vol. 109, 12.
26. Concerning the question of continuity in economic administration and corporate policy see Werner Plumpe, *Vom Plan zum Markt. Wirtschaftsverwaltung und Unternehmerverbände in der britischen Zone* (Düsseldorf, 1987).
27. Statement by von Menges at the sixth meeting of the Allied Control Committee at GHH Oberhausen, 17 February 1948, DvMA vol. 109, 12.
28. Concerning the central importance of the currency reform for foreign trade see C. Buchheim, *Die Wiedereingliederung Westdeutschlands*, 51ff. Buchheim asserts that "through it [i.e. the currency reform], the preconditions were met for the full realization of the large, already present growth potential of the West German economy." Ibid., 62.

for the new beginning. But the currency reform was also a decisive turning point in the international economic arena. Even though the full convertibility of the D-Mark on 1 January 1959 was still a long way off and the dollar clause still impeded the development of foreign trade, the stabilization of the wartime inflation and the creation of a stable currency had laid the foundation for wide participation of West German industry in an export offensive in foreign markets.

ECONOMIC INTEGRATION INTO WESTERN EUROPE

The hypothesis often presented in the relevant literature is that the economic integration of German industry into Western Europe opened up new markets, which then formed the basis for the export boom. But this was not really the case.[29] It is more accurate to say that in the years after 1945 the percentage of exports going to Western European countries was much higher than before the war (76.8 percent in 1949 compared with 54.8 percent in 1936) because overseas business had been disrupted by the war and Germany had not yet reclaimed fully its old place in the world economy. After 1949, it became the explicit goal of West German policy to reduce the proportion of exports going to Western Europe, that is, to increase the absolute quantity of exports going elsewhere.

In 1952, the countries of the Organization for European Economic Cooperation (OEEC) accounted for 48 percent of Germany's $326 billion in imports. While the Federal Republic showed in 1949 a current account deficit of more than $1 billion, it achieved in 1951 a trade surplus of $150 million. This was the first such surplus since the war, primarily due to an export surplus of $405 million with the countries of the European Payments Union (EPU).[30]

Undoubtedly, the step toward the German return to the world market took place in the West European market. The successful development with the neighboring states on the one hand reflected the traditional bonds of pre-war Germany. On the other hand, the entry into the European market was made possible by Ludwig

29. For a critical assessment of the West European "integration legend," see Alan S. Milward, "Entscheidungsphasen der Westintegration," in: Ludolf Herbst (ed.), *Westdeutschland 1945-1955. Unterwerfung, Kontrolle, Integration* (München, 1986), 231ff. Also important in this context is Hanns Jürgen Küsters, "Zollunion oder Freihandelszone? Zur Kontroverse über die Handelspolitik Westeuropas in den fünfziger Jahren," in: Helmut Berding (ed.), *Wirtschaftliche und politische Integration in Europe im 19. und 20. Jahrhundert* (Göttingen, 1984), 295ff.
30. Bundesminister für den Marshallplan (ed.), *Wiederaufbau im Zeichen des Marshallplanes 1948-1952* (Bonn, 1953), 84-85.

Erhard's so-called "big gate"[31] of the EPU and the OEEC. Participation in the Marshall Plan, Schuman Plan, World Bank, the International Monetary Fund, and the London Debt Agreement of 1953 was rooted in the desire to be politically integrated in the West.[32] These institutions were like "wings"[33] in the return of Western Germany to the world market.

The important thing to note here is that the economic integration of Western Europe after 1945 and in the first years of the Federal Republic was a political goal. Even the policy of liberalization was pursued by the federal government mostly out of political motivations. For example, as Otmar Emminger, leader of the German OEEC delegation in Paris, noted in 1949, liberalization was

> ... the calling card, so to speak, with which Germany can reenter the European community of nations as an independent member on economic grounds. With a good-faith effort, much distrust could be overcome in the outside world, not just by German politics, but also by German economic policy and economic practice.[34]

Similarly, the industry of the Ruhr saw in the foundation of the European Coal and Steel Community (ECSC) in 1952 a political instrument to push through the reconstruction of its own plants and organizations.[35] This was also true of the founding of the Common Market in 1955 through 1957. As with the ECSC, the West German position was determined not by economic considerations alone, but by higher priorities of foreign policy.

In evaluating the integration of Europe, there were fundamental conflicts between the Chancellery and the Foreign Ministry on one side and the Minister of Economic Affairs, Ludwig Erhard, on the

31. Erhard, *Deutschlands Rückkehr zum Weltmarkt*, 22.
32. Alan S. Milward, *The Reconstruction of Western Europe 1945-1951* (London, 1984); Michael J. Hogan, *The Marshall Plan. America, Britain and the Reconstruction of Western Europe 1947-1952*, (Cambridge, Mass., 1988); Hans-Jürgen Schröder (ed.), *Marshallplan und westdeutscher Wiederaufstieg, Positionen-Kontroversen* (Stuttgart, 1990); Klaus Schwabe, *The Beginnings of the Schumann-Plan 1950/51* (Baden-Baden, 1988); Hans-Jürgen Küsters, *Die Gründung der europäischen Wirtschaftsgemeinschaft* (Baden-Baden, 1982); Herbst (ed.), *Vom Marshallplan zur EWG. Die Eingliederung der Bundesrepublik in die westliche Welt* (München, 1990); Charles S. Maier and Günther Bischof (eds.), *Deutschland und der Marshall-Plan* (Baden-Baden, 1992).
33. Erhard, *Deutschlands Rückkehr zum Weltmarkt*, 41.
34. Memo by Otmar Emminger, "Liberalisierung des Außenhandels," November 29, 1949, cited in: Christoph Buchheim, "Einige wirtschaftspolitische Maßnahmen Westdeutschlands von 1945 bis zur Gegenwart," in: Hans Pohl (ed.), *Wettbewerbsbeschränkungen auf internationalen Märkten* (Stuttgart, 1988), 213-226, here 218.
35. Werner Bührer, *Ruhrstahl und Europa. Die Wirtschaftsvereinigung Eisen- und Stahlindustrie und die Anfänge der europäischen Integration 1945-1952* (München, 1986); John Gillingham, *Coal, Steel, and the Rebirth of Europe, 1945-1955. The Germans and the French from Ruhr Conflict to Economic Community* (Cambridge, 1991).

other. Erhard disparaged the European Economic Community (EEC) as "economic nonsense" and judged the customs union of the six to be a retreat from world-wide multilateral trade. For his part, Adenauer considered West European integration an "indispensable springboard for us to get back into foreign policy at all." In addition, the United States, whose assistance Adenauer held "absolutely necessary for us," saw in the integration of Western Europe "the starting point of its entire policy in Europe."[36] In January 1956, Adenauer pushed through his "order of integration" (according to Article 65 of the Basic Law) against the opposition of Ludwig Erhard and his Economics Ministry.[37] This outcome demonstrates clearly the primacy of foreign policy goals in a most important decision of trade policy.

In the conflict between Erhard and Adenauer, the business community stood on the side of the Economics Minister. For export industry, the customs union meant an unwanted unity with a market that, while not negligible, was hardly of cosmic importance (29.2 percent of West German exports in 1957). For their part, West German farmers saw the opening of the common market through the EEC agricultural policy as the road to confrontation with cheaper products from France and the Netherlands. Even the iron and steel industry foresaw above all an "essential sharpening" of competition in the home market.

At the beginning of the 1950s, the leading actors in industry and business viewed the policy of West European integration – at least insofar as it pertained to the politically motivated formation of trading blocks and intervention in free trade flows – with justifiable hesitation and skepticism. The extraordinary dependence of German foreign trade on Europe was seen as a warning signal: According to the Economics Ministry's view, the high proportion of exports going to Europe indicated merely that the "easily grasped" had been quickly achieved. However, this only served to compensate for considerable losses on the world market, that is, in those countries overseas that traditionally had been supplied by the German export industry.[38]

This interpretation is supported by the export statistics of Ferrostaal AG. From 1948 to 1950, more than 71 percent of the firm's total exports ended up in the West European bloc. But this atypically high (in comparison to the pre-war years) proportion of exports to Western Europe abruptly fell to 33.9 percent in 1950 and to 28.1 percent in 1951. The data are consistent with the conclusion that the for-

---

36. Adenauer to Erhard, 13 April 1956, cited in: Daniel Koerfer, *Kampf ums Kanzleramt. Erhard und Adenauer* (Stuttgart, 1987), 134ff.
37. Ibid., 134ff.
38. Erhard, *Deutschlands Rückkehr zum Weltmarkt*, 22.

mation of the ECSC had remarkably little influence on the immediate export strategies of the German iron and steel industry, at least as regards the member countries of the Union. By contrast, the economic talks between chancellor Adenauer and French Prime Minister Pierre Mendès-France that accompanied the negotiations over the "Germany Treaty" and "Saarland Statute" in Paris in October 1954 triggered a noticeable response.[39]

Against this background, various plans sprouted for cooperation between French and German industry for the cultivation of foreign markets, especially in North Africa. In December 1954, Ferrostaal AG signed a cooperation agreement with the Paris-based *Association européenne minière et industrielle* (ASSEMI). This association took up its work on 1 January 1954 and pursued the goal of "commissioning the necessary studies for carrying out individual industrial projects in Africa, taking part in the establishment of producer firms in Africa, and contributing where possible to the delivery of facilities and their financing."[40]

Although the intended Franco-German cooperation in Africa was never realized, cooperation in other third markets, such as South America, proved considerably more fruitful. Among other things, Ferrostaal AG worked closely together with French economic and financial circles on the financing of the Brazilian metallurgical plant COSIPA.[41] It was essentially this goal of cooperation in third markets that motivated Ferrostaal AG in 1957 to consider opening a branch in Paris. The conclusion of the Treaties of Rome on 1 January 1958 and the impending customs union played a key role in these considerations.[42] According to von Menges, the acquisition of a stake in Aciers & Tubes Spéciaux (A.T.S.) in Paris-Saint Dénis promised the following advantages:

1. A chance to get a foothold in the French iron trade within the framework of the Common Market;
2. The ability to supply our own foreign apparatus with materials from the French market;

---

39. See Vollrath Frhr. von Maltzan, "Fünf Jahre deutscher Handelspolitik. Bestandsaufnahme und Plädoyer für eine liberale Handelspolitik," 30 April 1955, in: *Die Auswärtige Politik der Bundesrepublik Deutschland* (Köln, 1972), 288.
40. von Menges to Reusch, 13 January 1954, "Memorandum zur deutsch-französischen wirtschaftlichen Zusammenarbeit in Afrika," enclosure to "Deutsch-französische Zusammenarbeit in Nordafrika," Haniel-Archiv Duisburg No. 400101410/343 (hereafter cited as HA).
41. von Menges to GHH Sterkrade A.G., 11 July 1956, HA No. 400101410/344. See also von Menges, *Unternehmensentscheide*, 133ff.
42. Memo by von Menges "DM-Aufwertung bzw. Franc-Abwertung," 12 August 1957, DvMA vol. 147.

3. The creation of a base in France for the almost up-and-running cooperative ventures with French industry and trade groups in third countries. Here I am thinking not so much of French Africa, as these things are probably still a long way from fruition, but rather of the existing cooperation in South America and Asia, for example, COSIPA, Argentine steel works, several projects in Ecuador, Colombia, the Chinese market, etc.[43]

Taken as a whole, the founding of the EEC made at first no noticeable impact on the export business of Ferrostaal AG. It was not until the 1960s that a clear change became apparent: The French market, which played practically no role in the 1950s, took on considerable importance in the 1960s, as a comparison with the traditionally important Dutch market shows. But this was only one side of the coin of European integration. On the other side, firms in the German export industry watched with dismay the development of a protectionist agricultural policy that increasingly hindered the importation of products from non-European countries, especially Latin America.[44] In 1964, six years after the founding of the EEC, the Federation of German Industry, in its first assessment of the Community's impact, warned against abandoning other options in favor of the EEC:

> The stronger orientation of German foreign trade toward the EEC market is a natural consequence of progressive integration. The fact that internal EEC trade is taking on more and more the character of a purely domestic market is to be welcomed, most of all because of the associated minimization of risk. Nevertheless, this must not be permitted to lead to a neglect of traditional markets.[45]

PROBING CENTRAL AND SOUTH AMERICAN MARKETS

The first targets of the West German export offensive in overseas markets were primarily Central and South American countries. West Germany was soon able to exert competitive pressure on other countries, especially Great Britain. By 1951, 10.8 percent of West German exports were going to South America; this meant that the pre-war level of 10.6 percent (1935 to 1937) had been met and surpassed just two years after the founding of the Federal Republic.

---

43. von Menges to Reusch, 14 November 1957, HA No. 400101410/344.
44. Memo by von Menges "Besprechung mit von der Groeben/EWG Brüssel," 13 April 1962, HA No. 400101410/344.
45. Bundesverband der Deutschen Industrie (ed.,) *Die deutsche Industrie im Gemeinsamen Markt. Bericht über die bisherigen Auswirkungen der europäischen Wirtschaftsgemeinschaft–1958 bis 1963*, Drucksache No. 71, (Köln, 1964), 16.

The conclusions that Dietrich Wilhelm von Menges, then board chairman of Ferrostaal AG and one of the pioneers in dealings with South America, drew after his first journey to all the important Central and South American countries from September to November 1949 contain interesting information about the background behind the success of German industry on this market. Von Menges saw good reason for optimism for German business in the region: A scarcity of dollars in almost all of South America had led to a stagnation of American private business there, and the English influence was "declining everywhere" because of "their very long delivery times" and because of the frequently poor quality of goods delivered by English industry after the war. In South America there was a strong general desire to do business with Germany again. According to von Menges, three things were responsible for this:

1. the realization that Germany is a better sales outlet for many products from South American countries than the United States;
2. the quality of German products, which had stood the test during the war when there was no service or new deliveries;
3. the ability of German companies to adapt commercially and technologically to the customer's individual requests.[46]

There was a clear double connection between the German overseas export offensive, especially in South America, and the Dollar-Saving and Embargo Policy: The reduction of the US import surplus improved the German dollar-balance, and as an expansion of trade in East European markets was not possible to the extent desired, Latin America became an attractive alternative. At the same time, the South American countries were keenly interested in remedying their chronic dollar shortages by expanding trade with Europe, most of all with the Federal Republic.[47] This goal was simultaneously a political one: a diversification of foreign trade was intended to free these countries from their perceived dependence on the hegemonic powers the United States and Great Britain.

As von Menges correctly ascertained, German exporters could not truly succeed, despite the auspicious initial conditions, as long as the conclusion of trade deals was restricted by the Dollar Clause. Thus, the exporters reasoned, it was imperative that the D-Mark become an

---

46. von Menges, Report on a Journey to South America from 12 September to 26 November 1949, 5 December 1949, HA No. 4001012022/20; printed in: Neebe, *Überseemärkte*, 90-155.
47. *A Study of Trade between Latin America and Europe.* Prepared by the Economic Commission for Latin America, the Economic Commission for Europe and the Food and Agriculture Organization, ed. UN Department of Economic Affairs (Geneva, January 1953); see Erhard, *Deutschlands Rückkehr zum Weltmarkt,* 157.

internationally accepted currency as soon as possible. Transit and barter deals could only be accepted as temporary solutions.

The strategic thrusts into the South American market by Ferrostaal AG and other German export firms proceeded parallel to independent trade and political moves by the federal government and the Economics Ministry. In 1950, trade agreements with running "offset accounts" were negotiated for the first time between the Federal Republic and various Latin American states, first with Uruguay, and then with Brazil and Argentina, among others.[48] An offset account was agreed upon with Argentina, one of the most important countries, for $124 million with a permissible "swing" of first $31 million, and later $50 million.[49]

In Argentina, the Ferrostaal AG chalked up its single biggest success in its postwar dealings with South America – the so-called trolley-bus deal of 18 January 1952. Acting as the leader of a consortium of German firms that included Daimler Benz AG, Henschel, and MAN, Ferrostaal AG made an agreement – approved personally by Argentine President Juan Peron – to deliver 700 trolley buses to Buenos Aires. Although the United States dominated the motor vehicle market in South America, a "technological gap in the market" for trolley buses, namely the "Kobold" electronic steering mechanism, gave the Europeans the edge.[50]

Clearly in the case of the trolley bus deal, the advance financing of such large orders still posed serious problems for German firms in 1951 to 1952. After the Argentine government had approved the agreement on the condition that the German government guarantee covering funds, open conflict broke out in Bonn between the security-minded banks and the market-hungry producers. The dispute went so far that Economics Minister Erhard had to intervene personally in order to prevent a collapse of the agreement. In a discussion at the Economics Ministry on 25 March 1952, Erhard prevailed upon the Bundesbank and the participating private banks to extend to the firm the necessary credit for the deal:

> The importance of the South American market for Germany makes it imperative to follow through on the trolley bus deal with Argentina under any circumstances. Considering that the highest authorities in Argentina have concerned themselves with this affair, the consequences for the entire South American market of a retreat from this deal if we do not suc-

---

48. Erhard, *Deutschlands Rückkehr zum Weltmarkt*, 161ff.
49. Ibid., 167-68.
50. von Menges, *Unternehmensentscheide*, 86-87. The steering equipment had been developed by the Kiepe company in Düsseldorf. See also Neebe, "Technology Transfer and Foreign Trade in the Early Years of the Federal Republic of Germany," in: *German Yearbook on Business History*, 1992, 133-55.

ceed in arranging the financing would be incalculable .... It is therefore in any case necessary ... to find a solution to the problem of the financing.[51]

GERMAN-AMERICAN TRADE

By the middle of the 1950s, such problems had been overcome. The first phase of the "return to the world market" had been concluded successfully and the initial barriers facing the West German export industry had been almost completely dismantled. Like many other firms, Ferrostaal AG had reestablished a presence in traditional markets and simultaneously laid the groundwork for expansion into new ones. The time when pragmatic maneuvering had to stand in the foreground of corporate strategy in foreign markets was over. At this point, a new phase began that was characterized by the consolidation of that which already had been achieved and by the systematic expansion of existing business relationships and long-term planning for the future.

In the case of the dollar, West German industry, apart from a few branches, did not make any appreciable effort to establish itself in this market in the early 1950s.[52] Many branches of the German export industry saw little opportunity to sell their products, which were made to a high standard of quality according to an American consumer market geared to the mass consumption of low-priced products.

A report by the Hamburg Chamber of Commerce on the New York industrial fair of April 1949 gives a very good insight into the differences in business mentality. This report is also interesting because it was in New York that the German export trade had its first opportunity to present itself after World War II. The experience formed the guiding principles for future reactions to the US market. The Chamber's report stated:

> One of the most interesting experiences ... is the fact that the American market prefers the cheap standardized mass product. If we in Germany believed that we could open up the largest market with the greatest purchasing power using durable quality products, this assumption has been

51. Minutes of the Federal Economics Ministry, "Kurzbericht über die Besprechung am 25. März 1952 im Bundeswirtschaftsministerium über die Finanzierung des Trolleybus-Geschäftes Ferrostaal–Daimler-Benz, Argentinien," 26 March 1952, B 102, vol. 7142b, 1, Bundesarchiv Koblenz (hereafter cited as BA).
52. In earlier literature the development of the West German foreign trade offensive on the North American market after 1949 was portrayed too smoothly. See, for example, Manfred Knapp, "Politische und wirtschaftliche Interdependenzen im Verhältnis USA-(Bundesrepublik) Germany 1945-1975," in: M. Knapp et al. (eds.), *Die USA und Deutschland 1918-1975* (München, 1978), 187ff.

proved wrong. For most consumer articles it is important that they are fashionable, have the appearance of quality rather than genuine quality and that they substitute low price for durability ... .The branches of industry affected will have to consider whether they are in a position to make a qualitative adjustment and whether such an adaptation is in fact desirable.[53]

The distinguishing features of the American market stood in clear contrast to the traditional philosophy of quality adhered to by German firms. In the self-assessment of the German export trade, quality but not the price was the critical factor in the success of a product on the foreign markets. According to a survey by the IFO-Institute in 1958 on the "Causes of West German Export Successes in the Opinion of Industrialists,"[54] 85 percent of those polled thought quality was the dominant factor in the production and capital goods industry. Even in the consumer goods industry, the quality factor came first for 77 percent of the exporters, while "value for the money" only was a poor second (41 percent). Value for the money was considered only to be more important in the leather and shoeware industry. Ability to deliver and service facilities (especially in the capital goods industry) also were considered crucial criteria for the success of German firms.

In the first phase of the revival of trade with America, mechanical and precision engineering and products from the optics industry played a large role.[55] After 1953, immediately following the breakup of the IG Farben conglomerate, the chemical industry undertook significant direct investment activity in the United States. Thus it was able to regain quickly its prewar position.[56] The rapid rise of the motor industry to the most important West German exporter on the North America market, by contrast, first began in the second half of the 1950s. In 1952, Germany earned just DM 19.4 million from motor vehicle export to the United States; in 1959, automobile

53. Report by the Hamburg Commerce of Trade, Department of Foreign Trade (Dr. Stephan), "Eindrücke von der New Yorker Industrie-Ausstellung 9.-24. April 1949," 12 May 1949, Archiv der Handelskammer Hamburg, V 30 70e/4 (XIII b).
54. *IFO Schnelldienst.* Articles on the economic situation. A 9 No. 1/2, 9 January 1958, "Die Ursachen der westdeutschen Exporterfolge im Urteil der Unternehmer."
55. In 1952 the mechanical engineering industry exported goods worth DM 142.0 million to the United States, the precision engineering and optical industry goods worth DM 121.0 million. In 1952 the total export to the United States was DM 1,049.0 million. *Statistisches Jahrbuch für die Bundesrepublik Deutschland,* 1953, 317.
56. B 102, Vol. 6938, No. 1, BA: This volume of documents gives a very good insight into the rapid expansion of the IG-Farben successors Farbwerke Hoechst AG and Farbenwerke Bayer AG between 1953 and 1957 on the US market; see also Raymond G. Stokes, *Divide and Prosper. The Heirs of I.G. Farben under Allied Authority 1945-1951* (Berkeley/Los Angeles/London, 1988).

exports amounted to more than DM 1.2 billion and represented just about a third of all German exports (DM 3.8 billion) to the United States.[57] Despite successes in particular sectors, the proportion of exports going to the United States did not exceed 6 to 7 percent of total exports until well into the 1960s and remained below the levels that prevailed before World War I and between the wars. It was not until 1968 that West German exporters achieved an export surplus with the United States.

It would be misleading to assess the importance of the US market for German export trade in the 1950s solely on the basis of the export percentages. For a number of major firms (for example, Siemens & Halske AG)[58] an outlet in the United States was a practical precondition for organizing deals for large-scale industrial units in other countries, especially in South America. As the financing of such projects was usually the primary problem, cooperation with American banks was often imperative.

Considerations of this sort also influenced the American strategy of Ferrostaal AG in the early 1950s. Ferrostaal AG, like other German enterprises, saw the renewed cultivation of a corps of representatives abroad as a task of cardinal importance if its export strategy was to have any hope of success. To remain competitive over the long term, a company had to have on site at its disposal a "combat-ready organization."[59] Two things were important here: a qualified technical staff, including the necessary German personnel, and the provision of the foreign bases with adequate services, storage for consigned goods, and repair shops. Ferrostaal AG consciously cooperated with other German companies in the interest of a "sharp concentration of German interests," as the cost of maintaining outposts abroad made it economically infeasible for even giant German firms such as Siemens AG, GHH, and Demag to operate them alone.

Especially important was the question of a presence in the United States. As von Menges recognized as early as 1949, the support of US banks was a crucial precondition for the financing of large-scale export deals. In New York, the springboard to his 1949 trip to South America, von Menges negotiated with various bankers and exporters, but was forced to admit that, in the short run at least, there just was not sufficient interest in foreign investment in steel and machinery.

57. *Stat. Jb.* 1960, 307.
58. E.g. Siemens, see Bavarian Ministry for Economic Affairs and Trade to the Federal Minister for Economic Affairs, 22 January 1954, B 102, vol. 6935, No. 1, BA.
59. See von Menges (from Caracas) to Hermann Reusch, 27 September 1949, HA No. 400101410/341.

Just one year later, the situation abroad had changed dramatically. The outbreak of the Korean War in June 1950 fueled an unexpected boom, not least in the international iron and steel industries. Whereas Ferrostaal AG had been hardly represented in the North American market between 1 January 1948 and 30 June 1950 (deliveries accounted for only DM 136,106 of the firm's DM 37.9 million in sales), sales in the second half of 1950 jumped to DM 3.5 million and climbed further in 1951 to DM 11.1 million. Within the space of a single year, the United States went from "negligible quantity" for Ferrostaal AG to its largest customer. The opening of an office in the United States was for the GHH group closely connected with the goal of taking advantage of the boom to develop "normal dealings" with the United States, with New York as the hub for the group's international business. In autumn 1950, Ferrostaal Overseas Corporation, New York (FSO) was chartered and vested with the sole responsibility for representing Ferrostaal AG in the United States.[60] The initial stock offering of $197,000 was purchased entirely by banker Eric M. Warburg, a long-time friend of the Reusch family. At the end of 1954, after the New York base had been successfully established, Ferrostaal AG exercised its contractual option to purchase a 25 percent stake in the company in the form of stock worth $49,250. In its application to the Federal Economics Ministry for permission to obtain hard currency, Ferrostaal AG's management explained:

> Soon, we will doubtless have to reckon with heightened American efforts at export, which could easily lead to the loss of important export markets. The stock acquisition we seek will serve to prevent this, and most of all to couple the interests of German producers in international business with those of the Americans with the help of the Ferrostaal Overseas Corporation, and thus to widen the scope of our business opportunities. The fact of our part-ownership would encourage other important German firms to entrust their interests to the Ferrostaal Overseas Corporation and thus to form an effective weapon against American competition. The location in New York is, as regards financial, finance-political, and informational considerations, of such eminent importance for us and for German industry that simply the establishment of such a stronghold could offer us incalculable advantages. Our intended course of action would doubtlessly contribute to an increase in German exports and would for us specifically open up new sales outlets.[61]

---

60 Memo by von Menges, "Bericht über den Aufenthalt in den Vereinigten Staaten vom 19.9-12.10.1950," 26 October 1950, HA No. 400101401/75. Printed in: Neebe, *Überseemärkte*, 158-64. See also von Menges, *Unternehmensentscheide*, 90ff.
61. Ferrostaal AG to the Federal Economics Ministry, "Erwerb einer Beteiligung bei der Firma Ferrostaal Overseas Corporation, New York," enclosures, 22 September 1954, B 102, vol. 6933, file 1, BA.

REVIVING TRADE IN EASTERN AND SOUTHEASTERN EUROPE

It was in trade with Eastern Europe that the real structural changes are to be found in comparison with the prewar period. Before the war, about 15 to 17 percent of German exports went to Eastern Europe. In 1949 to 1950, exports were about 5 percent, and by 1952, had dropped to 2 percent. From a contemporary point of view, it was the breaking up after 1945 of the trade links in Central Europe that had developed over the course of centuries that posed the greatest problems for the West German export industry. The prevailing view among West German industrialists at the time was that expansion of trade with Eastern and Southeastern Europe was an indispensable condition for successful integration into the world economy.

In contrast, the United States followed their strategy of "Economic Defense Policy"[62] introduced by the Marshall Plan, and sought to stop the East-West trade and to shift fundamentally the German and West European trade to the Western Hemisphere and to the US market.[63] The Coordinating Committee of East-West Trade Policy (COCOM), upon its formation on 22 November 1949 in Paris, drew up ever more comprehensive lists of "strategic goods" that could not be exported to the Eastern Bloc. After the Battle Act came into force in 1952, East-West trade was brought almost to a total standstill.[64] A memorandum of the US National Security Council (NSC 68) of 14 April 1950 explicitly spelled out the internal relationship between the American Marshall Plan, the embargo policy against the Soviet Union, and the political desirability of a reorientation of West German and West European export trade[65] to

62. See Robert A. Pollard, *Economic Security and the Origins of the Cold War, 1945-1950* (New York, 1985), here 133ff., 161ff.
63. Essential for the presentation of the Western embargo policy: Gunnar Adler-Karlsson, *Western Economic Warfare 1947-1967. A Case Study in Foreign Economic Policy* (Stockholm, 1968). On the origins of the US economic security policy see Robert A. Pollard, *Economic Security and the Origins of the Cold War 1945-1950* (New York, 1985); Philip J. Funigiello, *American-Soviet Trade in the Cold War* (Chapel Hill, 1988). The divergent interests in trade with Eastern Europe of the Federal Republic and the United States are discussed in Hanns-Dieter Jacobsen, *Die Ost-West-Wirtschaftsbeziehungen als deutsch-amerikanisches Problem* (Baden-Baden, 1986) and in: Günther Mai, "Osthandel und Westintegration 1947-1957. Europa, die USA und die Entstehung einer hegemonialen Partnerschaft," in: Herbst (ed.), *Vom Marshall-Plan zur EWG*, 203-226.
64. In 1951, among DM 2, 721.5 million worth of US exports to the Federal Republic were included DM 713.8 worth of wheat, DM 237.4 million worth of corn, and DM 546.9 million worth of coal. *Stat. Jahrb.*, 1953, 344-345.
65. Documentation of the most important embargo regulations for West Germany between 1949 and 1955 can be found in: Hans Jürgen Lambers, *Das Ost-Embargo* (Frankfurt/Berlin, 1956).

the dollar.[66] In May 1951, the delegation of the European Cooperation Administration (ECA) in West Germany informed the West German Minister responsible for the Marshall Plan that counterpart funds from the Special Funds of the European Recovery Programme (ERP) subsequently would be denied to firms taking part in "illegal" trade with the Soviet Union and its satellite states.[67] In July 1951, the Marshall Plan authorities froze for the first time the allocation of ERP counterpart funds to a West German firm because of a violation of the embargo of strategic goods to the Eastern Bloc. By June 1952, the blacklist of West German firms accused by the United States of illegal practices in East-West trade totaled 87. Apart from freezing ERP counterpart funds, the sanctions consisted of refusing to deliver strategic goods from the United States (including licenses) and barring the firms involved from Marshall Plan delivery programs.[68]

Between 1950 and 1953, the German-American dispute grew so intense that it threatened to poison relations between the Truman administration and the Adenauer government. Economics Minister Ludwig Erhard and German industry preferred the concept of an "open, global trade policy." Erhard fundamentally rejected the use of trade policy as an instrument of foreign policy, common practice in the period between the wars. The political division of the world into two halves did not mean, in his view, that the West German economy had to withdraw completely from the Eastern markets.[69]

The American accusations that German leaders and businessmen did not take the Western Embargo policy seriously were partly justified. The case of Schloemann AG in 1952 illustrates the attitude of the responsible German authorities toward enforcement of the Battle Act. The affair began with plans of Schloemann AG, a subsidiary of the GHH group, to deliver a complete rolling mill to Hungary. Allied authorities had blocked the delivery of the plant in 1951. But shortly before the Battle Act took effect on 24 January 1952, the head of the East-West division of the Federal Economics Ministry, Dr. Kroll, gave instructions to hustle the plant across the Hungarian

66. A Report to the National Security Council by the Executive Secretary (Lay), 14 April 1950 (NSC 68), in: *Foreign Relations of the United States* 1950, 1:234-292. (*FRUS*) Detail on NSC 68 in John Lewis Gaddis, *Strategies of Containment* (New York, 1982), 89ff. See also Pollard, *Economic Security and the Origins of the Cold War*, 222ff.
67. Alexander F. Kiefer, Security Information HICOG Bonn: "Development of the Export Control Procedure in the Federal Republic of Germany during the Period 1945-52," 10 November 1952, RG 469, Mission to Germany, Box 2, National Archives, Washington (hereafter cited as NA).
68. Walter Trautman, *Osthandel Ja oder Nein?* (Stuttgart, 1954), 116ff.
69. See Neebe, "Optionen westdeutscher Außenwirtschaftspolitik 1949-1953," in: Herbst, (ed.), *Vom Marshallplan zur EWG*, 179ff., 185.

border covertly at night. Just two days earlier, while deliberately not informing the Allies, the Economics Ministry granted Schloemann AG an export permit valid until midnight, 23 January. The chair of the East-West Trade Subcommittee of the High Commissioner for Germany (HICOG), Alexander F. Kiefer, protested energetically to the Federal government and declared that the affair had generated "great displeasure" in the United States. Just how high up in the US government this displeasure reached became clear during Adenauer's first visit to Washington one year later in April 1953. The Americans presented the German delegation with an ultimatum (characterized by a tone of "unmistakable severity," according to the protocols) demanding the definitive impoundment of 10,000 tons of scrap and the remaining rolling mill parts that Schloemann AG still had to deliver to Hungary.[70] Secretary of State Dulles's remarks to Adenauer contained a barely veiled threat: "The American public and the Congress are especially sensitive when it comes to questions of East-West trade, and any country that fails to abide by essential tenets of our East-West trade program will have to reckon with the cancellation of all foreign aid."[71]

In the view of German Big Business, an important precondition for a successful reintegration into the world economy lay in the expansion of trade with Eastern and Southeastern Europe. Trading West German manufactured and semi-manufactured goods for raw materials and foodstuffs meant a reduction in the high level of imports from the United States and an improvement of the dollar balance (dollar saving). To the Federation of German Industry (BDI), the umbrella organization of German industry, and to the foreign trade department in the Finance Ministry, this seemed to be the right way of solving certain foreign trade problems.[72]

Ferrostaal AG also saw the revival of its pre-war markets in Eastern and Southeastern Europe as one of the most important components – after the foray into South America – of its postwar export

70. Internal confidential minutes of the Foreign Ministry, "Bericht über die wirtschaftlichen Besprechungen mit der amerikanischen Regierung anläßlich des Kanzlerbesuchs in den Vereinigten Staaten (April 1953)," II-304-06/80, Politisches Archiv des Auswärtigen Amtes, (hereafter cited as PAAA).
71. Konrad Adenauer, *Erinnerungen 1945-1953* (Stuttgart, 2nd ed. 1973), 576.
72. For direct evidence it suffices here to mention: confidential meeting of BDI in Cologne "Der Handel mit ost- und südosteuropäischen Ländern" (minutes, 17 pages), 3 March 1950, HA No. 400101401/85; "Aufzeichnung über den gegenwärtigen Stand und die weiteren Perspektiven der Handelsbeziehungen der BRD mit der sowjetischen Besatzungszone und den Ostblockstaaten," 9 June 1952 ("Strictly confidential!"), circulated by Minister of Economic Affairs Erhard as a discussion paper for the cabinet meeting on June 16, 1952 and approved by the cabinet on 24 June 1952, B 102, vol. 7204, BA.

strategy. Between 1 January 1948 and 30 June 1950, the Eastern Bloc came in third in the regional export statistics, albeit a distant third, behind Western Europe and South America. In 1950, Eastern Europe advanced to second place with 26 percent of German exports (behind Western Europe with 33.9 percent). In the same year, trade with the GDR accounted for 19.8 percent of Ferrostaal AG's export business, putting it in first place, well ahead of Peru (11.8 percent) and Sweden (10.96 percent).[73]

Whereas political problems caused bilateral economic relations at the state level between the Soviet Union and the Federal Republic to proceed very slowly (the first regular trade treaty was not signed until 1958), direct business contacts between West German companies and Soviet foreign trade authorities quietly developed much earlier. In dealings with the East, "business marched in front of the flag," and politics and economics were decoupled in light of mutual commercial interests.

To anchor institutionally the two-track character of foreign trade and foreign policy and simultaneously secure the influence of organized interest groups in the field of Eastern trade, economic organizations agreed in April 1952 to establish an "Eastern Committee of the German Economy," analogous to the previous "Russia Committee." The timing of this event was no coincidence: In the Germany Treaty, signed on 26 May 1952, which ended the occupation status and dissolved the Allied High Commission (HICOG) and JEIA, the Allies forfeited their special rights to interfere in the foreign trade of the Federal Republic.[74]

The establishment of concrete commercial relations between the Federal Republic and the Soviet Union had already received significant stimulus from the Moscow International Economic Conference (MIEC)[75] of April 1952 and an official offer of DM 2 billion worth of business that the Germans received there. At this point, a regular race ensued in the Federal Republic to settle the first business agreements with the Soviet Union.[76]

At the Moscow World Economic Conference, political considerations allowed only "second rank" German businessmen to take part "in a private capacity." Four months later at the Hotel Richmond in

---

73. Neebe, *Überseemärkte*, 378.
74. Because of the later failure of the European Defense Community (EDC), sovereignty was reached when the Paris treaties had been introduced in May 1955. Documentation in: Lambers, *Das Ost-Embargo*, 28ff., 39.
75. RG 59, Box 1480-81, NA.
76. See Documents in RG 59, Box 1481, e.g. 398.00-MO/6-1352, NA; B 102, vol. 7214b, BA.

Copenhagen, a delegation of German businessmen of the highest standing met, with the blessing of the responsible ministries in Bonn, with the leadership of the Soviet Foreign Trade Ministry. Alongside Dietrich Wilhelm von Menges were Ernst Wolf Mommsen, Otto Wolff von Amerongen, Gerhard Bruns, and six other leading German industrialists.[77] With the meeting in Copenhagen in August 1952, the ice had been broken and the first official contact with the USSR had been secured. A short while later, in March-April 1953, the first direct government-to-government negotiations between the Federal Republic and the Soviet Union began in connection with the Geneva conference of the Economic Commission for Europe (ECE) on East-West economic relations.[78]

From the beginning of the 1950s, Ferrostaal AG was able to get started right away in dealings with the Soviets, a business most closely associated with the Otto Wolff firm. The importance for Ferrostaal AG of the opening of the Soviet market can be seen in the figures between 1955 and 1965. Whereas the Soviet Union in 1956 stood in sixth place among the company's export markets with 4.18 percent, deliveries in 1959 and 1960 amounted to more than 12 percent of total exports, making the USSR the firm's second largest export market in the world. This peak, however, could not be maintained over the long term, and the 1960s saw a clear drop in business with the Soviet Union.

This happened mostly because of a fundamental change in the structure of foreign trade. When the obstacles in East-West trade started to fall at the beginning of the 1960s, it became evident that the pre-war pattern of Central European trade currents had lost its attractiveness for West Germany and the other industrial countries of Western Europe. The politically initiated redirection of trade flows at the end of the 1940s and the beginning of the 1950s toward the Western hemisphere put increased pressure on West German industry to modernize. The successful reintegration into the world economic system demanded an increasingly international division of labor. Therefore, the complementary division of labor, in which raw materials were exchanged for manufactured goods, lost more and more of its rele-

---

77. Memo by von Menges, "Vermerk über das Ergebnis einer Besprechung mit den Herren einer russischen Delegation über die Möglichkeiten der Aufnahme eines Warenaustausches zwischen Russland und der deutschen Wirtschaft am 4. August 1952, 10 Uhr, im Hotel Richmond in Kopenhagen", 5 August 1952, HA No. 400101401/342. Printed in: Neebe, *Überseemärkte*, 195-97.
78. Memo by Dr. Sartorius, "Wirtschaftsbeziehungen zwischen der Bundesrepublik Deutschland und der Sowjetunion", part 2 "Der Warenaustausch seit 1945", 10 April 1957, Abt. IV, Ref. 413, vol. 96, PAAA.

vance. This pattern was supplemented and eventually superseded by an intra-industrial network within the Western world.[79] East-West trade, which had faced a political barrier in the postwar years by the end of the 1950s and beginning of the 1960s, was simultaneously impeded by structural handicaps that became ever more obvious.

German illusions of unlimited possibilities for the expansion of trade with the East had by this time all but disappeared. Nevertheless, there was a marked consciousness at Ferrostaal AG, which had been a pioneer in the "Russia business" and which had maintained a small office in Moscow since 1960, of the "essential importance" of this market. As von Menges noted in 1963, although the Russia business could never be a "panacea," it could retain, considering the growing indebtedness of the developing countries and their ever-lengthening payment schedules, "an essential importance, even if the percentage figure is small, alongside export markets in the rest of the world."[80]

Conclusion

West Germany's rapid and successful return to the world market after 1945 took place against the background of auspicious starting conditions: the economic and political framework of the *pax Americana*, multilateralism, and liberalization in world trade were all favorable to the traditionally export-oriented German economy. The Korean War accelerated this development by creating an increased demand for capital goods. German industry, which possessed enormous slack capacity thanks to the shutdown of the armaments industry after World War II, was particularly well placed to meet this demand. At the same time, Allied production bans and restrictions on West German firms were speedily rescinded, reflecting the rapid restoration of German sovereignty and its acceptance into the Cold War anti-Soviet alliance.

From the point of view of the export industry, quality, not price, was of primary importance for success in foreign markets. Reliable

---

79. The proportion of raw materials among West German exports sank between 1950 and 1960 from 14.0 percent to 4.6 percent, while the proportion of manufactured goods during the same period rose from 64.8 percent to 82.4 percent. For imports the proportion of manufactured goods rose from 12.6 percent to 32.2 percent, while the proportion of raw materials sank from 29.6 percent to 21.7 percent and the proportion of foodstuffs fell from 44.1 percent to 26.3 percent of the total imports, in: Statistisches Bundesamt (ed.), *Bevölkerung und Wirtschaft 1872-1972* (Wiesbaden, 1972), 192ff.
80. Memo by von Menges, "Bericht über allgemeine Eindrücke während eines Besuches in Moskau vom 22. bis 26. Juli 1963," 30 July 1963, DvMA, vol. 138. Printed in: Neebe, *Überseemärkte*, 354-56.

delivery and service (especially in the capital goods industry) were also considered crucial criteria for German firms. Thus, the demands of the dollar market stood in contrast to the traditional philosophy adhered to by German firms, and it was not until after the end of the 1950s that America became a significant market for German exports.

The first patterns of foreign trade that appeared after the war show an essential continuity from the pre-war period. The return to the world market was in this respect also a return to old markets. And the West German economy had few difficulties in quickly recapturing its traditional position, especially in competition with Great Britain in the South American market. The attempt to rebuild and further develop the traditional markets in Eastern and Southeastern Europe, by contrast, met with only limited success, as it increasingly ran up against political barriers after 1949-1950. The United States sought to instrumentalize foreign trade for the purpose of waging economic warfare against the Soviet Union and its satellites, a policy that was widely and unambiguously opposed by the German business community. German export industry found an ally in this matter in Ludwig Erhard and the Economics Ministry, which advocated a policy of "open global trade policy" without political restrictions. Out of this conflict between American political and German economic interests arose the strategy of "decoupling" trade policy and foreign policy. Concretely, this strategy meant that German trade marched in front of the flag into the Eastern markets.

In the West, the situation was in some respects exactly the opposite; the economic integration into the West European market was driven primarily by foreign policy goals – often against the wishes of the business community and the Economics Ministry, which saw the EEC as a step backward from the goal of multilateralism and free trade. It was Adenauer's politically motivated decision to bind the Federal Republic firmly to the West that initiated the dynamic process of economic integration that has gone on since the sixties. Though industry initially hesitated to follow the chancellor's lead, German trade since then has been increasingly directed toward the European Common Market.

Chapter 5

❖

"RECONQUERING OUR OLD POSITION"
West German Osthandel Strategies of the 1950s*

Robert Mark Spaulding, Jr.

The process of restoring the traditional patterns of trade between West German industry and Soviet state agencies in the postwar period was an enormously complicated task that required the full decade of the 1950s to complete. By 1959 the Federal Republic had assumed a traditional German role in the modern European economic order as the premier Western trade partner for Russia/Soviet Union.[1] With the largest share of the Soviet import market in its hands already by 1960, West German industry was, and is, uniquely poised to benefit from any expansion of East-West trade. Since the Federal Republic's leading position in Soviet trade emerged as one of the enduring features of the European cold war order, and will

---

* Portions of this essay are based on a presentation "'Organized Capitalism vs. Planned Economy' German Responses to the Soviet State Monopoly in Foreign Trade, 1918-1960," made at the Colloquium on the European Strategies of German Big Business, Brown University, November 1992; I am grateful for the many helpful comments received there.

1. The West German-Soviet "Long Term Agreement on Trade and Payments," signed in April 1958 and covering the period 1958-60, serves as another important marker for the completion of this restoration process. For data on West German and Soviet trade in the 1950s see *United Nations Statistical Papers*, Series T, *Direction of International Trade*, vols. I-XI (Geneva, 1950-).

likely continue as a feature of the new post-cold war order, we ought to look more closely at the decade in which German industry claimed that leading position.

Undoubtedly, the unique political legacy of German economic policies toward the East contributed to the complexities of restoring West German trade with the Soviets and the Soviet bloc. The highly politicized cold war atmosphere surrounding East-West trade in general and the political legacy of interwar German-Soviet economic cooperation in particular made the restoration of earlier trade patterns between Central and Eastern Europe an especially problematic area of postwar reconstruction. The Osthandel could not be separated from *Politik*, or perhaps even from *grosse Politik*, with all the ominous overtones carried by the latter phrase in the context of German-Soviet relations.[2]

Yet because of German economic structures, i.e., the private ownership of economic property, the Osthandel never could be a purely political issue. Ultimately, the West German private sector provided the material wherewithal for any type of trade policy toward the East. For that reason, political considerations (no matter how vital) could never completely eclipse business calculation in any West German discussion of Eastern trade policies. "Osthandel als Politik" could never be divorced completely from "Osthandel als Geschäft." Whatever its special political motives, trade with the East was always in the end a business activity; a "kaufmännische Angelegenheit" just as surely as it was a "diplomatische Angelegenheit." From the 1920s through the 1950s and beyond, the German private sector generally referred to trade with the Soviets as "Rußlandgeschäft" – a telling revelation of the primary concern of the German business community (and of the German perception of the Soviet state). Fully aware that Chancellor Konrad Adenauer and Foreign Office bureaucracy viewed the Osthandel primarily from the political angle, many West German private sector participants nevertheless continued understandably to view their own activities in the East primarily from a business perspective.

How then did the West German business community in its various sub-groupings view the business of Germany's Eastern trade? Specifically, what business goals did German private sector groups

---

2. For treatments of the Osthandel as a factor in West German Ostpolitik see Angela Stent, *From Embargo to Ostpolitik* (Cambridge, Mass., 1981); Hanns-Dieter Jacobsen, *Ost-West Wirtschaftsbeziehungen als deutsch-amerikanisches Problem* (Baden, 1986); Günther Mai, "Osthandel und Westintegration 1947-1957," in Ludolf Herbst, Werner Bührer, and Hanno Sowade (eds.), *Die Eingliederung der Bundesrepublik Deutschland in die westliche Welt*, (München, 1990), 203-25.

set for themselves as they approached the Soviet Union in the postwar world? Which strategies did the West Germans choose in pursuit of these goals? Finally, how successful was West German business in achieving its goals in Eastern Europe, and what role did conscious business strategies play in West German successes and failures? This essay explores these questions with the aim of illuminating the important and only incompletely understood business side of the Osthandel in the 1950s. The political significance that all parties attached to West German-Soviet economic agreements often overshadowed the entire process of trade with the East, obscuring German business strategies in approaching the Soviet Union. In addition to the generally recognized goal of increasing West German trade with the Soviets, the German business community had detailed and explicit views of how that trade should be pursued.

"HEUTE IST DIE LAGE UNGEFÄHR DIESELBE": INTERWAR EXPERIENCE AND POSTWAR STRATEGIES[3]

West German Osthandel strategies of the 1950s grew directly out of German business experiences with the Soviets in the interwar period. Lenin's April 1918 proclamation of a state monopoly over Soviet foreign trade had presented German business with a fundamentally new strategic challenge: recovering its profitable position in what had been a one billion mark export market (1913) in the face of the Soviet state monopsony.[4] Most fundamentally, this meant restoring the pre-World War I trade volume between the two countries with German credits for purchases by the war-ravaged Soviets. These German efforts produced mixed results. In February 1926 a German government guarantee of RM 30 million in export credits to Soviet Russia failed to boost German-Soviet trade. Leading private sector interest groups such as the industrial Reichsverband, the German Chamber of Commerce, and the Union of German Iron and Steel Industrialists began to question whether Germany could effectively influence the value, volume, or direction of Soviet foreign trade.[5] On the other hand some

---

3. Erwin von Carnap (Executive Secretary [Geschäftsführer] of the Ost-Ausschuß), "Memorandum über die Bildung eines Ost-Ausschusses," 13 February 1951, OA 4, Archiv des Bundesverbandes der deutschen Industrie (hereafter cited as BdI).
4. *Statistik des deutschen Reiches*, N.F. vol. 271, V, 1; *Statistisches Jahrbuch für das deutsche Reich*, 35 (1914), 252. Walther Kirchner cites pre-1914 profit rates on German sales in Russia of 5-42 percent depending on the industry, *Die Deutsche Industrie und die Industrialisierung Russlands 1815-1914* (St. Katherinen, 1986), 341-42.
5. See, e.g., the negative assessment offered at the Reichsverband's Hauptausschuß meeting, 19 May 1927, 62/10.5, vol. 1, Bayer-Archiv Leverkusen (hereafter cited

RM 600 million in German credits provided between 1930 and 1932 were followed closely by RM 1,389 million in German industrial exports to the USSR in 1931-32, reviving German hopes that Soviet trade policies did not lie beyond the influence of the outside world.[6]

A second business challenge grew out of the revolutionary organization of Soviet foreign trade in a state monopoly and the negotiating tactics employed by the new Soviet foreign trade representatives.[7] By early 1922 the Soviet Foreign Trade Office (Handelsvertretung) in Berlin had begun to use its monopsonist position as a means of seeking unusually generous price concessions and credit terms from many of Germany's largest industrial enterprises. In June 1922 Hans von Raumer (AEG) complained to Hermann Bücher (Union of German Iron and Steel Industrialists and industrial Reichsverband) that the Russians were asking for credit terms beyond what AEG gave to its best customers! In a complaint repeated by a wide range of German industrialists over the next 40 years, Raumer noted how "by being played off against each other, the firms negotiating with Russia were being driven down."[8] For German businesses engaged in sales to the new Soviet state, devising an organizational response to the Soviet state trade monopoly that could prevent German firms from being "played off" against each other became the overwhelming issue of the 1920s.

Only after the leading German interest groups brought their members into a single organization, the newly formed "Rußland-Ausschuß der deutschen Wirtschaft," in August 1928 could the situation of destructively competitive intra-German underbidding in prices, payment, and delivery terms on Soviet orders begin to improve.[9] Working closely with the Brüning government in the

---

as BAL); also Reichsverband Executive Secretary (Geschäftsführer) Hans Kraemer's pessimistic forecast for economic relations with the Soviets, Reichsverband Presidium meeting, 29 March 1928, 62/10.3, Bd. 2, BAL.

6. The exact amount of German credit provided in 1931-32 is difficult to determine because the Germans began "revolving" portions of the RM 330 million credit from March 1931 as it was repaid in early 1932.

7. On Soviet foreign trade organization and the state monopoly see Alexander Baykov, *Soviet Foreign Trade* (Princeton, 1946), 7ff.; Glen Alden Smith, *Soviet Foreign Trade: Organization, Operations, and Policy, 1918-1971* (New York, 1971); Hubert Schneider, *Das sowjetische Aussenhandelsmonopol 1920-1925* (Cologne, 1973); Franklyn D. Holzman, *Foreign Trade under Central Planning* (Cambridge, Mass., 1974).

8. Guggenheimer (MAN) to Paul Reusch (GHH), 15 June 1922, 300193024/4, Haniel Archiv, Duisburg (hereafter cited as Haniel).

9. Founding members of the Russland-Ausschuß included the Reichsverband der deutschen Industrie, the German Chamber of Commerce (DIHT), Reichsverband des deutschen Gross- und Überseehandels, Centralverband des deutschen Bank- und Bankiergewerbes, Deutsch-Russischer Verein; for a history of the Russland-

spring of 1931, the Rußland-Ausschuß reached agreement with the Soviet government on a set of standard payment and delivery terms for German industrial goods delivered to the USSR as part of the Reich government's guarantee of RM 300 million in export credits for the Soviets.[10] Six months later the Russland-Ausschuss gained an even better position from which to enforce a common German approach to the Soviets when the Reich government (Economics Minister Hermann Warmbold) gave the Committee the right to approve or reject contracts that used the Reich loan guarantees.[11]

Supported by Hjalmar Schacht and other Economics Ministry officials in the 1930s, the Russland-Ausschuss eventually regulated all aspects of the intra-German competition for Soviet orders. When the Russland-Ausschuss managed to sign a formal agreement with the Soviet Handelsvertretung in Berlin on generally applicable payment and delivery terms (Allgemeine Lieferbedingungen) in 1935, it could do so only because the Reich government insisted on this type of agreement as part of the arrangements for a new 200 million Mark export credit.[12] The standardized terms were then enforced by orders of the Economics Ministry to the Export Control Offices. That same arrangement was repeated with another 200 million in trade credits in the 19 August 1939 German-Soviet Economic Agreement which paved the way for the notorious Non-Aggression Pact of 21 August.[13]

For West German suppliers to the Soviets, the dual lesson of German-Soviet trade in the interwar period appeared straightforward. First, German government and business groups together must con-

---

Ausschuß see Hans-Jürgen Perrey, *Der Russland-Ausschuss der deutschen Wirtschaft. Die deutsch-sowjetischen Wirtschaftsbeziehungen der Zwischenkriegszeit* (Munich, 1985).
10. The terms for the new Soviet orders were set by the Piatkov Agreement of 14 April 1931, signed by G. Piatkov (Vice-Chair of the Gosplan) for the Presidium of the Soviet Supreme Economic Council and members of the Russland-Ausschuß: Hans Kraemer (RdI), Karl Köttgen (Siemens-Schuckert) and Wolfgang Reuter (DEMAG). A copy of the agreement as circulated confidentially by the Russland-Ausschuß can be found in 20-1100-1, Rheinisch-Westfälisches Wirtschaftsarchiv zu Köln e.V.. (hereafter cited as RWWA).
11. H.-J. Perrey, *Der Russland-Ausschuss der deutschen Wirtschaft*, 191.
12. Ibid., 243; copies of these agreements in *Documents on German Foreign Policy* (Washington, 1959), Series C, IV, No. 21 [hereafter cited as DGFP].
13. H.-J. Perrey, *Der Russland-Ausschuss der deutschen Wirtschaft*, 297; DGFP, D, VI, No. 346; Erlass of the Economics Ministry to the Export Control Offices (No. 177/39), R7/4699, Bundesachiv (hereafter cited as BA). A subsequent agreement between the Russland-Ausschuß and the Soviet Trade Office in Berlin on 12 December 1939 finalized delivery terms and arbitration procedures. Revealingly, copies of that December agreement can be found in the files of the West German Foreign Office from the late 1950s, 413.85.00/101, Politisches Archiv des Auswärtigen Amtes (hereafter cited as PAAA) and in the Otto Wolff Nachlass (available since 1990), also in files from the late 1950s, 72-189-17, RWWA.

tinue to pursue every means for increasing the value and volume of German-Soviet exchanges if Germany hoped to preserve its traditional position as Russia's premier Western trade partner. Second, without some organizational defence against the "unfair" trade practices of the Soviet state monopoly, German producers would be played off against one another in an expensive bidding war for Soviet orders that would reduce German profits to the very thinnest margins. Further, by bringing German exporters together in a single organization (Russland-Ausschuß) and having that organization work closely with the German government, it was possible to negotiate standard payment and delivery terms with the Soviets and to enforce these terms on the German exporters, thereby reducing intra-German competition and preserving profits. In view of this legacy, it could come as no surprise that the West German private sector sought to "recreate" the old Russland-Ausschuß in some new form as part of the larger revival of private interest groups seeking to influence West German foreign economic policies in the new Federal Republic.

Almost as soon as reconstituted economic interest groups began to emerge in the Western zones of occupied Germany in 1945-46, they turned their attention to the crucially important question of West German foreign trade relations. In June 1948 Germany's most powerful industrial and commercial associations combined their resources on the study of foreign trade problems in the new Arbeitsgemeinschaft Aussenhandel. This tremendously influential group sought "common ground" in the private sector on the "fundamental questions" of trade policy that "interested all economic sectors."[14] In October 1949, 35 industrial interest groups joined together in the new suprasectoral industrial interest group, "Ausschuß für Wirtschaftsfragen der industriellen Verbände," with a committee on foreign trade. In 1950 this powerful group adopted the name Bundesverband der deutschen Industrie, in obvious reference to the Weimar-era Reichsverband der deutschen Industrie. Wilhelm Mann (IG Farben) chaired the first meeting of the Bundesverband's foreign trade committee in May 1950.[15]

14. Maltzan memorandum on a conversation with Beyer and Petersen (German Chamber of Commerce), 24 February 1951, B102/2262, H.1, BA. Among the founding members were virtually all of the Federal Republic's most powerful interest groups: the new Bundesverband der deutscher Industrie, German Chamber of Commerce, the Bundesverband des Deutschen Groß- und Außenhandels, the Bundesverband deutschen Banken, and the Außenhandelsvereinigung des Deutschen Einzelhandels.
15. On the origins of the industrial Bundesverband see Braunthal, *The Federation of German Industry in Politics* (Ithaca, 1965): George Brodach, *Der Bundesverband der deutschen Industrie* (Düsseldorf, 1987); Raithel, *Wirtschaft und Außenpolitik*, 77 ff. and the literature cited there.

In this context of rebuilding private sector interest groups, the question of (re)creating an exclusive private sector organization to handle issues of trade with the Soviets (and their new East European dependencies) was opened. In February 1950 Edgar H.P. Meyer, Executive Secretary (Geschäftsführer) of Mann's foreign trade committee, first in the Ausschuß für Wirtschaftsfragen and then in the BdI, had several communications, including a personal meeting with Gerhard Schauke (Mannesmann Export, Berlin), the former Executive Secretary (Geschäftsführer) of the old interwar era Russland-Ausschuß. Schauke talked openly about the "creation of an Ost-Ausschuß" to succeed the Russland-Ausschuß, even drafting an organizational plan and a membership list.[16] In response the BdI established an "Ostreferat" in the summer of 1950, but concluded, apparently on its own, that "for political reasons" the new unit could not be "activated" at that time.[17]

Unaware of the BdI's activities in this area, Christian Kuhlemann (CDU), Chairman of the Bundestag Committee on Foreign Trade, suggested in November 1950 that the Federal Republic establish an Eastern Trade Office (Osthandelskontor) to regulate material exchanges with the Soviet bloc.[18] When Kuhlemann's suggestion became public, the BdI immediately obtained a private meeting with him to "discuss the coordination of West German interests in East-West trade [Geschäft]." Although the BdI agreed with Kuhlemann's goal of "avoiding mutual price underbidding in deals with the Soviet zone and Eastern countries," it "rejected" the creation of any state agency – either a Foreign Trade Office or a Treuhandstelle – for channelling East-West trade. Instead, the BdI revealed its plan to sponsor a "fusion of West German interests vis-à-vis the state trading organizations in the East bloc countries" just "as soon as the political situation has changed." Meyer told Kuhlemann that the BdI's still dormant Ostreferat would "when necessary be transformed into an Eastern Committee analogous to the earlier Russia

16. Schauke to Meyer, "Bildung eines Ost-Ausschusses" and "Zusammensetzung des Ost-Ausschusses," 8 February 1950, OA 4, BdI.
17. Meyer's internal BdI memorandum to Wilhelm Beutler, 19 January 1951, OA 4, BdI. Schauke also acknowledged that the "political situation" in March 1950 had "not allowed" more extensive discussions and that "it appeared advisable to handle the entire matter with a certain caution and to wait." Schauke to the BdI, 10 February 1951, OA 4, BdI.
18. Kuhlemann was not alone in government circles proposing active state management of East-West trade. On 13 July 1950 Erhard had written to Adenauer on East-West trade matters raising, among other issues, the question of "whether a special office similar to the Treuhandstelle for interzonal trade should be erected," B136/7807, BA.

Committee." In addition, "more active" trade with the Soviet bloc countries remained a goal.[19]

A month after the January 1951 meeting with Kuhlemann, the BdI produced an internal memorandum on the "necessity" of an Eastern Committee as well as the "duties" and organization of the proposed group. The necessity for a new Eastern Committee was drawn from the "experience" of the 1920s, which "taught" that business between the free market West and Soviet-style "state capitalist economy" will "develop disadvantageously for the exporters from states with free economies unless a certain [degree of] control over prices and delivery and payment terms takes place on the part of the Western exporters or at least can be begun at any time." As the "best example" of "proper direction and oversight of business with the USSR," the BdI cited the Russland-Ausschuß of the interwar period. The memorandum continued with an explicit connection of the interwar and postwar periods: "Today the situation is roughly the same, centrally directed buyers playing off one supplier against the other with either truthful or false statements."[20] German exporters should move beyond striking occasional deals with the Soviets based on "substantial [German] price concessions" and should instead think about a "useful, real, and constantly developing business relationship" with the East. That relationship required "centralized steering and advising for business with the USSR, and if necessary also with the satellite states, through a committee based on the cooperation of the sectoral interest groups [Fachverbände]."

This same BdI memorandum went on to list the "duties" [Aufgaben] of a new Eastern Committee; these, too, were drawn directly from interwar experiences. First, the new Ost-Ausschuß would promote trade between the two countries by "advising and disseminating information" [Auskunftserteilung] on the German side and "especially by making business connections" between Germans and Soviets. Second, the Ost-Ausschuß would "set certain guidelines for delivery and payment terms by using the old terms negotiated by the Russia Committee with the Soviets."[21]

19. BdI internal memorandum to Beutler on the upcoming meeting with Kuhlemann, 16 January 1951; Meyer's notes on the meeting with Kuhlemann, 19 January 1951, both in OA 4, BdI. This was a genuine representation of the BdI's position. Nearly identical views were expressed by Carnap and Meyer to Schauke on 23 January 1951, i.e., that "our efforts to activate the Osthandel are still impeded [gehemmt] by political developments," but efforts continue to "expand West German direct exports to the East [Ostländer]," OA 4, BdI.
20. The extensive and explicit references to the earlier Russland-Ausschuß may be explained in part by the arrival of a new letter from Schauke on 12 February 1951 that discussed the organization and functions of that earlier body, OA 4, BdI.
21. The paragraph continues: "Only mutually recognized terms set down in black and

In fulfilling its two major functions of increasing trade and limiting intra-German competition, the Ost-Ausschuß would investigate possible methods of financing business deals with the East, either through paper credits [Wechselkredite] or by arranging compensation deals. The interwar financing method – credit provided by a bank consortium and guaranteed by the government through the "Hermes" export credit insurance program – was also mentioned as "possible." Financing arranged through the Ost-Ausschuß would both promote trade and serve as a means of preventing radical underbidding by "irresponsible" German firms since "the use of financing options created by the Ost-Ausschuß has as a prerequisite an appropriate price posture [angemessene Preisstellung] on the part of the supplier." Determinations of an "appropriate" price would be made by the sectoral interest groups.

This important BdI memorandum concluded with von Carnap's suggestion to Meyer that a "small working group" drawn from the West German steel, machine, and chemical industries meet to discuss the creation of an Ost-Ausschuß and other issues of East-West trade.[22] These ambitious plans remained in limbo through 1951 as the expanding Korean conflict, American efforts further to restrict Western exports to the Soviet bloc, and the continuing role of the Allied High Commissioners as supervisors of West German trade with the East precluded the activation of a new Ost-Ausschuß.

Not until the spring of 1952 did political and economic developments combine to bring the Eastern trade issue to the forefront of German politics. In the context of West German-Allied negotiations for the General Treaty and the Contractual Agreements, and the impending return of full commercial sovereignty to the FRG in the spring of 1952, the SPD launched a parliamentary inquiry into the government's East-West trade policies and the alleged "discrimination" against the FRG within pan-Western export control policies. At the same time Soviet export agencies began offering supplies of wood, grain, and oil to West German import firms as part of the propaganda

---

white guarantee the suppliers protection against pressure on prices [Preisdrückerei] and disadvantageous differences of opinion between the contracting parties."

22. Carnap's list included Karl Lange (VDMA) and Richard Carstensen (MAN) for the machine industry; Wallenhorst (Exportausschuss Eisen und Stahl), Kraus (Otto Wolff), Gerhard Schauke (Mannesmann), and Schulz (Ferrostaal) for the steel industry; Vogel (Bayer) for chemicals; and Herbert Gruhner (AEG) for the electrical industry. On all these plans, Carnap's internal BdI "Memorandum über die Bildung eines Ost-Ausschusses," 13 February 1951, BdI, OA 4. Carnap's vision of the Federal government providing state guarantees for private West German bank loans to the Soviets in the near future reveals a fantastically optimistic and ultimately unrealistic view of West German-Soviet international relations and the larger context of East-West relations in the 1950s.

effort surrounding the Moscow "World Economic Conference" in April 1952.[23] Even before the debate over these developments came to a head in the Bundestag, Hans Kroll, head of the "East-West Trade Group" in the Federal Ministry for Economics, understood that the combination of political pressure from the SPD and economic pressure from the business community would compel the government to improve trade relations with the Soviets.[24]

On 6 May 1952 the Bundestag resolved unanimously that "the remaining limits on German freedom of action in the control of merchandise trade and – so far as is legally possible – in the conclusion of trade treaties with East bloc countries must be eliminated as soon as possible."[25] By removing those remaining limits, the General Treaty and Contractual Agreements confronted the Federal government with the new task of devising some means by which the West Germans could negotiate with the foreign trade organizations of those Soviet bloc countries that did not yet officially recognize the Federal Republic. With the scheduled abolition of the Allied High Commission, the question arose as to how the Federal Republic planned to negotiate any new trade agreements at all with those Soviet bloc states with which it had no diplomatic ties.[26] In response to a question from the chairman of the Bundestag's Economic Policy Committee on this point, Erhard admitted that "the establishment of diplomatic relations and international recognition is not to be expected in the foreseeable future," and therefore "a way must be found that makes possible the conclusion of trade agreements after the General Treaty is in force, yet that does not prejudice our negative position on international recognition of these countries."[27] The federal government

23. In June 1952 the Soviet wood exporting agency, EXPORTLES, offered pit-props and plywood to a West German import firm. At the same time E. van Hazebrouck, one of Germany's oldest Hansa trading firms, negotiated to buy DM 15 million in grain and seedcake from the Soviets.
24. Kroll's "Memorandum on the Results of the Moscow [Economic] Conference," 19 April 1952 and "Memorandum on the SPD Inquiry Regarding Eastern Trade," 2 May 1952, both in B136/7807, BA.
25. SPD inquiry, 17 January 1952, *Verhandlungen des deutschen Bundestages*, I. Wahlperiode 1949, Stenographische Berichte (Bonn, 1952), 10: Drucksache Nr. 2935, 7933. For the debate on 6 May 1952, ibid., 11: 8961-8967. The report of the Bundestag Committee on the Occupation Statute and Foreign Affairs supported the idea of an Ost-Ausschuß by noting that "existing arrangements" in the FRG "are not sufficient to offset the superiority of the Eastern trade monopolies;" ibid., 11: Drucksache Nr. 3282, 9011-2.
26. With countries where old JEIA treaties were in place (Poland, Czechoslovakia, Hungary, and Bulgaria), a simple solution was found in the extension of these treaties without any mention of their previous legal basis. However, relations with the Soviet Union, Romania, and China required some other solution.
27. Draft response of Erhard to Wilhelm Naegel (Christian Democrats), November 1952, 411.22, 1, PAAA.

found its solution to this diplomatic dilemma in the Ost-Ausschuß, which would now perform the double duty of protecting private economic interests and representing the Federal Republic. This private sector group would assume the task of "making trade policy contact with those East bloc countries with which JEIA agreements do not exist."[28] Private West German citizens would substitute for government officers from the Foreign Office and Economics Ministries while an agreement between the Ost-Ausschuß and some subordinate agency in the Soviet foreign trade bureaucracy would substitute for a full trade treaty between the two countries.

Just three weeks after the Bundestag resolution of 6 May, Kroll drafted plans for a submission to the Cabinet that reflected the dual role envisioned for the Ost-Ausschuß by authorizing the Economics Ministry to begin the "resumption or expansion of economic relations with the East bloc countries" and to "arrange for the organizational consolidation of participating German economic groups for the purpose of protecting their economic interests vis-à-vis the East bloc countries (Ost-Ausschuß)."[29] On 30 June the BdI informed its member groups that "in cooperation with the appropriate government offices" the BdI and other leading interest groups would "create" [ins Leben rufen] an Ost-Ausschuß on 3 July 1952. The new Committee would "advise" the government and "coordinate measures to avoid macroeconomically damaging underbidding" by German suppliers.[30]

On 14 July 1952 a "small circle of leading experts in Ost-Geschäft" gathered in Frankfurt for a "preparatory meeting" on the Ost-Ausschuß. Two days later the BdI solicited nominations from the Verbände for "leading figures from industry" with experience in

28. Reinhardt to Westrick and Erhard on "Organization and Function of the Eastern Committee," 23 March 1956, B102/58158, BA.
29. Kroll draft to Erhard, 26 May 1952, B102/57785, BA; Erhard's cabinet submission, 16 June 1952, B102/7204, BA. In the Chancellor's Office, Dossmann (Referat 6: "Cabinet Coordination" of economic policy) recommended approval of the plan on 23 June 1952, B136/7808, BA. On the following day, 24 June 1952, the Cabinet, with little discussion, approved Erhard's plan to set up the Eastern Committee, B136/7808, BA, available in *Die Kabinettsprotokolle der Bundesregierung* (Boppard am Rhein, 1982-), 5 (1952), 403.
30. Beutler's "Mitteilung," 30 June 1952, OA 4, BdI. On 3 July the Economics Ministry (Seeliger) informed the BdI and other groups that the government was "thinking" of an "organizational consolidation of all interested firms," although a BdI Aktenvermerk from 26 June notes that Mann as Chairman of the Foreign Trade Committee already had the permission of the Economics Ministry to call together an Ost-Ausschuß; both documents in OA 4, BdI. The formal decision to "follow the government's initiative" [!] and call for the creation of an Ost-Ausschuß was made by the BdI's Foreign Trade Committee on 3 July 1952, BdI "Aussenhandels-Mitteilung" 78/52, 16 July 1952, OA 4, BdI.

Eastern trade to join the Committee.[31] After some months of self-interested wrangling among the sectoral interest groups, retired Bremen Senator H. Wenhold (C.F. Corssen) and Hermann J. Abs joined Menne and Reuter on the Vorstand. Otto Wolff von Amerongen chaired the important "working group" on the USSR.[32] On 9 October 1952 the Ost-Ausschuß held its first, well-publicized "konstituierende" assembly, meeting with Erhard and his "closest advisers" to discuss the "duties and organization" of the new Ost-Ausschuß.[33] The Committee as it emerged was a product of the larger "Arbeitsgemeinschaft Aussenhandel," which included the BdI, the German Chamber of Commerce, the Bundesverband des Deutschen Groß- und Außenhandels, the Bundesverband deutscher Banken, and the Außenhandelsvereinigung des Deutschen Einzelhandels. In fact the BdI dominated the Ost-Ausschuß by providing the Chairman, Reuter; one of the three Deputy Chairs, Menne (after 1956, two of four); the Chairman of the important working group on the USSR (Wolff); and the Executive Secretary (Geschäftsführer) of both the Ost-Ausschuß as a whole and the working group on the USSR (von Carnap).

The Eastern Committee had come into being as a neocorporatist mechanism for the pursuit of two enduring West German trade strategies vis-à-vis the Soviet Union. Most fundamentally, the Eastern Committee could serve as a way of conducting trade negotiations with the Soviets in the immediate postwar framework of international relations that prevented any official contacts between the two countries. For both the government and business, trade negotiations were part of a larger strategic goal: an "expansion of trade with the East bloc" with the "possibility of reconquering our old position" in the Eastern trade, as Hans Kroll explained to a

31. BdI "Aussenhandels-Mitteilung" 78/52, 16 July 1952, OA 4, BdI. Nominations from the Verbände would add members to the core group of industrial representatives already "recommended" [vorgeschlagen] by the BdI: W. Alexander Menne (Hoechst), Hans Reuter (Demag), Director Leipersberger (Siemens), Carl Haiblen (Felten & Guilleaume), Richard Carstensen (MAN), Karl Lange (VDMA), Curt Schilde (Ernst Krause & Co.), and Gerhard Schauke (Mannesmann Export GmbH). A draft of introductory remarks for the 14 July meeting described the new Ost-Ausschuß as "having been planned by us [BdI] for some time already," OA 4, BdI.
32. According to Wolff, his selection as Chairman was made at Erhard's personal insistence based on the reputation Otto Wolff Sr. had made as a pioneer in German trade with Soviets in the early 1920s. Otto Wolff, personal interview with the author, Cologne, 3 July 1991.
33. On this meeting see the nearly identical statements issued by the Economics Ministry (Tages-Nachrichten of the Federal Minister for Economics, Nr. 1419, 10 October 1952, Ludwig-Erhard-Archiv, Bonn) and by the BdI in its *Mitteilungen*, October 1952.

group of West German industrialists in early 1952.[34] The Ost-Ausschuß was also a means to a second strategic goal: preventing the centrally directed foreign trading companies of the Soviet economy from exploiting the competition between private German firms to gain excessive concessions on prices, credits, and delivery terms. Drawing on experience with Soviet buyers in the interwar period, the new Eastern Committee hoped to get uniform "terms of delivery, acceptance, and payments" for trade with all East European countries – a project insistently advanced by the business community and supported by the government.[35]

In pursuing the twin goals of West German commercial strategy toward the Soviets – expanding trade and defending profits by restricting intra-German competition – the Ost-Ausschuß occupied a singularly advantageous position. Viewed by the Federal government as "the sole representative of the entire business community for Eastern trade questions," the Ost-Ausschuß possessed the unambiguous backing of the state.[36] As the product of a broad coalition of Spitzenverbände in the "Arbeitsgemeinschaft Außenhandel," the Ost-Ausschuß occupied an unchallenged position within the private sector. In spite of these formidable assets, the Ost-Ausschuß was not able to secure the immediate, well articulated West German commercial objectives in the Soviet trade.

"UNTER DEN HEUTIGEN UMSTÄNDEN IST EINE BEFRIEDIGENDE LÖSUNG NICHT ZU FINDEN:" ORGANIZING A WEST GERMAN RESPONSE TO THE SOVIET STATE MONOPOLY IN FOREIGN TRADE.[37]

Since early 1950 portions of the West German business community had placed the standardization of business practices toward the Soviets in order to avoid excessive intra-German competition at the very top of German priorities for a successful return to the Eastern trade. Several extensive rounds of negotiations with the Soviets on this issue ran through the end of the decade without producing the agreements sought by the Ost-Ausschuß. By the early 1960s the realization set in

34. "Memorandum to the Files" on an 18 January meeting at the Economics Ministry, OA4, BdI.
35. Reinhardt to Westrick and Erhard on "Organization and Function of the Eastern Committee," 23 March 1956, B102/58158, BA.
36. Tages-Nachrichten of the Federal Minister for Economics, Nr. 1425, 16 October 1952, Ludwig-Erhard-Archiv, Bonn.
37. Wallenhorst summation, 7 June 1960, PR5 73 10.3, Mannesmann Archiv.

that a binding agreement with the Soviets on terms of delivery, credit and payment, and arbitration procedures would not be forthcoming. At the same time the Ost-Ausschuß was unwilling and unable to impose unilaterally a standard set of terms on German exporters.

A first round of preliminary discussions between the Ost-Ausschuß and Soviet trade representatives took place in 1953-54 in the background of United Nations trade development meetings held in Geneva. Wolff, von Carnap, and von Ziegesar (VDMA) met with members of the Soviet Ministry for Internal and Foreign Trade and established a working relationship with the Soviet trade attaché normally stationed in Bern, Kurepov; they presented their idea for the conclusion of a "Rahmenabkommen" that would set the basic terms for all West German industrial sales to the Soviets.[38] Over the following two years, political uncertainties first inside the Soviet Union (the first phase of the Stalin succession struggle) and then within the Western alliance (the EDC debâcle) prevented sustained negotiations between the Soviets and the Ost-Ausschuß, so that no real progress was achieved until 1953-54.

When Adenauer's September 1955 visit to Moscow failed to produce any official trade agreements, the Ost-Ausschuß again took up the pursuit of a private agreement. However, Ost-Ausschuß plans for a private-level understanding with the USSR were thwarted by the Soviets, who wanted an official treaty and were not willing to accept a private understanding in its place. As a result of these conflicting aims, both sides spent 1956 in a non-productive circle of negotiations.

Bulganin's February 1957 letter to Adenauer finally served as the impetus to break this deadlock and begin formal treaty negotiations between the two governments.[39] Yet even the resulting agreement, signed in Bonn on 25 April 1958, did not resolve the issue of general terms for Soviet contracts that the Ost-Ausschuß considered so pressing. Instead, an exchange of letters between German chief negotiator Rolf Lahr and Soviet Deputy Minister of Foreign Trade Kumykin indicated that both sides would pursue an agreement between the Soviet Union and the Ost-Ausschuß on "general delivery terms and questions of arbitration."[40]

Despite their written promise of April 1958, the Soviets refused to commit themselves to any generally applicable set of terms for Ger-

---

38. Memoranda by Wolff, 20 April 1953 and by Zahn-Stranik (desk officer for East-West trade in the Handelspolitische Abteilung of the West German Foreign Office), 21 April 1952, both documents in OA 1, BdI; "Ergebnisprotokoll" signed by Wolff and other Ost-Ausschuß members, 3 July 1953, OA 1, BdI.
39. For the text of the Bulganin's 5 February 1957 letter, *Dokumente zur Deutschlandpolitik*, III. Reihe, 3, 299-315.
40. 413.85.00/101, PAAA.

man-Soviet business. This Soviet refusal began first as a postponement of discussions on the matter until after the new Soviet Trade Office in Cologne had opened, and then until after the Bundestag had ratified the trade agreement between the two states (February 1959).[41] Then, on 8 April 1959, Medvedkov, the senior officer of the Soviet Embassy's Trade Department, told Wolff and other members of the Ost-Ausschuß that the Soviets were not considering the "obligatory" delivery and payment terms being advanced by the Ost-Ausschuß, but rather were thinking of voluntary "guidelines" for future West German-Soviet deals. Medvekov repeated that message to Wolff at meetings on 23 June and 4 September.[42] The Soviet Foreign Trade Ministry made the same point to West German Ambassador Hans Kroll in Moscow on 2 November.[43]

By this time, November 1959, the West German Foreign Office came to the accurate assessment that the Soviet position had "hardened" in a refusal to sign any obligatory general terms for Soviet purchases that would regulate West German-Soviet trade in the manner long sought by the Ost-Ausschuß.[44] In January 1960 the Federal Republic entered into a new round of routine negotiations with the Soviets over the annual "commodity list," which helped shape trade for the upcoming year, although the issue of standard terms for business contracts with the Soviets remained unresolved. Approval of the new commodity lists for 1960 in late February served as an admission by the West Germans that they no longer expected a resolution of the general terms issue.[45]

Unable to obtain Soviet cooperation for a bilateral agreement on general terms for deliveries and payments, the Ost-Ausschuß was forced to consider a unilateral West German imposition of such terms on all Soviet contracts. Not only the Ost-Ausschuß itself, but also the key government ministries whose cooperation would have been necessary to enforce any self-imposed terms (Foreign Office and Economics Ministry) were deeply divided internally over the wisdom of such a move. Influential voices within each of these agencies argued that any set of business terms unilaterally imposed by the Germans without the agreement of the Soviets would drive the Sovi-

41. Carnap to Herbert Gruhner (AEG), 19 May 1958, 72-189-15, RWWA; Carnap's notes on a 15 July 1958 conversation with Shalashov (Deputy head of the Trade Department at the Soviet embassy in Bonn), forwarded by Wolff to the Foreign Office on 17 July, ibid. and 413.85.00/106, PAAA.
42. 72-189-15, RWWA.
43. 413-85.00/101, PAAA.
44. Zahn-Stranik's memorandum, 7 November 1959, ibid.
45. Notice of the West German-Soviet negotiations for the 1960 commodity lists was published in the *Bundesanzeiger*, No. 52, 16 March 1960.

ets into the arms of German competitors in Britain, France, Italy, and Sweden. In addition, both the Ost-Ausschuß and Erhard's Economics Ministry balked at having the state assume such a commanding position in controlling foreign trade.

The Ost-Ausschuß itself had long been ambivalent on this issue. When the Ost-Ausschuß Hauptausschuß first considered the question on 23 May 1956, Wolff said he hoped that a set of unilaterally imposed West German terms could "be avoided," but that this would have to be considered if negotiations with the Soviets failed. That same meeting revealed the Ost-Ausschuß as deeply divided over whether a unilateral solution was "desirable or realizable."[46] As late as August 1958 the Ausschuß could not articulate a definite stand on the question in discussions with the West German Foreign Office.[47] Ost-Ausschuß indecision may have provided some comfort to the Foreign Office, which was itself divided on the question. In March 1956 both Albert Hilger van Scherpenberg, head of the Trade Policy Department, and Zahn-Stranik, at the East-West Trade desk, favored another attempt to negotiate with the Soviets rather than any unilateral West German action. Yet at a 28 April 1956 meeting on Eastern trade questions, Hallstein, "after extensive discussion," rather incomprehensibly claimed to favor further negotiations with the Soviets, but urged the Ost-Ausschuß to develop on its own a set of obligatory "minimum terms" as a solution to the problem.[48] Opinion at the upper levels of the Economics Ministry was similarly divided. Hermann Reinhardt, head of the Foreign Trade Department, favored an "autonomous" West German regulation of Soviet contracts, while Economics Minister Ludwig Erhard preferred a negotiated settlement with the Soviets.[49] With opinion divided among both businessmen and bureaucrats, it is not surprising that the government never took the bold step of instructing the Economics Ministry to use its power to enforce a set of binding terms on Soviet contracts.

Without either an agreement with the Soviets or obligatory terms imposed at home, West German industry lacked protection from the

46. OA 3/2, BdI; confirmation of Ost-Ausschuß indecision at this meeting from the perspective of the Economics Ministry, B102/57785, BA.
47. Ost-Ausschuß "Interne Notiz" on a 19 August meeting with members of the Economics Ministry and Foreign Office on how to proceed with negotiations for delivery and acceptance terms in West German-Soviet trade, 72-189-15, RWWA.
48. OA 3/1, BdI; B102/57785, BA.
49. Reinhardt at a meeting with Hallstein and OA members, 2 May 1956, B102/57785, BA; Wolff's account of Economics Ministry positions given at an Ost-Ausschuß meeting with Hallstein, 7 May 1956, OA 3/1, BdI. At the 19 August 1958 meeting cited above, the Economics Ministry representative (Schauenburg) declined to voice an opinion on the issue because the Economics Ministry "did not consider the question as belonging to the competence of the Foreign Office," 72-189-15, RWWA.

"unfair" trade practices of monopolistic Soviet foreign trade organizations. With the gradual decontrol of West German foreign trade after 1954 and the arrival of a freely convertible deutschmark in 1958, few regulations remained that might limit competition in the Eastern market.[50]

Those few industrial branches in which exports remained under state control, e.g., refined steel, had minimum prices and other standards imposed on them by the Economics Ministry (through the Bundesstelle für Warenverkehr), for which they were grateful.[51] Otherwise, it was a rare exception that private sector organizations could impose a settlement on competing firms. Even the generally well-organized iron and steel industry lacked the internal cohesion necessary to restrict competition in Soviet sales, as the discussions inside the iron and steel producers interest group (Wirtschaftsvereinigung Eisen und Stahlindustrie) in the late 1950s show.[52] Speaking for the important Walzstahl-Vereinigung, Dr. Wallenhorst admitted reluctantly that producers and exporters would be unwilling to commit to either a fullblown "syndicate" or to the "softer solution" of an organization that would "set offering prices."[53] In 1960 the Association of German Machine Building Institutes (VDMA) was repeating almost verbatim the old German complaint of the early 1920s: "Thanks to their monopolistic position, it is easy for the [Soviet] companies to play off one [West German] supplier against another."[54] Nor was this complaint restricted to industrial producers; West German insurance com-

50. For example, beginning in February 1959 West German exporters were free to arrange non-DM credits for buyers in the East, thus reopening intra-German competition in supplying credit to the Soviets. Earlier 1954 regulations of Economics Ministry (RA 89/54, based on powers granted under the Außenwirtschaftsgesetz of 1953) had prevented completion in this area by imposing a 90-day maximum on East European payments for West German exports. The prospect of renewed competition in this area was the subject of the "streng vertraulich" Vorstand meeting of the Ost-Ausschuß, 4 June 1959, OA 5/1, BdI.
51. Dr. Blankenagel's (Edelstahl-Vereinigung) comments at the 28 January 1959 meeting of the Wirtschaftsvereinigung Eisen und Stahlindustrie as recorded in the memo of H. Schulz (Phoenix-Rheinrohr), 29 January 1959 and in the Wirtschaftsvereinigung's own summary of that meeting ("Diskussionsgrundlagen zur Frage einer Neuorientierung des Eisen- und Stahl-Außenhandels gegenüber Staatshandel treibenden Ländern"), both documents in PR5 73 10.3, Mannesmann Archiv.
52. H. Schulz (Phoenix-Rheinrohr) understatedly characterized the 28 January 1959 meeting of the Wirtschaftsvereinigung Eisen und Stahlindustrie as revealing "substantial differences of opinion about the supervision of sales and the maintenance of prices" vis-à-vis countries with state monopolies in foreign trade. Schulz memorandum, 29 January 1959, PR5 73 10.3, Mannesmann Archiv.
53. Wallenhorst's summation, 7 June 1960, PR5 73 10.3, Mannesmann Archiv.
54. Memorandum from the Economics Ministry's desk for "Maschinen-, Fahrzeug-, und Stahlbau," 26 July 1960, B102/18492b, BA.

panies complained that Soviets unfairly used the "Übergewicht" of their "monopolistic economy" against individual private trade partners to insist that all freight insurance be covered by Soviet agencies.[55]

A decade of unsuccessful West German business strategy toward the Soviet bloc can be summed up in Wallenhorst's June 1960 lament: "Since 1953 the necessity of confronting the centralized buying system of the East bloc countries with a centralized sales system in order to prevent the Eastern side from playing off the exporters against each other has been repeatedly emphasized in numerous meetings, press reports, etc. Despite repeated attempts, a practical solution has not yet been found."[56]

"INSGESAMT KANN DIE BUNDESREPUBLIK MIT DER ENTWICKLUNG DES OSTHANDELS ZUFRIEDEN SEIN:" THE SOURCES OF WEST GERMAN SUCCESS.[57]

Ironically, the West German private sector's long-term inability to create an institutional framework that would limit intra-German competition in exports to the Soviet bloc overlapped in time with West German industry regaining its traditional position as the primary supplier of value-added merchandise to Eastern Europe. What does this coincidence of failure and success in the 1950s say about West German business strategies and their role in regaining the Soviet market?

Most fundamentally, these events indicate that West German business circles grossly overestimated the organizational and negotiating advantages that Soviet agencies held as a result of the state monopoly in foreign trade. In 1951 the BdI had warned that West German-Soviet trade would "develop disadvantageously" for the exporters from the free market economy if Soviet tactics were not countered by centralized West German structures. Instead, the growth of trade accelerated through the end of the decade and West German producers and exporters participated eagerly in the Soviet market. West German profits might well have been higher if exporters had succeeded in some price-fixing arrangement on the West German side. Yet even without that artificial cushion, profit

---

55. Edgar Schnell (General-Direktor of Nordstern Allgemeine Versicherung) on the need for a "general agreement" with the Soviets on transport insurance questions, 12 May 1958, RWWA 72-189-15.
56. Wallenhorst (Walzstahl-Vereinigung) to Sendler, 7 June 1960, PR5 73 10.3, Mannesmann Archiv.
57. Otto Wolff at a meeting of the Haupt-Ausschuß of the Ost-Ausschuß, 16 December 1958, OA 5/1, BdI.

margins were comfortable enough that West German suppliers filled 90 percent of the industrial orders proposed by the Soviets in the annual commodity lists of 1958-60.

The BdI had made some grievous errors in extracting the lessons for a West German strategy for the 1950s from the German experiences with the Soviets in the late 1920s and early 1930s. The two periods did not compare well. The late 1920s and the 1930s were characterized by overproduction, depressed demand, and a uniquely advantageous buyer's market for capital equipment. In postwar Europe, by contrast, a strong seller's market for capital goods prevailed, keeping the Federal Republic out of recession until the mid-1960s.[58] In working to recover the Soviet market after 1945, German business did not need a centralized counter-organization to maintain prices and preserve profits – the global forces of supply and demand (to which the Soviets were also subject when they ventured into the world market) performed those functions through high demand for German investment goods.

The advantages that propelled West German industry to the top of the Soviet import market in the 1950s were much broader and deeper than the organizational tactic that often preoccupied the Ost-Ausschuß. Underneath any short-term strategy for countering the Soviet organizational advantage, lay enduring German business practices, larger political arrangements of the Federal Republic, and traditional German economic structures.

First and most fundamentally the West Germans displayed a broadly based, long-term commitment to regaining a leading position in the East European and Soviet markets. The West German private sector began planning an Ost-Ausschuß in February 1950 – just five months after the founding of the FRG and well before the new state recovered full commercial sovereignty. Looking back on these years, Otto Wolff cited the West German commitment to "our natural markets" in the East and "determination" and "patience" in regaining those markets as the starting points for West German success in the Soviet market.[59] Businessmen and bureaucrats shared the assumption that West German industry could, should, and would regain its former dominance in the Soviet market. In a June 1950 let-

---

58. Alternatively, one must at least consider that BdI members intentionally exaggerated the Soviet organizational advantage in an effort to foster creation of a West German counter-organization, for which support would not otherwise have been forthcoming. I have seen no evidence that this was the case, and none that the BdI intentionally misled any government or private group in its sometimes overly optimistic and sometimes overly pessimistic assessments of the Soviet and East European markets.
59. Otto Wolff, personal interview with the author, Cologne, 3 July 1991.

ter to Chancellor Adenauer on East-West trade issues, Erhard cited West German industry's "oldest traditional" economic contacts and "centuries old relationships" in assuming that the new FRG would come to occupy a "special economic position" vis-à-vis the Soviet bloc.[60] When Hans Kroll mentioned "reconquering our old position" in the Eastern market as a goal of West German commercial policy, he did so with the casual confidence that this objective was taken for granted in both government and business circles.

This shared view of West Germany's ultimate commercial mission in the East led to a second source of West German success in the East: the intimate working relationship forged between the Federal government and the business community in this issue area. Assured that Adenauer, Erhard, Kroll, van Scherpenberg, and other members of the ministerial bureaucracy were committed to the ideal of maximizing trade with the East within the existing political limits, the BdI backed its government on every aspect of its Ostpolitik, even when that support required short-term economic setbacks.[61] As a result, Soviet and East European governments were never able to set economic interests against political interests or to find a fissure between the Federal government and its private sector that might be exploited for political or economic gain by the East. The Ost-Ausschuß played a central role in forging and maintaining this West German consensus; it was here that leading industrial, commercial, and financial representatives met with upper level members of the ministerial bureaucracy to assess the political and economic trade-offs of policy decisions. As a corporatist structure that balanced private desires with public duties, the Ost-Ausschuß was well suited to handling the inextricably connected political and economic facets of the Osthandel. In this larger sense the Ost-Ausschuß did serve as the counter-organization to the Soviet structures of a state monopoly in foreign trade.

Ultimately, West German commercial success in the Soviet Union and Eastern Europe rested on a material basis. Most fundamentally, West German industry had the advanced capital and investment goods that the East needed. These quality products were supported by market knowledge, short delivery times, punctual delivery, reliable installation (when required), and toward the end of the decade, by short-term credits. In assessing the process by which West Ger-

60. Erhard to Adenauer, "Betr.: Ost-West-Handel," 13 June 1950, B136/7807, BA.
61. I have explored the emergence of a West German government-private sector consensus on Osthandel goals and policies in the 1950s elsewhere, most recently in "Die (Wieder) Geburt der westdeutschen Wirtschafts-Diplomatie in Osteuropa 1950-1960," in Rolf Steininger (ed.), *Die doppelte Eindämmung: Die deutsche Frage und europäische Sicherheit in den 50er Jahren* (Munich, 1993).

man industry regained its leading position in the Soviet market, Otto Wolff emphasized the material basis of success, particularly the "trust" that Eastern trade partners placed in the abilities of the German economy to deliver quality goods.[62]

These sources of West German success in the East – commitment to the Eastern market, corporatist consensus via the Ost-Ausschuß, and high quality products – were not strategies and structures unique to the West German experience in Eastern Europe. Rather, each component of success in the East was a regionally applied variant of more general and more enduring German export strategies. Determination to regain the East European and Soviet markets was the regional version of a traditional West German commitment to market knowledge and patience. The Ost-Ausschuß was the regionally specific version of larger West German corporatist structures that fostered government-business cooperation, particularly in trade policy.[63] The dynamos, generators, pipes, fittings, and food processing equipment that moved from West Germany to the Soviet Union was a regional subset of a larger flow of advanced capital goods that went from the Federal Republic to other parts of the world.

Market knowledge, government-business cooperation at home, and first-rate products – these are what German business used to offset the state monopoly in foreign trade and regain the Soviet market. These strategies were not unique to the Soviet market, but were the same material advantages that underlay West German success in other export markets as well: Western Europe, Latin America, North America. Nor were these qualities new to the postwar era. Some of these same enduring attributes had made German products dominant in the Russian market prior to 1914 and in the Soviet market in the 1920s.[64] This was the perhaps too obvious lesson of the past – a lesson that West German industry needed to relearn in the 1950s. It was then that unconscious Osthandel strategies were already laying the groundwork for a new era of German economic success in the East – an era that entered another phase in the 1970s and even more so in the 1990s and after the collapse of the Soviet Union and its East European empire.[65]

---

62. Otto Wolff, personal interview with the author, Cologne, 3 July 1991.
63. E.g., the Economics Ministry's "Foreign Trade Council," the "Länder Committee on Foreign Trade," and the "Parliamentary Council on Trade Agreements."
64. A Soviet foreign trade report of 1921 listed the following German qualities as reasons Soviet trade officials gladly placed their orders with German suppliers: geographic location, good knowledge of the Russian market, and the high quality of German manufactures; cited in Günter Rosenfeld, *Sowjetunion und Deutschalnd 1922-1933* (Berlin [East], 1984), 66, note 208.
65. See above and below the contributions by V.R. Berghahn.

Chapter 6

❖

LOWERING SOVIET EXPECTATIONS
West German Industry and Osthandel during the Brandt Era

Volker R. Berghahn

*I*n the previous chapter, Mark Spaulding has analyzed, on the basis of new archival material, West German Osthandel strategies during the 1950s. He did so largely from the perspective of industry and of those of its branches that were particularly interested in trade with Eastern Europe and the Soviet Union. What is so striking about this story is the strong German desire to reconquer traditional trading positions that had been lost at the end of World War II; for without Hitler's attempt to establish a brutal formal empire in the East and his subsequent defeat in 1945, the commercial links that had been forged between the Weimar Republic and Stalin's Russia before 1933 might well have survived the Great Slump. Indeed, with the Western trading system – since World War I in virtually a permanent state of instability anyway – being swept by a wave of protectionism and economic nationalism in the early 1930s, the Soviet Union became one of Germany's best customers. Ironically, without Stalin the German depression with its millions of unemployed might have been even worse. Hitler's aggressive policies and ultimately his invasion of

Eastern Europe and the Soviet Union changed all that, and in 1945 Germany and the vast territories its armies had conquered and ruthlessly exploited lay in ruins.

The year 1945 was supposed to be a 'new beginning.' Yet given the many continuities in managerial personnel and attitudes that were also in evidence in other fields of West German industrial politics after the war,[1] it is not surprising that parts of the German business community would be looking east again in their quest to lift their companies out of the rubble in which the Hitler regime had left them. There were other factors that were also propelling them eastward. Although the evidence is less tangible, it apparently took many industrialists some time to accept that Germany's traditional power position in Europe, which still looked so invincible in 1941, had been completely destroyed.[2] Equally, they were slow to realize that they were now supposed to find a place under the large, though still poorly defined roof of the Western Pax Americana, just as the East Germans were to be included in the Pax Sovietica. In its economic ramifications, the "American Peace" meant that German business was expected to integrate itself into a liberal-capitalist "Open Door" Western world trading system and to recast its traditional restrictive organizational structures, above all their elaborate cartel system, in such a way that it was compatible with American notions of multilaterialism.[3]

The initial reluctance to face these new postwar realities was reinforced by resentments at Allied de-Nazification, decartellization, and dismantling policies. The beginning of the cold war, which resulted in a shift in American occupation policy away from primarily punitive measures, thereby exacerbating the inequalities that had already occurred in the treatment of former Nazis, confirmed many industrialists, who had been interned and de-Nazified, in their feelings of righteousness. They were convinced that their interpretations of their roles in the Third Reich had been all along more accurate than those of the "dogmatic" Americans who, motivated by a missionary zeal, had put "innocent" colleagues in the dock. They also insisted that their predictions about the course of postwar history had been right: communism was the real enemy, and fighting it was more important than hunting suspected Nazis. Still, it is important to emphasize that we are only just beginning to appreciate how deeply internment, de-Nazification, and the trials of prominent industrialists

---

1. See V.R. Berghahn, *The Americanisation of West German Industry, 1945-1973*, (New York, 1987), 40ff.
2. See, e.g., V.R. Berghahn and P.J. Friedrich, *Otto A. Friedrich. Ein politischer Unternehmer* (Frankfurt, 1993), 57ff.
3. See V.R. Berghahn, *Americanisation*, 155ff.

at Nuremberg traumatized an entire older generation of German entrepreneurs and managers.

While, with the acceleration of the East-West confrontation, these resentments and feelings of bitterness were gradually overwhelmed by a desire to cooperate with the Allies in the defense of Western Europe against communism and the Red Army, another reservation about Washington's grand strategy lingered on well into the 1950s. Many German managers continued to be skeptical that the Open Door the U.S. were working so hard to establish would work and survive. They believed that it would, if nothing else, be vulnerable to crises, when nations would quickly relapse into the economic nationalism and protectionism of the 1930s. As they saw it, where then would a country like Germany, whose industries were vitally dependent upon raw materials from overseas, find itself? If confidence in the viability of multilateralism had been greater, it would be difficult to understand why German industry was so keen, in the 1950s, to revive production facilities for synthetic rubber and gasoline – just in case the Open Door in natural caoutchouc and fossil fuels might be slammed shut again in a crisis. It is the prevalence of such worries that explains, at least in part, the renewed look in the 1950s toward those countries, now under communism, with which Germany had traditionally exchanged manufactured goods for raw materials and foodstuffs.

The outbreak of the Korean War is a case in point. At the start it very much looked like precisely another dreaded crisis of the Western world economy. By the end of 1950 the Americans began to press for a system of priority allocations for raw materials and steel among the industries of the NATO countries, and Bonn was strongly urged to regulate certain industries. Otto A. Friedrich, an industrialist from Hamburg-Harburg and a member of the presidium of the Federation of German Industries (BDI), was appointed Raw Materials Advisor to the Federal Government.[4] Fortunately, this time the crisis was quickly overcome and the postwar boom of the Western economy resumed. Even now German skepticism did not disappear completely and, indeed, received a fresh boost when West German business discovered that moving into the American market on a larger scale was not as easy as liberal-capitalist ideology proclaimed. While Washington loudly urged other countries to remove or lower their trade barriers, the U.S. domestic market was fenced in by many restrictions, as protectionist sentiment had remained much stronger in other parts of the continent than among the East Coast liberal-cap-

---

4. See V.R. Berghahn and P.J. Friedrich, *Otto A. Friedrich*, 134ff.

italist Establishment. And time and again Congress proved to be a powerful guardian of protectionist interests.

West Germany's Economics Minister Ludwig Erhard gained firsthand experience of this when he visited the U.S. in 1953 and met, among others, Clarence B. Randall, the chairman of a mixed commission, appointed by President Eisenhower and charged with looking into U.S. trade and tariff policies.[5] Although Randall was himself a freetrader, about half of his commission members were protectionists, and Randall feared that the latter might gain the upper hand, unless Erhard could show some progress in his fight against cartels and restrictive practices in the Federal Republic, on whose behavior as a pacemaker of economic change in Europe American eyes were fixed. As Erhard reported on his return to Bonn, for this reason it was important that "the call for security did not ring [through German industry] at this moment."

Finally, there was Washington's rigid embargo against the Soviet Union during those pivotal years of the cold war. This embargo included a range of manufactured goods that, in the eyes of West German industry, were not necessarily of strategic importance. Why could the Americans not be a bit more flexible about certain exports to the Soviet bloc? In short, West German business was thought to have some reason to feel aggrieved, and such feelings influenced moods and attitudes. Tradition, but also the above mentioned perceptions and experiences of the postwar period, thus caused industrialists to think of re-establishing their former trading links with the East. And trade there was, even if it must be stressed that the actual figures remained small when compared with West Germany's rapidly expanding links with Western Europe and the rest of the world. In 1952, some 62.3 percent of exports went to the OEEC countries; some 6.5 percent were sent to the U.S. A mere 5.5 percent was shipped to the countries of Eastern Europe.[6] In 1937 this figure had been three times higher. Meanwhile, the Federal Republic imported 48.3 percent of its goods from OEEC countries, while 13.4 percent came from the U.S. The Eastern European share was a barely 5 percent, trailing even behind Latin America and the countries of the Sterling bloc. Karl Lange, the secretary general of the Association of German Machine Tool Manufacturers (VDMA), was therefore objectively exaggerating (though personally probably convinced of the truth of his statement) when he declared in March 1950 at a closed meeting of top industrialists that improving trade relations with the East was "a question of survival for German industry."[7]

5. Ibid., 120ff., also for the following.
6. See R. Neebe, 'Optionen westdeutscher Aussenwirtschaftspolitik, 1949-1953', in L. Herbst et al. (eds.), *Vom Marshallplan zur EWG* (Munich, 1990), 193.
7. Ibid., 175.

Nevertheless, as Mark Spaulding has shown, the desire to rebuild traditional ties with Eastern Europe remained strong throughout the 1950s and beyond. By the 1960s the hitherto unfavorable political climate of Osthandel was becoming considerably more clement. Toward the end of the Eisenhower era, the idea had slowly been gaining ground that sooner or later the hardline policies of cold war confrontation, of non-recognition of the postwar territorial status quo, and of a Western "roll-back" of the Soviet Union would have to be replaced by detente between the superpowers. In the era of megatonne hydrogen bombs and Intercontinental Ballistic Missiles, there was no other way if a nuclear holocaust, by accident or by miscalculation, was to be avoided.

The rethinking of East-West relations was reinforced by the Kennedy administration, whose advent in 1960 slowly also began to affect the basic orientation of Ostpolitik in the Federal Republic. Although Chancellor Konrad Adenauer found adaptation very difficult, Social Democrats around Willy Brandt, the mayor of West Berlin, responded more flexibly to the incipient change in superpower relations.[8] They began to discuss a new-style Ostpolitik that would work for German reunification not on the basis of Adenauer's "policy of strength," but in the wake of American efforts at detente; they were also prepared explicitly to recognize the territorial status quo in the East as a precondition of gradual change in relations with the Soviet Bloc. Finally, it was hoped that a strategy of improvements in the diplomatic sphere would pave the way for a relaxation of political conditions inside East Germany: "Change through rapprochement." There is no need here to recount the evolution of Ostpolitik during the 1960s, as it has been quite well analyzes by other authors.[9] By 1969, when Brandt competed for the chancellorship and eventually won it, he campaigned, inter alia, on a specific program of settling the cold war disputes with West Germany's Eastern European neighbors.

These developments were bound to affect West German Osthandel, and those businessmen who had continued to look east for commercial opportunities were, not surprisingly, excited by them. Even if most of their trading partners were by now in the West, the boom of the 1950s had long since come to an end. So developing new markets meant spreading the risks of harder times, such as the Federal Republic had experienced in 1965-66. They also perceived a vast

---

8. See, e.g., H.-J. Grabbe, *Unionsparteien, Sozialdemokratie und Vereinigte Staaten von Amerika, 1945-1966* (Düsseldorf, 1983), 256ff.
9. See, e.g., W.F. Griffith, *The Ostpolitik of the Federal Republic of Germany* (Cambridge, Mass., 1978); R. Tilford (ed.), *The Ostpolitik and Political Change in Germany* (Farnborough, 1975).

potential for development, not least in the Soviet Union, and they thought to have the edge in Eastern European markets over their foreign competitors. No less encouraging was a new openness on the Soviet side. It also helped that in the Kremlin, the euphoria over sputnik and a sense that the communist East was outrunning the capitalist West had once again been replaced by a resurgence of the old inferiority complex. By the late 1960s it was clear that the Soviet bloc had fallen behind in cutting-edge technologies. There was potential, but it remained untapped. Moscow's huge planning bureaucracy not only lacked the dynamism, but also the capital to start or expand the large industrial development projects that were on the drawing boards. At the same time, the worldwide shift from coal to oil and natural gas as a primary source of energy had made the development of Siberia very attractive. The Soviet Union had plenty of oil and gas as well as other raw materials that, if tapped and offered on the world market, would yield much needed revenue with which to finance other industrial projects.

It is against the background of intensified Ostpolitik contacts and the start of negotiations by the newly elected SPD/FDP coalition government in Bonn under Chancellor Brandt, which in turn changed the Osthandel climate, that top West German industrialists prepared to journey eastward. One of them was Otto A. Friedrich, whose reports on his experiences in the Soviet Union in 1970 and 1973 form the basis of the subsequent analysis. Friedrich had meanwhile become an important figure in the Osthandel game. He was a partner of the Flick Group, one of the most powerful industrial conglomerates in the Federal Republic still run by the aging Friedrich Flick and a few close associates. In 1969 he had also been elected president of the German Employers' Federation (BDA). Flick, who had been tried by the Allies after the war for his involvement with the Nazi regime, had rebuilt an empire that gave him a major stake in a number of key enterprises. One of them was Daimler-Benz, the crown jewel of West Germany's powerful automobile industry. The Stuttgart company had in the meantime been approached by Moscow about the building and running of a large truck assembly plant, known as the Kama Project.

While the project was no doubt important in itself, its conception also signalled a change in the traditional theme of Osthandel. In the past German-Russian economic relations had been based primarily on the exchange of goods. Kama went beyond this and hence required a deeper German involvement, i.e., technical cooperation and support in the running of new production facilities in the Soviet Union. It required direct investments rather than just government loan guarantees and the opening of sales offices in another country. We have seen that the West Germans had begun cautiously to move into this new stage in the internationalization of Western capitalism in the late 1950s, when they took participations in foreign companies, mainly in Western Europe, and prepared to set up production facilities overseas. Now the Soviets asked them to come to the East on a similar basis. Yet, given the large capital outlays required, and also remembering their earlier difficulties with Soviet bureaucracies, it is not surprising that the spokesmen of German industry should fall back on an idea the British Prime Minister David Lloyd George had put forward in 1922 at the Genoa Conference. Hoping to open up the economy of Leninist Russia during its NEP period after the end of the civil war, he had proposed the formation of an international consortium to mobilize the necessary resources for a revival of links with Russia, of course under British leadership. The plan was scuttled when the Weimar Government and Foreign Minister Walther Rathenau detached themselves from Lloyd George's scheme and signed a bilateral agreement with the Bolsheviks at Rapallo.[10] Whatever Rathenau's calculations and the domestic pressures upon him may have been, Rapallo led to the full-scale resumption of German industry's business links with Russia after World War I.

Because of these larger ramifications of Friedrich's trip to the Soviet Union both for the investment strategies of the Flick Group and of West German industry as a whole, he prepared himself with great care and over several months.[11] It was clear from the start that the Kremlin would see him as a spokesman of industry, and his papers therefore contain a variety of newspaper cuttings on the themes of Ostpolitik and Osthandel as well as notes on his discussions with Foreign Minister Walther Scheel, Defense Minister Helmut Schmidt, and Hanns Martin Schleyer of Daimler-Benz. Then, in August 1970, Bonn and Moscow signed a treaty that was seen by German business as a crucial step in the Soviet-German rapprochement. It was at this point that Hans-Günther Sohl, the head of the Thyssen trust and one of the most influential spokesmen of the Ruhr steel industry, raised the question of the future of Osthandel beyond the Kama Project and the earlier massive contracts to lay pipelines for oil and natural gas between Siberia and western Europe. Sohl's conclusions were far from euphoric. Irrespective of "the positive attitude of German business toward relations with the USSR," he wrote, "a spectacular increase of trade could hardly be expected in the next

---

10. See, e.g., H. Graml, *Europa zwischen den Kriegen*, (Munich, 1969), 126ff.
11. For details see V.R. Berghahn and P.J. Friedrich, *Otto A. Friedrich*, 35lff., also for the following.

few years." The differences between the two political and economic systems in East and West would stand in the way of such an increase. Moreover, Sohl added, the Soviet Union suffered from a severe shortage of foreign exchange. Meanwhile, on the German side, he invoked a shortage of capital and current high interest rates as an obstacle to financing large long-term ventures in the East.

Two weeks later Friedrich received an official invitation to visit the Soviet Union from G.M. Gvishiani, the vice president of the State Committee for Science and Technology. He went from 23-27 November 1970. The report on this trip is highly interesting not only as an account of his experiences and conversations in the Soviet Union, but also for what it had to say about the origins of the invitation. According to Friedrich it had been issued to him some time ago via France:

> This is why I paid a visit to Paris in February 1970 to inform myself. As is well-known, it was back then that major fears arose in France that German industry would go it alone in Russia; I therefore thought it appropriate to explain that German companies (like Daimler-Benz) were, when it came to such agreements, rather anxious to obtain the cooperation of French industry or that of other West European countries.

Indeed, in order to make certain that the French got this point, his visits in Paris also included a conversation with the French Minister for Industry, Xavier Ortoli, and with Marc Jacquet, the chairman of the Gaullist caucus in the National Assembly.

These impressions from his trips to France help to explain why Friedrich thought it wise to delay his acceptance of a Soviet invitation until November 1970. There were other reasons, above all his own unease about the evolution of Brandt's Ostpolitik. In June 1970 these qualms persuaded him to write a letter to Brandt in which he wondered if the chancellor was making too many concessions in his negotiations with Moscow. He admitted that it was difficult for him to fathom the pro's and con's of Brandt's strategy since he was not familiar with all its intricacies. However, he was certain that the Americans would, over the next few years, withdraw their troops from the European continent. This prospect alone, he conceded, certainly required "a new orientation of Ostpolitik at the right time." But Friedrich was apparently unsure when this would be. His discomfort also explains why he sought further information from Rainer Barzel, the parliamentary leader of the CDU which – as the main opposition party – had become very critical of Brandt's foreign policy.[12] In this conversation Friedrich gave a new reason why he was now slowly coming to

---

12. See A. Baring, *Machtwechsel* (Stuttgart, 1982), 197ff.

feel that a trip to Moscow would be timely, after all; he "considered it dangerous that [the Soviets] might have illusions about the scope of a possible co-operation with German industry" and that this might lead "to negative repercussions if they are disappointed later on." He then corrected the last half sentence to read that it might result "in an even more tense relationship than in former years."

This was the message Friedrich took to Moscow at the end of November. Fortified by further preparatory discussions with Economics Minister Karl Schiller, State Secretary in the Foreign Office Paul Frank, Horst Emcke (Minister in the Chancellery), Hans Leussink (Minister for Research), Ernst-Wolf Mommsen, a fellow industrialist and state secretary in the Ministry of Defense, and others, he labored hard to put across to his Soviet hosts "*that the tempo and scope of an engagement of German industry* in the field of technological co-operation and in an expansion of the volume of trade with the Soviet Union *must not be overestimated.*"[13] Otherwise there would be disappointments and relations with the Federal Republic would only "deteriorate rather than improve." Friedrich also stressed "that German companies were completely free in their entrepreneurial decision-making." They could not be "pressured by the state or by their own associations to behave in a certain way." Moreover, all companies were subject to the free-wheeling capital market, where the interest rates charged for loans influenced their room for maneuver. Finally, Friedrich used every discussion with his Soviet hosts to point out "that no increased commitment of German firms could be expected without a satisfactory *solution to the Berlin Problem* and without a *recognition of the EEC as a reality*" of European politics. These two questions, he added, were "of fundamental importance to German business."

According to his later report, these remarks at first greatly disappointed his hosts. However, he also felt that "the Russians are more open to sincerely held, though uncomfortable views" than they would be to "unsubstantiated promises or even to exaggerated praises for what was being achieved and aimed at in the Soviet Union." Although Friedrich had quite a few criticisms of the Soviet system of planning, of productivity, and the provision of the population with consumer goods, he gained the general impression that "the GOSPLAN had achieved similar advances in respect of overall planning as had been made by the large trusts in the free economies of the West in the last 10 to 15 years." By this he meant that the Soviets, too, were learning from false starts "how much more flexibly planning must be handled, if it is to remain close to reality and that year after year the planning

---

13. V.R. Berghahn and P.J. Friedrich, *Otto A. Friedrich*, 353ff., also for the following.

of details had to be adjusted to new developments." Perhaps, he concluded, the Soviets had more experience in these matters than the West surmised, "just as the plans of larger trusts in the West are gaining in economic realism (*Wirtschaftsnähe*) from year to year."

Finally, Friedrich's report broached the "much discussed *question concerning a convergence of the [two] economic systems.*" He believed there was little of it, since the economic differences were simply too great. In the Soviet Union all decisions were subject not to the primacy of economic considerations, but to that of politics. Ultimately, all the Soviet leadership was interested in was the country's political power position secured by armaments that would give it parity with the United States and NATO and provide against dangers emanating from China. No economic or consumer interests would be strong enough to change these axioms of Soviet policy. In view of this, Friedrich added, all speculations about whether German deliveries of civilian goods would relieve the military sector or whether they would draw economic potential into the civilian sector became irrelevant. Neither development would influence the Soviets in their determination to remain militarily powerful at home and abroad, and thus cement their political dominance. Consequently, all German economic activity in Russia should be seen from just this angle: "What is serving detente and the prevention of dangerous crises in the world?" In this sense, he believed, a slow expansion that did not have negative effects on Bonn's Western allies might be realized.

Friedrich returned convinced that his trip had had a sobering effect on his hosts. He reported that Helmuth Allardt, the West German ambassador to Moscow, had expressed to him "his deep satisfaction" that the realities of the situation had been so clearly explained to the Kremlin. This had acted as an antidote to "the euphoria" that had infected the leading men of the Soviet government. Friedrich reiterated that this had been the main aim of his trip, and that it was certainly not connected to the Kama Project in which, he added, Daimler-Benz found itself in competition with Klöckner-Humboldt-Deutz, Renault, and British Leyland. Nor did he wish his trip to be seen as "a political aid [mission] for the current Federal Government." He was therefore also relieved that he "had not seen any friendly commentaries in the socialist newspapers," while he was not aware of any objections that had appeared in the papers that were "close to the BDA."

Friedrich maintained this reserved attitude during the following two years, as the debate on Ostpolitik reached its crisis point, pushing Osthandel into the background. Arnulf Baring has retold in great detail the story of the ratification of the various Eastern Treaties the

Brandt government negotiated in the early 1970s.[14] These agreements ran into fierce opposition from the CDU/CSU, which perceived them as a sell-out of vital West German national interests. The crisis reached its climax in April 1972, when Barzel introduced a vote of no-confidence in the Bundestag against Brandt that, had it been successful, would have installed him as Ccancellor of a new CDU/CSU government. Barzel failed, but the country remained in turmoil thereafter because Brandt asked the Federal president to dissolve Parliament and to hold fresh elections. These elections of November 1972 fetched Brandt an enlarged majority and a renewed mandate to bring his Ostpolitik to a conclusion.

Friedrich kept his distance from this battle among the political parties and was careful not to continue his contacts with the Soviets. Only Sohl had the independence of mind to undertake another trip to the Soviet Union in June 1972, accompanied only by his personal assistant and his son as his interpreter.[15] He wanted to look beyond the upheavals in West German domestic politics to see if there were still opportunities for Osthandel, whatever the outcome of Brandt's Ostpolitik. His impressions were apparently more positive than Friedrich's some 18 months earlier. He warned of underestimating the Soviet economy and pleaded for close cooperation between the Federal Republic and the USSR. In making this point it is unlikely that he, the steel manager, did not also have in mind Russia's vast raw materials reserves and trading opportunities for his trust.

However, Friedrich's reluctance to go himself before the elections of November 1972 should not be construed to mean that he had lost interest in Osthandel questions. Nothing demonstrated this more clearly than the fact that a new round of talks began just a few weeks after the victory of the Brandt coalition at the polls.[16] In January 1973 he had a visit from the Soviet chargé d'affaires at the Soviet embassy in Bonn-Rolandseck. The diplomat wanted to know whether German business had any "strong political reservations" about Osthandel. Friedrich denied this "generally," adding that there were no doubt "exceptions." Instead, he mentioned another obstacle, i.e., that "a fully employed and strongly export-oriented economy which over the years [and] with great sacrifice has built up its markets" could not within a short period provide additional export goods and additional technological cooperation. Still, he concluded, the traditional positive attitude of German industry toward Osthandel was undiminished. There existed, in his view, a solid basis for cooperation even if it had been neglected for many years.

14. A. Baring, *Machtwechsel*, 361ff.
15. V.R. Berghahn and P.J. Friedrich, *Otto A. Friedrich*, 355ff., also for the following.
16. Ibid., 355ff., also for the following.

It appears that the chargé d'affaires was testing the waters in advance of Leonid Breshnev's visit to Bonn in May 1973, which Friedrich was invited to attend. Later he gave his impressions in a letter to his brother Carl Joachim Friedrich, the well-known Harvard political scientist. He had been particularly struck by Breshnev's "mixture of joviality and genuine Russian cordiality," on the one hand, and his "brutal will to power," his continued awkwardness over the Berlin problem, and his "impatience with German industry's slowness in promoting the large-scale projects of Russia in Siberia," on the other. These observations and his sense of Germany's precarious position between the huge military and political potentials of the two superpowers left Friedrich uneasy, and it seems that it was also with these apprehensions that he set out on his second trip to Moscow in October 1973.

Briefed by Ulrich Sahm, Bonn's ambassador to Moscow, he also met Minister President Kossygin at this time. He learned that the negotiations with Daimler-Benz and the Gildemeister Machine Tool Co. were judged as "quite positive." But he also felt that his hosts had meanwhile gained the impression that Western interest (and that of the Federal Republic in particular) in cooperation with the Soviet Union had declined. Friedrich granted that progress had been slow, but this was not because of political problems; rather, because West German industry was busy meeting demand for its goods at home and in the West. He left feeling that these arguments had been accepted by his hosts – an impression that was later confirmed by Joachim Zahn, Daimler-Benz's top executive, who had been in Moscow on business at the same time as Friedrich.

Moving on to more specific items, Friedrich then summarized in his report his discussions on the exploitation of Siberia's energy sources and raw materials, about which Franco-Russian negotiations had taken place a few months earlier. He repeated his familiar view that these projects were too large and required such massive amounts of capital that they could not be mastered by a single country – not "at least as far as Europe is concerned." He thought it more sensible to turn this into a co-operative venture between several EEC countries. The Soviets should not hesitate to agree to "the formation of consortia of companies" from different European countries, instead of feeling that this solution would confront them with all-powerful capitalist "'monopolies.'" Friedrich was able to confirm that France would welcome such cooperations with German companies. Jointly they would also find it easier to solve the attendant credit problems. He was interested to see that Kossygin raised the question of the consortia himself, involving European firms with companies from America and Japan. He felt that the Minister President's queries may have been related to his recent negotiations with U.S. Treasury Secretary George Shultz and the impending visit to the USSR of the Japanese Prime Minister Tanaka. All in all, Friedrich left Moscow convinced that the Soviets continued to hold "strong hopes and expectations of a growing cooperation" with West German industry. Even if the tempo had been disappointingly slow, mutual trust had been strengthened. He thought he had contributed to this growing atmosphere of trust because he had been as open about the realities of the situation in the Federal Republic as he had been in 1970 during his first visit.

Although Ostpolitik since the 1960s had done much to smooth the path of Osthandel, West German industry's relations with the East continued to experience further ups and downs. On the one hand, the oil shock and the economic difficulties of the 1970s did much to invalidate Friedrich's argument that German business was too busy elsewhere to expand its markets in the East. On the other hand, the renewed tensions between the superpowers over Afghanistan and the arms race put a damper on Germany's trade with the Soviet bloc – at least until Michail Gorbachov came along. And with the collapse of that bloc and of communism, Germany's economic relations with the East became a different ball-game altogether – for the first time since World War I.

Chapter 7

❖

STRATEGIES OF GERMAN BIG BUSINESS IN THEIR INTERNATIONAL SETTING DURING THE 1980S

Margit Köppen

"Going global" is today's corporate strategy virtually worldwide, not only in terms of trading, but also of participations, joint ventures, and other alliances.

In Germany, however, the issue of international corporate strategies is frequently being reduced to what is called *Standortdebatte,* i.e., a debate on German competitiveness in comparison with the industries of other countries. In this context foreign investment is treated according to the notion that companies are forced to migrate to other countries because, in Germany, labor costs are too high and working hours too short. Management is using this argument as a means of exerting pressure on unions in wage negotiations. The following pages, therefore, also tackle the question of whether low wages and long working hours, which are primarily a feature of developing countries, but also one of peripheral European countries, are in fact as decisive for direct investment abroad as German management tends to argue.

The academic literature is somewhat more sophisticated and tries to identify specific patterns of internationalization. Following are just a few of the most common explanatory approaches. Starting out from automotive production, some have identified the international interlinked production as the current trend in production. Known as global sourcing, it means the worldwide exchange of product parts, components, and so-called CKD sets (e.g. dismantled or "completely knocked down" cars) between different production sites. According to this view, mass production of components is predominant in the world market and, as a consequence, the traditional linkage between products manufactured at a certain site and regional markets no longer exists.[1]

Other scholars have seen the opposite trend. In their recent book on the automotive industry J.P. Womack et al. of MIT assume that direct investment, decentralized in a flexible fashion and adjusted to specific regional markets, is the road of the future.[2]

There is yet another theory, represented in Germany by Konrad Seitz, according to which the world market will turn into one single integrated market that will eventually absorb domestic markets. As a result of this development "companies will globalize and set up worldwide production and research centers. Foreign investment will be the motor of the world economy and will replace traditional trading."[3] Seitz has formulated a bold theory that is far from reflecting German corporate reality.

In so far as his assumptions are based on statistical material, it is difficult to trace the corporate strategies behind the data found. It would require a detailed study and assessment of representative corporate activities, which go beyond the scope of this article. All I can do here is provide a glimpse of how German companies behave in the internationalization roundabout. Three aspects will be considered:

1. The strong market orientation of German direct investment, with the United States serving as a model.
2. The specific impetus provided by the European Internal Market of 1993.
3. The issue of wage costs as a decisive investment incentive.

INCREASE IN DIRECT INVESTMENTS AS A WORLDWIDE TREND

Foreign direct investment of companies from everywhere to everywhere boomed during the 1980s. Direct investment tripled in the years from 1984 to 1987, and continued to rise by another 20 percent

1. U. Bochum and H.-R. Meißner, "Im Tiefflug durch die Handelsschranken. Standortstrategien der großen Automobilkonzerne," in M. Muster and U. Richter (eds.), *Mit Vollgas in den Stau*, (Hamburg, 1990).
2. J.P. Womack, et al., *The Machine that Changed the World* (New York, 1990).
3. K. Seitz, *Die japanisch-amerikanische Herausforderung* (München, 1990).

between 1988 and 1989. With an annual 29 percent, the worldwide growth rate of direct investments since 1983 has been three times the growth rate of world trade and four times the growth rate of production (see Table 2.1, p. 226).

Meanwhile, in Germany, direct investment is being discussed almost exclusively under the ideological heading of "transfer of labor to low wage countries." In reality, the industrialized countries are more or less among themselves in this respect: between 1985 and 1989, 81 percent of worldwide direct investments went to the industrialized countries, and 70 percent of the direct investment capital flowing into foreign companies came from the five big metropolitan countries: Great Britain, United States, Japan, France, and Germany (see Table 2.2, p. 226).

Given the number of new investments per year, Japan has become the trendsetter in foreign investment since the mid-1980s. For the first time, Japan overtook Great Britain, which up to that date had traditionally provided the world's largest investment flow. As early as 1988 Japan as an investor had also overtaken the United States.

DIRECT INVESTMENTS OF GERMAN COMPANIES

So far, the German economy has been relying more on exports than on direct investment in order to supply world markets. Germany's total accumulated foreign investment accounts for no more than 30 percent of exports within a single year. The Federal Republic became the export champion of the 1980s; even in light of slackening economic activities, Germany still held its top position in 1990, with exports amounting to DM 641 billion, ahead of both the United States (DM 636 billion) and Japan (DM 436 billion).[4] But sales of foreign companies with German capital participation are also playing a substantial role in the world market. The turnovers achieved were about equal to those of Germany's total exports. In 1986 total German exports were DM 526 billion, while annual sales of foreign companies were DM 513 billion.[5]

In the 1980s German companies substantially increased their foreign investment activities. By the end of 1989 total foreign investment was DM 196 billion, with 5,400 German investors participating in international activities. This is a 132 percent increase compared to

4. United Nations, *World Investment Report 1991* (New York).
5. Deutsche Bundesbank, "Die Kapitalverflechtung der Unternehmen mit dem Ausland 1982-1988," in Statistische Beihefte zu den Monatsberichten der Deutschen Bundesbank, Reihe 3, Zahlungsbilanzstatistik, April 1990, No. 4.

1980 (see Table 2.3, p. 227). German industries, which are predominantly export-oriented, are also the frontrunners in direct investment. The chemical industry followed by electrical engineering, automobile manufacture, and mechanical engineering are the most powerful foreign investors. Exports are also distinctly higher in the three industries mentioned above. But even though they account for 45 percent of German exports, they contribute only 17.8 percent to foreign investment. Other metal industry sectors account for even less than 1 percent of the total of foreign investments. This leads to my first hypothesis: foreign investment supplements German exports, but is far from replacing them.

The regional structure of German foreign investment, too, reflects its market orientation: 74 percent of total investments went to the United States and the EC countries, i.e., to areas representing major sales markets. The United States and Canada continue to be the most important target countries of German direct investment, providing for roughly one-third of total investments. One major incentive to invest in the United States results from the strong exchange rate fluctuations of the deutschmark against the United States dollar, which hinder reliable export projections. In 1985, for example, the mark lost 38 percent in value against the dollar rate of 1980, and, in the annual average of 1990, outstripped again the level of 1985 by 82 percent. Of course, a strong mark aggravates exports in the dollar area, thus placing companies with their own production sites in the United States in a much better position.

A further incentive for direct investment in the United States is the option of opening up new markets. The geographical size of the United States alone is conducive to the setting up of production capacities, distribution, and service networks on site. Between 1980 and 1989 German direct investment in the United States tripled, with the chemical industry being by far the largest investor, followed by electrical engineering, the automotive industry, and mechanical engineering. Siemens tops all other German corporations in America investment activities, increasing the number of employed in the United States from roughly 1,000 at the beginning of the 1970s to some 30,000 in the 1990s. As early as in the mid-1980s about 85 percent of Siemens' American sales derived from performance achieved in that country. By taking over the American Bendix-Electronic Group, Siemens succeeded in establishing itself as a supplier of automobile electronics. Together with Corning, Siemens is today No. 1 in the glass fiber cable market. In 1987 the 50-50 joint venture SIECOR held a 45 percent market share in the United States. Strengthened by the acquisition of the former IBM company ROLM, Siemens aimed to become the third largest supplier of telephone communication systems after AT&T and Northern Telecom. Besides Siemens there is Bosch as a true German triad company, with its own United States-based production sites and joint ventures for car electronics and only very recently BMW and Daimler-Benz have followed suit. Two of Bosch's four joint ventures are managed by Japanese partners – a concept that makes some sense, as it facilitates efforts to supply other United States-based Japanese car manufactures. Bosch also has joint ventures with Japanese suppliers in Japan, for instance, who manufacture ABS Systems, based on Bosch technology.

The above mentioned examples provide evidence of the fact that capturing markets is the prime incentive to invest. All of Bosch's facilities, for example, are close to its big customers in the automotive industry. In order to adjust the systems of high-quality vehicle components to customer requirements, Bosch is setting up a wide range of development centers near its customers in several European countries, North and Latin America, India, and Australia. Bosch thus pursues the principle of customer proximity and regional production sites in the markets concerned. Yet 70 percent of the group's capacity is based in Germany. "Our biggest and our best plants are here and that's where they are going to stay," confirmed Bosch-boss Bierich in August 1991 in the German journal *Manager Magazin*. Bierich's view applies, in principle, to the whole of German industry. The home base remains the most important center of production and technological development. To quote the renowned American competition theorist Michael Porter: "The home base is the place where competitive advantages start out from and where they must be maintained. Global strategies supplement and consolidate the home base. It is the frosting, not the cake itself."[6] I would like to adopt this as my second hypothesis.

The technology issue plays an outstanding role in German investment. German companies hardly ever set up their own businesses in the United States. Rather, German investors participate in or establish joint subsidiaries and, through them, cooperate also technologically. Of the 184 transactions made by major German production companies in the United States between 1985 and 1989, 86 percent were acquisitions and a mere 26 cases were business start-ups. Which of the partners eventually benefits from the technology surplus of such a cooperation differs from case to case. Siemens, for example, succeeded in being the worldwide market leader in med-

---

6. M. Porter, *Nationale Wettbewerbsvorteile. Erfolgreich Konkurrieren auf dem Weltmarkt* (München, 1991).

ical technology before General Electric by establishing its business where it could be sure of finding the most demanding customers for medical equipment – in the United States. By taking over American firms it could further develop its own technology.

It is, on the other hand, by no means coincidental that IBM and Siemens chose IBM's supermodern laboratory in East Fishkil as the location for their joint development of 64-megabyte chips, rather than Siemens' Munich-based facility. In this case, the emphasis of the strategic alliance is evidently on IBM, which supports my third hypothesis: In cooperations between major industrial countries in the triad there is no fixed definition as to who supplies or receives technology. Most probably, business cooperations, too, reflect national competitive advantages or weaknesses in the industrial sectors concerned. The weaker partner in such strategic alliances, however, is frequently exposed to the risk of being absorbed by the stronger one.

While the United States is the place where German investors hold their largest investment on a countrywide scale, the most sizeable investment on the regional level was made in the European Community. EC countries in 1989 accounted for 43 percent of the total German foreign investment, which is fairly close to exports: some 55 percent of all goods produced in Germany were exported to EC-neighbor states. Foreign investment activities have gained enormous momentum due to the 1993 project. The German investments in EC countries alone tripled in the course of the 1980s (see Table 2.4, p. 227).

Investments are accompanied by an increase in concentration.[7] Five hundred sixty-one cooperations, participations, and take-overs, involving 1,000 of the biggest EC-companies, were recorded by the EC Commission in the 1985-86 period. Some 1,384 such transactions were registered in 1989-90. Only 40 percent of these alliances were formed on a national level, while the remaining 60 percent concerned operations between EC member states or EC member states and outside states (see Table 2.5, p. 228). In the EC, too, almost all companies preferred majority participations and mergers in working together. Since business start-ups played only a minor role, direct investments were hardly ever linked to a growth in employment. According to management survey findings, the main reason for German investors' capital spending in the EC countries was the expected market growth after implementation of the Internal Market. Adjustment of industrial standards and removal of trade barriers

7. European Commission (ed.), *Bericht über die Wettbewerbspolitik,* various annual editions up to 1991, Brussels.

in the EC facilitated the establishment of intra-group European coordinated production. In many cases the uniform market allowed economies of scale.

It is, however, not always easy to determine whether the 1993 project is indeed the decisive factor for companies' propensity to invest. The automotive industry, for example, has long operated under the conditions of worldwide interlinked production. GM Europe and Ford Europe, for instance, produce the same type of cars at different European production sites. In addition, there are plants producing car parts and aggregates, and thus a constant flow of components is linking European production sites to one another. To provide another example: after VW acquired a majority participation in the Spanish automobile company SEAT, the total European demand for the Polo model could be met from manufacture in Spain. Higher-quality models are still being produced in western Germany, while other VW models may soon be built in eastern Germany and at Skoda in Czechoslovakia. In this example, too, production is centered on regional markets, with the small Polo car expected to dominate in southern European markets and Skoda in the eastern European markets.

Global sourcing was therefore not necessarily the dominant strategy of the automotive industry. Rather, corporate concepts aimed at regionally oriented intra-group coordinated production in Europe, on the one hand, and for the North and Latin American markets, on the other. In other cases, the fear of intensified competition is the reason for the concentration efforts of European business. Nixdorf, the German computer company, could not retain its competitiveness and was acquired by Siemens in 1989. Some years ago the German typewriter manufacturer, Triumph Adler, was bought by Olivetti. Strategic alliances are also increasing in the badly hit computer business. Siemens in Germany, Bull in France, and Olivetti in Italy began to work on establishing a European computer infrastructure. The rising tendency to conclude cooperative arrangements also affected companies with very high R&D expenditure, for example in the aerospace industry. In the civilian sector of this industry, four states became involved in the production of the Airbus. Military projects, too, have become increasingly internationalized.

According to the European Commission in Brussels, growing international competition, in particular from Japan and United States, emerged as one of the major reasons for the promotion of European company mergers. The model of European stock companies, for instance, is meant to establish a suitable legal form for truly European companies. So far, however, neither the legal form of a "Europe Inc."

has been implemented, nor has there been a general trend of national capital being replaced by truly European companies.

Evidently, there is still sufficient scope for action with respect to the Europeanization of German companies. Whether and to what extent this trend increases will depend not least on the speed with which the legal, political, economic, and monetary conditions planned by the Commission are implemented. In any case, it will be necessary to transfer additional national functions to Brussels. The absence of a European central bank and of a uniform currency and monetary policy, for example, makes itself felt in differing capital-market interest rates. Furthermore, a uniform corporate tax system is required, and the field of a "social Europe" and management-labor relations also show only meager signs of advancement. It should be said in this context that, if the Commission aims to promote company mergers for competitive reasons, the competition of countries outside the Community must also be endured since building a "fortress Europe" hardly provides the answer.

WAGE COSTS AS AN INVESTMENT INCENTIVE?

German trade unions are frequently faced with the question: Are we in Germany, with high labor costs and short working hours, virtually pushing companies out of the country? Obviously, low wage costs are not a serious factor in companies' readiness to invest in the United States or France. In order to answer this question I would like to draw attention to German investment in southern Europe and the developing countries.

Take Portugal – an EU member state with considerable wage cost advantages – as an example. In 1988 metal companies in Portugal had to pay only one-fourth of the labor costs per working hour spent in Germany. Yet in 1987, a mere 0.4 percent of total of German direct investment capital was concentrated in this country. Portugal has just begun to establish its own industry. The focal point of German investment in the metal area is the electrical engineering industry which attracted 40 percent of total capital spending. German companies that produce in Portugal nevertheless use the wage cost advantage in order to export from there.[8] This is particularly true of the clothing and shoe industry and, to a smaller degree, also of elec-

---

8. M. Wortmann, "Produktionsverlagerungen aus der Bundesrepublik Deutschland an die euopäische Peripherie," in Friedrich-Ebert-Stiftung, *Vierteljahresberichte*, No. 122, 1990.

trical engineering. The vast majority of the total of 6,650 people employed in German subsidiaries in the electrical engineering sector works in the exports sector. Grundig, a TV and entertainment electronics manufacturer, started the first larger-scale investment on the basis of cost-oriented considerations. Recently, Siemens has been the most important electrical engineering company in Portugal, manufacturing car accessories for export in two different plants.

An investment guide for Portugal put it this way: "From the very start, industrial development has been based on the low wage factor, and low wages still correspond to low average productivity."[9] Portugal remains suitable as a production site for relatively simple but labor-intensive products since the country lacks a well-trained labor force. It is to be feared, however, that in the medium term Portugal will be exposed to strong competition from eastern Germany and eastern Europe. Spain, by contrast, has a much larger domestic market and a significantly superior industrial development in comparison to Portugal.[10] Spain has become an important site for European corporations such as VW, Renault, and Peugeot. General Motors and Ford, too, benefit from Spain as a production site for small and medium-size cars. The country is firmly integrated in corporate strategies for the regional market of Europe. It is, therefore, of special significance to the supply industry. Automotive firms are pressing suppliers to move close to Spanish production sites. In addition, the intense competitive pressure exerted in particular on suppliers to the car industry has forced many of these firms to internationalize production and to exploit the cost advantages provided by southern European countries.

The share of developing countries as target regions for German foreign investment declined from 15 percent in 1980 to 10 percent in 1989. Vehicle construction is the only metal industry sector where production from affiliated companies in developing countries contributed substantially to turnover.[11] Latin America, in particular Brazil and Mexico, accounted for 73 percent of the approximately DM 20 billion that German companies invested in developing countries. With its production site in Pueblo, VW is the largest German investor in Mexico. In Mexico, VW had a 38 percent market share in motor vehicles and also used Mexico as a supply base for the United States market. In the field of assembly, wage costs, which rep-

9. R. Franke and F. Stollberg (eds.), *Investitionsstandorte in den Ländern der EG* (Frankfurt/Main, 1990).
10. M. Wortmann, *German Direct Investment in the Spanish Economy following Spain's Entry into the EEC* (Berlin, 1991).
11. R. Jungnickel, *Neue Technologien und Produktionsverlagerungen* (Hamburg, 1991).

resent only 3 percent of total costs, are virtually immaterial. German investors' efforts are geared to domestic demand and the new free trade zone, making Mexico the gateway to the American market.

To summarize it can be said that simple, work-intensive, and non-automated production procedures are constantly declining in modern industrial production – and with them declines the wage cost advantage as an argument in favor of companies' activities abroad. For the production concept of "lean production," labor costs are of no real significance. The decisive requirements of today, such as high quality and variety of product lines, cannot be met on the basis of the former Taylorist mass production in low-wage countries.

Conclusion

There is no such thing as one global strategy for all companies. Global strategies must be part of corporate strategies, which in turn are oriented toward a holistic optimization of corporate activities.[12] Worldwide competition, and in some cases stagnating markets, provide the current scope for corporate activities. Efforts of large-scale companies are directed at opening up the three big economic regions, the triad, in terms of both the markets and production sites. From the viewpoint of optimization of corporate activities, capital spending abroad could be a suitable tool if the following applies:

- when transportation costs for exports of finished products are disproportionately high (for this reason, commercial vehicles of Mercedes Benz are assembled in different parts of the world);
- when exchange rate fluctuations or import restrictions must be taken into account;
- when the conditions for production are more promising; this could be wages in simple production, or R&D facilities in the case of more complex production;
- when products and delivery periods are adjusted totally to customer requirements, for example in the case of car suppliers; and
- when customer tastes and wishes in different parts of the world demand differences in product design. (This argument, by the way, seems to lose ground as fashion styles around the world start to resemble each other more and more.)

---

12. H.-R. Meißner and W. Oesterheld, "Unternehmenskonzentration und EG-Binnenmarkt," in M. Heine, et al. (eds.), *EG-Schwarzbuch Binnenmarkt* (Berlin, 1991).

In addition to these traditional reasons, there are some new factors that promote foreign investment. Micro-electronics as a key technology is playing a dominant role here. Micro-electronics accelerates technological development, shortens product cycles, and, on the other hand, makes new investments and R&D expenditure more expensive. As a consequence companies are increasingly willing to merge or cooperate with others.[13] At the same time, micro-electronics facilitates communications and the dissemination of standard techniques in the triad. It is a means of integrating economic activities in different sites all over the world, and it thus improves the preconditions for worldwide corporate activities. If however, as I have tried to show, capital abroad is largely spent in the form of company acquisitions and participation takeovers – as is the case at least in the triad countries – then this type of internationalization bears some risks as well. Buying the technology and buying the competitor involves the risk that innovation is replaced by stagnation and dynamic economic processes by size. Such alliances tend to support mediocrity.

One last word about the currently fashionable strategic alliances. Alliances are no magic recipe. Porter puts it very clearly: "Maintaining and improving the competitive position demands from companies the development of internal capabilities in those areas which are material to the competitive advantage. In the long-term, global industry leaders seldom rely on partners when it comes to protecting facilities and know-how essential for gaining an edge over the competition."[14] Some German companies, too, which in the past have relied on external diversification and have made acquisitions in other sectors of industry, are now looking for international partners for their subsidiaries. It remains to be seen which one is the right strategy.

---

13. H.E. Müller, "Unternehmenskonzentration in Europa," in R. Welzmüller (ed.), *Standortpoker und Ressourcenverteilung in Europa*, (Köln, 1990).
14. M. Porter, *Nationale Wettbewerbsvorteile*, 100.

Chapter 8

❖

GERMAN INDUSTRY AND THE EUROPEAN UNION IN THE 1990S*

Jeffrey J. Anderson

German industry has profited from the European common market in the past, and by all indications will continue to do so. Although "Project 1992" has sparked strategic readjustments across all sectors of the economy, only a handful of industries appear to suffer in a barrier-free market.[1] Yet the European Union is more than an economic market. It is also a source of costs and benefits that are political in origins. Regulatory frameworks and distributive programs administered by the EU shape the incentive structures within which firms operate, and have assumed increasing importance alongside – indeed, over and above – the rules of the game established by national governments. How does German industry approach the EU

---

* Research for this paper was funded by the Younger U.S. Scholars to Germany Fellowship Program of The German Marshall Fund of the United States. I also would like to thank the research institute of the *Deutsche Gesellschaft für Auswärtige Politik* in Bonn for its support.
1. Exceptions include the information processing and telecommunications industries. A. Herrmann, W. Ochel, and M. Wegner, *Bundesrepublik und Binnenmarkt '92: Perspektiven für Wirtschaft und Wirtschaftspolitik* (Berlin, 1990). For an excellent discussion of the origins of the Single European Act, see D. Cameron, "The 1991 Initiative: Causes and Consequences," in: A. Sbragia (ed.), *Euro-Politics* (Washington D.C., 1992), 23-74.

as a set of political institutions? What does it seek from Brussels, and how does it set about achieving its aims? Are there significant differences across sectors and, if so, to what can these be attributed? What are the implications of German industry's political relations with the EU for the broader international, institutional commitments of the Federal Republic?

These questions take on added importance in light of recent history. German unification, which exploded onto the international agenda in 1989 with a force that astonished participants and observers alike, contributed to an acceleration of the European integration process.[2] Germany's neighbors, fearful of its economic potential and a return to unilateralism, sought to embed the Federal Republic even deeper within the web of international institutions it had called home since the late 1940s. For their part, German leaders sought to meet these concerns half way, and along with the French championed a deepened and widened Community. As a result of these joint efforts, significant commitments to further European integration were negotiated at the Maastricht summit in December 1991. Unification also has left visible imprints at the domestic level. The mounting economic costs of unity have placed strains on the German polity that are unique in its postwar history. Have the domestic and international ramifications of unification influenced the interests, objectives, and strategies of German business vis-à-vis the EU?

On the basis of a brief review of the general attitudes of German business toward the EC prior to unification and an examination of the post-1989 activities of peak associations and selected industry groups, the dominant theme is one of continuity. Although European integration and, to a far lesser extent, unification have placed new issues on German industry's EU agenda and have required additional commitments of institutional resources by industry associations to their Brussels operations, their interests and objectives remain bound up positively and constructively with the existing framework.

HISTORICAL BACKGROUND

Business associations have been a perennial feature of the Community landscape, although they have never played the role ascribed to

---

2. See K. Kaiser, "Germany's Unification," *Foreign Affairs* 70 (Winter 1991), 179-205, and J. Anderson and J. Goodman, "Mars or Minerva? A United Germany in a Post-Cold War Europe," in: R. Keohane, J. Nye, and S. Hoffmann (eds.), *After the Cold War: International Institutions and State Strategies in Europe, 1989-91* (Cambridge, MA, 1993).

them by neofunctionalist theories of integration.[3] Instead of acting as one of the driving forces behind a cumulative transfer of sovereignty from national governments to the EC, business interest associations (BIAs) have been content to perform the same membership services in Brussels that they do at home. They gather and exchange information, monitor Community developments, and attempt to influence the myriad decisions undertaken by the Brussels bureaucracy.[4] Indeed, contrary to neofunctionalist predictions, BIAs have pursued their interests in a flexible manner, working both ends of the national-supranational continuum to achieve their specific objectives.

Beginning with the European Recovery Program in the late 1940s, European business interests sought to create and maintain a presence at the doors of the increasingly important institutions for (European) international cooperation.[5] Within five years of the signing of the Treaty of Rome in 1957, European-wide BIAs had set up shop in Brussels to represent the craft industries, agriculture, banking institutions, and chambers of commerce.[6] Perhaps the most significant of these organizations was and is the *Union des Industries de la Communauté Européenne* (UNICE), which formed in 1958 to represent the general interests of European business. Thereafter, BIA activity in Brussels matched the ebb and flow of Community integration, increasing in both frequency and intensity since the mid-1980s.[7] The principal beneficiaries of this interest group revival have not been the European peak associations, which historically have been hamstrung by internal differences of opinion among national members. Rather, national peak associations, industry groups, and individual firms, particularly the larger corporations, have responded to the increasing political weight of the EC with the creation and/or expansion of representational capacities at the European level. Business dominates the group scene in Brussels; in 1985, BIAs comprised 583 of the 695 registered interest groups in Brussels.[8]

3. See P. Taylor, *The Limits of European Integration* (New York, 1983), Chapter 1.
4. N. Nugent, *The Government and Politics of the European Community* (Durham, N.C., 1989), 194–206.
5. H-W. Platzer, *Unternehmensverbände in der EG: Ihre nationale und transnationale Organisation und Politik* (Kehl am Rhein, 1984), 37–41.
6. P. Schmitter and W. Streeck, "Organized Interests and the Europe of 1992," in: N. Ornstein and M. Perlman (eds.), *Political Power and Social Change* (Washington, D.C., 1991), 51.
7. B. Kohler-Koch, "Vertikale Machtverteilung und organisierte Wirtschaftsinteressen in der Europäischen Gemeinschaft," in: U. von Aleman, R. Heinze, and B. Hombach (eds.), *Die Kraft der Region: Nordrhein-Westfalen in Europa* (Bonn, 1990), 226–30.
8. Figures taken from Schmitter and Streeck, "Organized Interests and the Europe of 1992," 52.

Business associations have adjusted to shifts in the institutional balance of power in Brussels. Until the mid-1980s, decision-making rested firmly in the hands of the member nations, acting through the Council of Ministers on the principle of unanimity. Under these conditions, BIAs focused their lobbying efforts almost exclusively on their respective national governments, which were in a position to protect vital national interests by means of the national veto in the Council.

The European Community Commission came into consideration for BIAs as well, largely due to its agenda-setting prerogatives. Since then, the Commission's powers have expanded, the European Parliament (EP) has grown modestly in importance, and voting procedures in the Council have begun to shift away from unanimity to qualified majority voting; the most significant watershed here was the Single European Act (SEA). Although the national governments remain key participants in the policy-making process and therefore targets of BIA lobbyists, both the Commission and the EP have assumed greater significance in the eyes of industry representatives in Brussels. Combined with the general weakening of the representational monopolies enjoyed by European peak associations, these developments have produced a much more fluid, competitive interest group environment in Brussels: the advent of American-style pluralism at the heart of the EC.[9]

German business associations have been key participants in these complex developments. Three separate peak associations represent business interests in the Federal Republic of Germany, and each has been very active in Brussels since the inception of the Community: the *Bundesverband der Deutschen Industrie* (BDI), which represents industry interests not directly tied to collective bargaining; the *Bundesvereinigung der Deutschen Arbeitgeberverbände* (BDA), which represents employers' interests in collective bargaining; and the *Deutscher Industrie- und Handelstag* (DIHT), which represents the chambers of industry and commerce.

Of these three organizations, the BDI played the most active role on EC issues prior to 1989.[10] It was an early supporter of a European customs union and the general goal of integration, calling for bold action on the part of European leaders a mere six months after its formation in October 1949. The organization applauded the formation of the European Coal and Steel Community (ECSC) despite the intense opposition of Ruhr industrial interests. It warned of the inefficiencies of partial integration, and encouraged German and other

---

9. See ibid., 59–67, and Kohler-Koch, "Vertikale Machtverteilung und organisierte Wirtschaftsinteressen in der Europäischen Gemeinschaft," 230.
10. The following is based largely on Platzer, *Unternehmensverbände in der EG*.

European governments to move beyond the ECSC to more encompassing forms of political and economic cooperation. The BDI's rationale for supporting the European Economic Community (EEC) reflected a faith not only in the benign and powerful effects of market forces, but also in the capacity of German industry to benefit disproportionately from these forces.

Up through the 1980s, the BDI advanced a consistent set of general policy positions, which were echoed by the other German peak associations. It maintained a fiercely liberal outlook on trade. The BDI was an early and enthusiastic supporter of Project 1992. It also backed the various initiatives to promote economic and monetary union, most recently EMU, although on this issue it sounded a more cautious note, warning of the dangers of inadequate coordination of national economic policies and the need for an absolutely independent European central bank. While the BDI approved of Community efforts to aid disadvantaged regions and groups via the structural funds, it pointed out the need for the efficient targeting of fund resources. It vehemently opposed any moves toward an interventionist industrial policy at the EC level, arguing that sectoral policies that seek to pick winners inevitably become politicized, and degenerate into protectionism and the conservation of noncompetitive economic structures.

To secure these interests, the BDI devoted substantial organizational resources to inject a European component into its internal administrative structure and to maintain a presence in Brussels; much the same can be said of the other German industrial peak associations.[11] The BDI played a dominant role within UNICE, but its limited capacity to act independently in Brussels became a subject of concern among its membership and association administrators. The BDI, with the BDA and DIHT, pursued conventional influence strategies at the Community level; the *sine qua non* of an effective Brussels lobbying campaign was to have the Bonn government on one's side, while a sympathetic Commission and support in the European Parliament were also of considerable value.[12]

How – if at all – have the European interests of Germany's industrial peak associations and of individual industry groups changed since the dramatic events of November 1989? The implementation of the Single European Act is an ongoing process that will continue to stretch beyond the target date of 31 December 1992; not only will it generate an increasingly barrier-free market, but it accords to the

11. For details, see ibid., 73–80.
12. Ibid., 94–101.

Community broad, new competences in a variety of policy areas of intense interest to business, including research and development, environmental regulations, structural policy, and social policy. The SEA has been joined by the more expansive and ambitious Maastricht treaty, which establishes a fixed timetable for the introduction of economic and monetary union, including a single European currency, and carves out new spheres of competence for the EU in the areas of foreign and defense policy, interior ministry cooperation, energy, and industrial policy. Community members are also expanding the membership of the EU to include willing EFTA candidates and, in the longer term, certain Eastern European countries (e.g. the Czech and Slovak Republics, Poland, and Hungary). Beside (or rather, underneath) these seismic changes in the EU, the wrenching process of German unification continues. In terms of both financial costs and political conflicts, the integration of the five new *Länder* (states) into the Federal Republic is proving to be far more burdensome than politicians and experts alike originally had predicted.

The question is whether the perceptions of the earlier EC framework held by German business have changed in response to one or more of these developments. Indeed, these developments have the potential to pull German industries in opposite directions. On the one hand, the growing importance of the EU would appear to raise the stakes for German business: the potential benefits of lobbying activities increase, if only because industry has more to gain *and* more to lose from EU decisions.[13] On the other hand, the economic challenges and opportunities posed by unification may draw German industry inward and possibly eastward, but in any event, away from its longstanding postwar western orientation. The outcome is not likely to be quite as stark as these alternatives suggest; any change in the interests, objectives, and strategies of German industry in relation to Europe is likely to be a nuanced mixture of these competing pulls.

GERMAN INDUSTRY IN THE 1990S

As defined and represented by the major peak associations, German industry attitudes toward the EU have not changed dramatically in the context of unification and deepening integration. The BDI and the DIHT acknowledge the far-reaching market adjustment imperatives that have confronted their members since the passage of the

---

13. For a similar point regarding the Single European Act, see Schmitter and Streeck, "Organized Interests and the Europe of 1992."

Single European Act, and maintain that on balance, German firms are well prepared to succeed in a barrier free market.[14] They express their continuing support for the goals and instruments of the Single European Act, providing that deregulation at the national level is not accompanied by a re-regulation at the European level, and voiced concerns that the 1992 deadline would not be met unless concerted action was taken by national governments and the Commission to ensure rapid approval and implementation of the remaining Commission directives. On the subject of trade, the BDI and the DIHT remain ardent supporters of free trade and an open EU, pointing to Germany's unchanged export orientation. To this end, they underlined the absolute importance of a successful conclusion to the Uruguay Round. The ambiguous position of the Community, not only in the GATT negotiations but also with respect to past and present trade issues like Japanese automobiles and bananas from Latin America, has sparked concerned criticism. To facilitate the creation of firms able to compete on international markets, they recommend additional transfers of regulatory competence to Brussels in the area of mergers and acquisitions.

The massive restructuring efforts underway in eastern Germany and the clearly desperate position of many large employers situated in the new *Länder* notwithstanding, the industrial peak associations have maintained a highly skeptical attitude toward industrial policies at both the national and supranational levels. They argue that the EU should adopt more stringent controls on national state aid practices, including sensitive sectors in Germany such as coal and shipbuilding. The new industrial policy powers granted to the Community at Maastricht (Article 130) are viewed as opening the door to the distortions of competition, unnecessary and undesirable state intervention, and protectionism.[15] According to a BDI official, "what we fear are the small, seemingly harmless steps that become irreversible and lead to full-scale sectoral policies." As for the long range goals of economic and monetary union and the expansion of the Community, the BDI and DIHT positions are in harmony with the general stance of the Bonn government: yes to EMU and to new members, including those from Eastern Europe, and no to large increases in the EU budget.[16]

14. The BDA has focused on issues relevant to collective bargaining and social policy.
15. The BDI has encountered criticism from members more positively disposed toward targeted intervention from Brussels, specifically the electronics industry. See "Politik für die Industrie, keine Industriepolitik," *Frankfurter Allgemeine Zeitung*, 2 July 1992, 15.
16. See the "Gemeinsame Stellungnahme zur Weiterentwicklung der Europäischen Gemeinschaft," released in June 1991 by the BDI, DIHT, BDA, and three other major industry associations.

As organizational actors in Brussels, both the BDI and the DIHT have been influenced by the increase in the volume and content of Community policy-making. Since the European peak associations to which they belong – UNICE for the BDI, Eurochambres for the DIHT – are generally incapable of developing effective positions on many substantive issues,[17] they have sought to compensate by working to enhance the effectiveness of these Euro-groups and by upgrading their own operations in Brussels. Although the former initiatives are unlikely to bear fruit in the near future, the importance of strengthening the European peak associations is clear to German industry representatives. The DIHT has encountered cases in which its policy positions have not been taken into account by the European Commission because of the inability of Eurochambres to arrive at a common position. In the words of a DIHT official in Bonn, "when we say one thing, and the Italians come along and say something else, this does not present a very compelling case before the Commission, which would prefer to incorporate 'the position' of the European chambers in its decisions."[18]

Recent shifts in the institutional balance of power in Brussels have led to subtle changes in German industry association lobbying strategies. The principal target remains the Bonn government, while the European Parliament continues to take a back seat to all other actors, since its powers are still too limited to be of concern. With the gradual expansion of qualified majority voting in the Council, however, peak associations are finding that they need to rethink their standard methods of operation in Brussels. As a DIHT official remarked, "we stand virtually no chance of getting our way [in the Council], since Germany can always be outvoted. Under qualified majority voting, it is natural to expect our minister to seek to be on the side of the winners. Therefore, we have to try to build cross-national alliances to be sure that our position lines up with the likely winners." This generally translates into closer contacts with other national peak associations, especially traditional allies like the Dutch and the British. Although BDI and DIHT officials know what it takes to influence the EU policy-making process, they are acutely aware of internal organizational constraints; they simply do not have enough people in Brussels to handle the increasing volume of Union activity. Officials speak of a *Kompetenzverlagerung* (competence transfer) to Brussels' advantage

17. A BDI official characterized UNICE, generally considered to be the most powerful of the European industry associations, as "a small shop, kept on a very short financial leash by its members."
18. Here and elsewhere, all unattributed quotations are from interviews conducted by the author in 1992 with German government officials and interest group representatives.

that is quickly spinning out of control, and institutional reform of BIA operations is therefore high on their agenda.

The economic consequences of German unification have had little if any influence on the positions of the BDI and the DIHT. Aside from strengthening an already wary attitude toward increases in Germany's contribution to the EU budget, the mounting costs of unification and the considerable problems encountered in managing the transition from state socialism to the social market economy have not sparked any major reassessment of European objectives and strategies. This is due largely to the confidence shared by these peak associations that over the medium to long term, the successful economic recipe implemented by West Germany in the 1950s, of which EC/EU membership was and is an important component, applies to the former GDR as well. Both associations acknowledge the difficulties experienced by eastern German firms and public authorities in taking on the stringent *acquis communautaire*, but evaluate these problems as transitional. Unlike some of the sectoral associations discussed below, the industrial peak associations have escaped internal east-west membership conflicts wrought by unification; as organizations pledged to represent the general interests of German business, the BDI and DIHT have stayed above the fray, and have maintained an orthodox social market economy approach to the problems in the new *Länder*.

Ironically perhaps, unification and European integration have contributed to a new edition of an old debate: the viability of Germany as a production location for industry. The business community and elements within the Christian-Liberal governing coalition question whether the country, which for many years has qualified as a high-cost production location, can afford to indulge in old habits under radically changed circumstances. They blame the unions and government policy for weakening *Standort Deutschland* to the point where Germany ranks number one in Europe on a variety of cost factors: the highest wages, the shortest work week, the most vacation days, the most burdensome business taxation system, the most stringent (and therefore expensive) environmental regulations, and so on. According to the industrial peak associations, domestic and international events have conspired to bring Germany to the brink of a *Standort* crisis. To finance the rising costs of German unification, the government found it necessary to postpone the oft promised and long awaited reform of the business taxation system. Moreover, Bonn's fiscal and monetary performance since unification have led to growing worries within the business community that many of the broader parameters that make Germany such an attractive place to do business – i.e. a sound budgetary policy, a strong currency, and a low inflation rate – are in jeopardy. Business associations want to use unification as an occasion to force policymakers to undertake a major reappraisal of "business as usual," particularly in the realm of state regulatory and taxation policy, as well as social policy.

The role of Europe in the *Standort Deutschland* debate is much more direct. According to the BDI, the Single European Act has touched off intensified competition not only between firms, but also between EU production locations. It notes that Germany typically has the strictest standards in Europe, whether with respect to product safety norms, technical standards, occupational safety, or environmental regulations. Thus, industry associations have called upon the government to converge unilaterally to the European norms. In short, the completion of the internal market places a new onus on the federal government to take account of current practice in other member countries when legislating, and to keep in mind the competitive needs of German industry. The BDI maintains national "solos" (*Alleingänge*) in these critical policy areas will be punished with an export of jobs and investment. While even the peak associations themselves are quick to point out that the country has not reached the end of its locational tether – there are many significant advantages of *Standort Deutschland* – they stress repeatedly that there is no time like the present to begin to address what they believe is an investment and employment crisis in the making.[19]

Automobiles

The auto industry exemplifies German postwar economic prowess. Its internationally renowned firms have progressed in strength, buttressed by a production strategy of sound engineering, a highly qualified workforce, and a dense network of vertically integrated components suppliers.[20] Recently, however, Japanese competition has grown more intense, targeting German product markets (e.g. luxury automobiles) thought to be relatively insulated. A sense of unease has taken hold in the industry. As in other German manufacturing sectors, the auto

---

19. A DIHT spokesperson stressed the need to distinguish rhetoric from reality in the *Standort* debate. Many German BIAs and firms are exaggerating the situation to generate political pressure for change: "This is standard fare in a democracy." This official went on to express concern about the danger of generating a self-fulfilling prophecy.
20. W. Streeck, "Successful Adjustment to Turbulent Markets: The Automobile Industry," in: P. Katzenstein (ed.), *Industry and Politics in West Germany: Toward the Third Republic* (Ithaca, 1989), 113–56. This section focuses exclusively on vehicle manufacturers.

industry lives by its ability to export; indeed, each of the major vehicle producers considers itself to be neither a German nor a European concern, but a global actor. This attitude shapes industry attitudes toward a variety of policy issues.

Unification has had little overall impact on the structure of the industry or on the industry association, the *Verband der Automobilindustrie e.V.* (VDA). The VDA operates a liaison office in Leipzig to provide services to producers located in the new *Länder*. Many of its western German members are active in the former GDR; an internal industry survey revealed that two of three members had already invested in eastern Germany or intended to do so in the near future.[21] Among the more well-known investment projects announced soon after unification were an Opel plant in Eisenach, Volkswagen (VW) production facilities in Chemnitz and Zwickau, and a Mercedes-Benz truck factory in Ludwigsfelde. Internal membership conflicts along east-west lines are insignificant; most friction arises among western firms seeking positional advantages in the eastern German markets.

To the VDA and its individual members, *Standort Deutschland* is a live issue. According to industry representatives, high production costs in Germany have already led to the export of low wage jobs. VW's takeover of the Spanish auto manufacturer SEAT in 1986 is an example; one could add the recent decision by BMW to build a plant in South Carolina, USA. In Germany, most firms are reducing workforce levels,[22] and those that can, like BMW and Mercedes-Benz, are accelerating the shift into qualitative growth strategies, involving technologically advanced automobiles and components. The VDA and

21. Verband der Automobilindustrie (ed.), *Auto 90/91* (Frankfurt, 1991), 34. The level of interest in eastern German production facilities is a function of the company's product line. For firms like VW and Opel, which manufacture affordable, mass production vehicles, the new *Länder* represent an important market as well as a springboard to Eastern Europe. For luxury automobile producers like BMW, interest is more modest. To date, BMW's investment in the new *Länder*, outside of a network of dealerships, include a DM 200 million greenfield development in Eisenach to produce machine tools for nearby auto factories, and a joint venture with Rolls Royce Plc to manufacture aircraft engines. Apparently not one for symbolic gestures, BMW ruled out the purchase of the company's original production facility in Eisenach. Dating from the late 1920s, the plant was used during GDR times to produce the (infamous) Wartburg. A VDA official explained that in view of the dilapidated conditions at the Eisenach site, the investment "would not have made economic sense."
22. In June 1992, Porsche announced plans to cut 850 jobs in the course of the 1992-1993 financial year, while Mercedes-Benz stunned financial markets with its plans to eliminate 20,000 jobs over the next several years. The VDA speculated that the number of jobs lost in the industry over the next several years could easily reach 200,000. See "200.000 Arbeitsplätze weniger?" *Frankfurter Allgemeine Zeitung*, 13 July 1992, 9.

individual managers have begun to voice their concerns publicly. They point to the completion of the internal market, which will intensify competitive pressures from other member country producers, and to the growing challenge from the Pacific Rim countries, especially Japan. Their catalogue of demands is indistinguishable from those advanced by the peak associations discussed above.

Although the VDA's effectiveness on domestic policy issues has been called into question,[23] it plays an important, multifaceted role in Brussels, where the VDA maintains an office in the building of the European automobile association, the ACEA.[24] Officials are able to move easily between their headquarters in Frankfurt, their lobby in Bonn, and Brussels to monitor developments and represent the industry's interests. The industry association has been joined in recent years by Daimler-Benz, Volkswagen, and BMW, each of which is represented independently in Brussels. The logic is straightforward; on most issues, a common front with other German producers is not only possible but desirable, but in certain cases, the firm must be in a position to press its own case. Volkswagen signed on to this logic later than the others, arriving in Brussels after 1992.[25] VDA and firm officials deny the existence of any coordination problems. They attribute their combined presence in Brussels to the accretion of powers by the Community in recent years.

Of the many EU issues that concern the German auto industry, perhaps the most central is the internal market itself. As a market, Europe is certainly not a novel phenomenon to these firms. According to the VDA, approximately two-thirds of total German vehicle output ends up in other EU members. As such, the completion of the internal market will not have as large an impact as in other sectors, at least in terms of a marked increase in demand. It is also difficult to attribute changes in firm-specific strategies, involving most significantly the spread of Japanese production innovations (group work and lean production) to the completion of the internal market; rather, they are directly linked to the Japanese challenge itself. Here imitation is the most sincere form of flattery.[26] Nevertheless, the implementation of

23. Streeck, "Successful Adjustment to Turbulent Markets," 136.
24. The ACEA is a relative newcomer to the Brussels scene, having replaced its two predecessors, one representing the individual European vehicle manufacturers and the other representing national umbrella associations. The former, the *Comité de Liaison de la Construction Automobile* (CLCA), dissolved in 1991 over the issue of Japanese imports.
25. A VW representative commented that it was easy to overestimate the value of an independent representation in Brussels. With recent EC moves to open up the European market for public procurement in vehicles, an independent monitoring capacity had become indispensable to VW.

the Single European Act is expected to improve preconditions for international competitiveness, and for this reason, the auto industry enthusiastically welcomed the single market initiative.

One of the potential benefits of the single market is a harmonization of technical standards for automobiles, or the WVTA system (whole vehicle type approval).[27] By the end of 1992, agreement on forty-one of the forty-four items had been achieved, while the remaining three were of no technical significance and became hostage to trade disputes between the EC members with Japan.[28] Countries such as France used these items, which are subject to national criteria, as non-tariff barriers to trade, not only against Japanese imports but also against automobiles produced within the EU. The resulting transaction costs are substantial, but industry officials were predicting that a fully harmonized regime was only a matter of time.

This optimism can be traced to the EU's automobile trade agreement with Japan, reached in the summer of 1991. It provided for a seven year period of voluntary restrictions on both Japanese imports and transplants (i.e. Japanese automobiles produced in Britain) beginning in January 1993. After 1999, Japanese automobiles produced within the Community will be treated as other domestic vehicles, and imports will be liberalized. This agreement is at some level protectionist in nature, but it provides explicitly for a set of deadlines to reduce the level of protectionism to zero, while giving the European industry a grace period in which to undertake necessary, and in all likelihood, painful adjustments.[29] As such, the compromise was supported by the VDA and its individual members, which have historically represented the liberal wing of the European automobile industry. This is a pragmatic wing, according to a VDA official:

26. The diffusion of these innovations in the German auto industry is by no means uniform. Mercedes-Benz, Opel, and Ford have adopted in whole or in part Japanese production methods, while others, notably Volkswagen, have been more reluctant to go this route.
27. For the background on the WVTA, see A. Smith and A. Venables, "Automobiles," in: G. Hufbauer (ed.), *Europe 1992* (Washington, D.C., 1990), 129.
28. In 1991, France offered a complete harmonization of WVTA, but laid down the condition that any automobile trade agreement with Japan would have to maintain the level of imports at the existing level indefinitely. The Commission, with the support of countries like Germany, rejected this offer as contrary to GATT regulations.
29. The potential dilemma facing German auto-makers was brought out in comments by a VW representative. After outlining "the fatal consequences" of European protectionism for the German auto industry, he commented on the 1991 EC-Japan agreement: "If the Japanese threat remains at its present level, we've set ourselves a damned tight schedule for meeting it."

> Protectionism cannot be done away with in a single stroke, but rather in steps, the fewer the better....The sooner we [the Europeans] realize that the Japanese, with their production and marketing systems, are practically invulnerable [to protectionist instruments], the better it will be for us, because we will be forced to embrace the challenge, with pay-offs in our international competitiveness.

In line with this philosophy, the German industry rejected the French approach, which advocated closing off the European market to create leverage against Japanese trade barriers in the auto sector.[30]

The VDA approaches other EU issues with an eye toward creating a level playing field for its members. The association has pushed hard for the harmonization of value-added taxes, since the large spread produces distortions in the sticker price of vehicles. A similar rationale underlies the industry's support for a harmonization of exhaust emissions standards. The auto industry supports economic and monetary union and the widening of the Union because these will lead to lower transaction costs (currency stability and a larger common market) and therefore more export opportunities for German auto manufacturers.

The VDA and its members have vigorously opposed the European Commission's proposal to adopt an industrial policy for the European automobile industry. Formulated with the Japanese challenge in mind, the initiative would *inter alia* provide financial assistance out of the European Social Fund for training and retraining schemes conducted by automobile manufacturers. The VDA argues that the EU should confine its activities to the provision of general market and regulatory parameters within which firms compete, and refrain from interventionist policies that invariably constrain competition, encourage protectionism, and conserve uncompetitive economic structures. With regard to the training dimension of the proposal, industry representatives maintain that German firms have been funding such programs for decades, and these have paid off in a highly qualified, flexible work force. A VDA official remarked scornfully that Germany's European partners, who have neglected this aspect of their businesses for years, are now in effect asking Germany, the net contributor to the EU budget, "to nourish its competitors."

CHEMICALS

The chemical industry, led by the three giants of Bayer, Hoechst, and BASF, is the largest in Europe, responsible for about 30 percent

---

30. This prompted the break-up of the European auto manufacturers association (see note 23), as well as the BMW decision to establish its own office in Brussels.

of total EU output in chemicals. The industry is heavily export-oriented; well over half of German sales take place abroad, and almost three-quarters of these sales occur in the EU market.[31] By means of cooperative strategies bringing together employers and unions, the industry successfully navigated a series of structural challenges in the 1980s, including a large increase in energy costs, excess capacity, the advent of new production technologies, and a heightened public sensitivity to the environmental costs of chemical production.[32]

The industry association is the *Verband der Chemischen Industrie* (VCI), which represents over 600 members from its headquarters in Frankfurt. While the VCI played a limited role in the firm-based adjustments mentioned above,[33] it has been very active across a range of political issues, many of which directly involve the EU. The VCI reacted quickly to the organizational challenge posed by unification; within a year of the Wall's demise, it had extended its reach into the new *Länder*. It established internal working groups to provide eastern German members with a forum to discuss their specific problems in economic policy, environmental policy, trade, quality control, and public relations. Unification has not created deep, new divisions in the membership, according to a VCI official. In a pattern reminiscent of other German industrial sectors discussed here, the most common tension unleashed by unification results from competition among western German firms for choice production locations and markets in the new *Länder*. Since these conflicts involved competing investment plans and strategies of member firms, the VCI remains studiously uninvolved.

According to the VCI, the new chemical production capacity located in the eastern *Länder* – e.g. BASF in Schwarzheide, Bayer in Bitterfeld – was superfluous at the time of its creation because western German firms were not operating at full capacity. Rather, the investments in eastern Germany were justified in terms of servicing markets in Eastern Europe, and of course these markets collapsed on the heels of unification. Shutting down these operations is out of the question for political reasons, the VCI admits. Industry representatives are concerned about the diversionary effects associated with unification. In terms of both material and intellectual investment, western German chemical firms are incurring opportunity costs by focusing on the new *Länder*. To cash in on the boomlet in the former GDR, Ger-

31. Source: Verband der Chemischen Industrie.
32. C. Allen, "Political Consequences of Change: The Chemical Industry," in: P. Katzenstein (ed.), *Industry and Politics in West Germany: Toward the Third Republic*, 157–84.
33. Ibid., 169.

man firms ignored lucrative, yet highly competitive markets, particularly in South-east Asia, and postponed work on product innovation. In the end, the VCI feared that the German chemical industry would lose ground to its competitors.

These concerns, specific to unification, were compounded by unease over the mounting production costs in Germany. VCI officials acknowledge that the German chemical industry is still basically healthy and strong. The threat to the successful economic recipe – cutting edge production technologies, infrastructure, dense networks of suppliers and industrial consumers, and a highly skilled workforce – comes from government policy, according to industry and firm spokespersons. While the VCI and its members complain about the general tax burden on manufacturing industry and inadequate government support for basic and product research, they concentrate their fire on *Standort* chemical production issues. Zoning and environmental laws lead to higher production costs, as well as long delays in the siting of new plants and in the release of new products. This is especially critical in the fields of biotechnology and genetic engineering, the new frontiers of the chemical industry. According to the VCI, virtually nothing is happening in these fields in Germany because of legal and administrative blocks. The larger chemical firms are responding to the situation by relocating production facilities abroad (Bayer has a facility in the United States), which means the export not only of jobs but also of research and development facilities. Small- and medium-sized firms in Germany, which cannot afford foreign production sites, are effectively shut out of what promises to be a very lucrative market.

On European issues, the VCI has worked through the European umbrella association for the chemical industry, the *Conseil Européen des Fédérations de l'Industrie Chimique* (CEFIC). The CEFIC, which formed in 1972 and includes non-EU members, represents not only national umbrella associations but also sectoral interest groups from the chemical industry. Like other European BIAs, it often has labored under paralyzing internal membership strains, particularly over trade and environmental issues. Indeed, the VCI recently came to the conclusion that it needs its own lobbying office in Brussels, in part because the CEFIC is not always able to represent German industry interests effectively and in part because of the general *Kompetenzverlagerung* outlined earlier. This organizational response has been matched by individual chemical firms. BASF, for example, has its own office in Brussels. The potential for coordination problems between industry association and members is downplayed by VCI officials; as one argued, "Brussels is such a big place and not easily surveyed. There is simply too much happening at any given time for one organization to follow adequately."

The past several years have witnessed a marked drop in earnings, the privatization of the eastern German chemical concerns, and growing worries about the future competitiveness of *Standort Deutschland*. These are not unrelated developments, and they have caused the industry association and its members to devote more attention to the EU political arena. With respect to the common market, the VCI points out that its members, especially the three largest, had been preparing for the completion of the internal market for quite some time. Hoechst, for example, has production facilities all over Europe.

German firms also invested heavily in EFTA countries. The German chemical industry, not surprisingly, has pushed a strongly liberal position in the EU; the VCI argues that Project 1992, which it supports, should not be used as an excuse to erect high tariff walls around the European Community. It pushed for a successful conclusion to the Uruguay Round, and maintains that Europe's protectionism on agriculture should not come at the expense of the manufacturing industry. As for EMU and the prospects of a widening of the Union, the VCI sees considerable economic advantages for the German chemical industry. In today's chemical industry, innovation rests on economics of scale that require markets larger than the common market of twelve or even fifteen.

The VCI has kept a close watch on a range of EU issues, including tax harmonization, export controls,[34] energy policy, patent law, product testing, and environmental policy. The VCI acknowledges that in many areas relevant to the chemical industry – e.g. biotechnology, environmental policy – the parameters are established in Brussels. The basic philosophy behind the VCI's lobbying approach at the Union level is to create a level playing field for all European chemical manufacturers. Whether it be environmental guidelines, taxation, or export controls, firms should suffer or profit equally under an EU-wide regulatory system. Where the German government's political objectives are more ambitious and stringent than those of its European neighbors, such as in the field of environmental regulation, the VCI often seeks EU-wide guidelines because it

---

34. In the wake of recent revelations about the involvement of European chemical companies, including German concerns, in Middle Eastern crisis regions, the UN, the EU, and individual nations like Germany have tightened up controls on the export of dangerous chemicals, particularly those used in the manufacture of weaponry. The VCI has been forced to walk a fine line between acknowledging the problem and combating it, on the one hand, and defending the export-oriented interests of its members on the other.

knows these would conform to a lower common denominator. Where prospects for harmonization at the EU level are dim, such as in the area of business taxation, the VCI pushes for unilateral convergence to the European norm in Bonn. The industry rejects any attempt to fashion a European industrial policy along French *dirigiste* lines; issues of capacity utilization and the allocation of state aids for product-related research should not be decided, either in whole or in part, by officials sitting in Brussels.

STEEL

The steel industry, along with coal and shipbuilding, represents one of the few perennial crisis sectors in the German economy. Highly capital intensive and open to price competition for an increasingly standardized product, steel production the world over is prone to deep, cyclical downturns characterized by large drops in prices and excess capacity. Although quite strong in comparative perspective, the German steel industry, dominated by such firms as Thyssen, Krupp, and Hoesch, has not been immune to this problem, and as a result has frequently turned to the state for assistance. The difficult years of the 1970s and 1980s necessitated the formation of "crisis cartels" in the main production centers of the Saarland and the Ruhr, which brought together employers, unions, and public authorities to manage reductions in capacity and attendant lay-offs.[35] This relatively consensual process of contraction, which since the 1970s has seen the workforce reduced from 340,000 to just over 150,000, is generally held as an example of the effectiveness of German corporatist models of industrial relations.[36]

Since 1989, an especially good year, the European steel industry has turned in a checkered performance. In other EU countries, industry problems have resulted from a drop in the demand for steel connected with global recessionary conditions. This does not describe the German case, however, where the *Sonderkonjunktur* in the new *Bundesländer* buoyed demand for steel. Rather, the problem confronting German steel producers was the considerable drop in

---

35. See J. Esser and W. Väth, "Overcoming the Steel Crisis in the Federal Republic of Germany 1974-1983," in: Y. Mény and V. Wright (eds.), *The Politics of Steel: Western Europe and the Steel Industry in the Crisis Years (1974-1984)* (New York, 1987), 623-91.
36. J. Esser and W. Fach, "Crisis Management Made in Germany: The Steel Industry," in: P. Katzenstein (ed.), *Industry and Politics in West Germany: Toward the Third Republic*, 221-48.

prices and correspondingly in earnings.³⁷ Industry officials attributed the resulting "uncomfortable situation" largely to the EU decision to open the common market to Eastern European steel imports.

The steel industry is represented by the *Wirtschaftsvereinigung Stahl* (WS). With unification, the association moved quickly to incorporate the indigenous steel producers in the former GDR into their organization. East-west membership conflicts arising out of unification have been minimal. As a WS official stated ruefully, "our association has never been known for its homogeneous membership."

Most of the strains have involved jockeying for position in the new *Länder* among the major western German firms.³⁸ These tensions are exacerbated by the general situation in the steel market – firms are fighting over a smaller pie. One issue that separates western from eastern steel firms involves state aids. The WS has always pursued a vehement anti-subsidy policy, both against the practices of European competitors and against the individual demands of its membership. The association has carried over this philosophy to the eastern *Länder*, which in turn has led to open disagreements with new members or with old members now investing in the east.

The industry association has generally watched the structural transformation unfolding in the former GDR from the sidelines. In 1989, the WS placed its services at the disposal of the Federal Ministry of Economics and the *Treuhandanstalt* (THA), offering to work out a "total concept" for the privatization of the eastern German steel industry. The government refused the offer, preferring instead to let the process of privatization unfold on a running, bilateral basis between the THA and prospective buyers.

Opinion is divided on the final impact of unification on the German steel industry and its place in Europe. Government officials downplay the long-term effects on industry structure and size, noting that the eastern part of Germany was never a significant location for the production of steel. They do not deny that there may be a sharpening of competitive relations among the western German firms, with the principle fault line dividing those that acquire production facilities in the new *Länder* and those that do not. WS representatives are more sensitive to the long-term implications of the competitive pressures

---

37. In early 1992, the industry association announced that steel prices had reached levels not seen in at least ten years. The loss in earnings for western German steel producers totaled DM 4 billion.
38. The most spectacular case involved the threat by Thyssen Stahl to lodge a formal complaint with the EC Commission if the Treuhand's package offer to Krupp Stahl for the EKO Stahl concern involved state aids. See "Thyssen erwägt Protest bei der EG," *Süddeutsche Zeitung*, 2 March 1992, 21.

unleashed by unification. They maintain that market forces did not demand new production capacity in the east, which has been maintained either for political purposes or for the long-term goal of servicing Eastern European markets. By 1992, the effect of steel production in the new *Länder* was readily discernible on the market, particularly since their traditional markets in Eastern Europe had collapsed and they had to turn westwards to sell their product. All agreed that the eastern German steel sector faced a wrenching shrinkage process, much of which had already taken place. Prior to unification, the GDR steel industry employed 80,000 workers, many of whom were not in any way connected with steel production, and produced 8 million tons of crude steel per year. By February of 1992, the respective figures were 22,000 (all actual steel workers) and 3.5 million tons.[39]

The industry as a whole finds itself under increasing competitive pressures from other EU countries and East Asian producers, notably South Korea and Japan. Although German steel firms historically have held the pole position in Europe, accounting for 29 percent of total EC production of crude steel in 1991, the gap separating them from their competitors has narrowed considerably in the past few years, and in some cases, they have been overtaken. For example, the French steel concern Usinor-Sacilor, which in 1988 lagged far behind the German productivity average, has now moved ahead; the firm requires 4.1 working hours to produce a ton of crude steel, while the German industry needs 4.8 hours. Between 1985 and 1990, productivity in the steel industry has increased in France by 70 percent, in Italy and Belgium by 40 percent, and in the UK by 33 percent. The comparable figure for West Germany was 19 percent.[40]

The steel concerns are aware of these facts, and the industry has been active in the general *Standort* debate. The considerable advantages of Germany as a production location are not lost on the industry; these include a qualified workforce not averse to technological improvements, and the proximity of major steel consumers to steel production sites, such as in the Ruhr Valley. These strengths are not easily reproduced abroad. According to firms and industry associations, however, the high costs of doing business in Germany are beginning to pinch. Business taxes and strict environmental regulations are identified as specifically German burdens that place them at a competitive disadvantage.

39. Figures from the Federal Ministry of Economics.
40. These and other statistics mentioned in the following paragraph are taken from W. Jaspert, "Von Auswanderung spricht in der Stahlbranche niemand," *Süddeutsche Zeitung*, 23 April 1992, 26.

Nevertheless, these drawbacks have not yet led to the export of steel jobs. A WS official argued that high wages and the regulatory frameworks imposed by the state serve as double-edged swords. Although they are an obvious handicap, they act as a constant spur to increase productivity and to rationalize production methods. A Thyssen official saw less of a silver lining in recent developments: "Germany has the shortest work week, the highest wages, and the longest vacations of any industrialized nation. These create monstrous disadvantages and huge burdens for industry, and the situation is fast approaching the critical point." To date, the relative deterioration in *Standort Deutschland* has prompted German steel companies to reduce workforce levels[41] and to engage in qualitative growth strategies, which focus on high quality specialty steels that are less prone to price competition from low-cost producers in the Far East.

Industry representatives have always operated with one eye on Brussels. Due to the provisions of the ECSC, the steel industry has been a barrier-free internal market for forty years. Therefore, the industry did not brace for momentous changes unleashed by the Single European Act. Long-standing competitive pressures, both international and domestic, prompted the wave of restructuring still under way in the industry; these include an internal reorganization at Thyssen and the decision by Krupp and Hoesch to merge steel production. The WS has maintained its own office in Brussels since 1968, when it moved from Luxembourg, the original seat of the ECSC. It works closely with Eurofer, the European umbrella association, although frequent internal conflicts have limited the latter's effectiveness.

There are indications that the representative monopoly held by Eurofer and the WS is coming under pressure. Individual steel producers in Germany see both organizations as plagued by internal paralysis, the result of their constant search for the lowest common denominator uniting their members. Krupp Stahl, for example, already has its own office in Brussels. A similar decision by Thyssen, which in 1992 had no EC office, was not far off, according to an official with the company. In view of the sweeping powers granted by the ECSC Treaty, the WS and individual firms like Thyssen have not noticed any great shift in competence from the national to the supranational level since the 1980s. Steel has always been a highly regulated sector.

41. Analysts predicted that by 1993, there would be 15,000 fewer jobs in the industry, 12,000 of these in eastern Germany alone. Many industry experts predict that by the year 2000, the steel sector will employ less than 100,000. See "Neue Rationalisierungswelle in der deutschen Stahlindustrie," *Frankfurter Allgemeine Zeitung*, 31 July 1992, 12.

From discussions with WS and individual firm representatives, a clear picture of the overall industry attitude toward the EU emerged, one that was decidedly Janus-faced. The EU is viewed as an absolutely vital and, at least in theory, effective mechanism to manage the cyclical overcapacity problems of the industry and to contain the strong political urge by member governments to subsidize inefficient, ailing steel concerns. In short, if the Community did not exist, something like it would have to be invented. Given that 40 percent of the steel that finds its way onto German markets is imported from other EU members, the room for distortions of competition has to be kept as small as possible.

Nevertheless, the German steel industry routinely expresses its dissatisfaction with the gap between theory and practice in the ECSC. Regarding state aids, for example, Article 4c of the ECSC treaty is very strict, and places narrow constraints on the ability of member governments to subsidize their steel industries. Exceptions to the exacting regulations must be approved unanimously by the Council. The 1989 codex on state aid to the steel industry, limited aid for steel to research and development programs, environmental improvements, and measures to reduce capacity. Regional aid for steel firms is no longer allowed.[42]

The WS is unhappy with the administration of these instruments. Historically, the German steel industry has been the least subsidized of EC member countries, and has objected bitterly to the levels of assistance doled out to European competitors.[43] In February 1992, WS President Dr. Ruprecht Vondran held a press conference in Brussels to protest the state aid practices of several EC member countries, and questioned the coherence of Community policy vis-à-vis the steel market. He argued that there was a contradiction between the Commission's lax enforcement of state aid prohibitions, and the dim view it took of the efforts of producers to adjust to the present slack demand for steel by exchanging information on production levels and deliveries. In short, the Commission was vigor-

---

42. The German government won an exception for the steel firms in the new *Länder*, which expired in 1993. Despite its general line on state aid for steel, the WS raised no objection to this special treatment for eastern German steel, although it would have preferred targeted, sector-specific measures of limited duration instead of the blunter instrument of regional aid.
43. The German steel industry resisted attempts by the ECSC in the 1970s and 1980s to erect trade barriers to protect the industry and to manage capacity reductions, arguing that the Community's approach imposed unfair burdens on efficient, non-subsidized producers in countries like Germany while shielding heavily subsidized firms in Italy and elsewhere. See Esser and Fach, "Crisis Management Made in Germany."

ously preventing firms from undertaking even modest private initiatives to reduce the oversupply of steel on European markets in the name of efficiency and competition, while implicitly allowing the inefficient losers of this process to be bailed out by their concerned governments. The result was a prolongation of the crisis in the industry, according to Vondran.

A recent flashpoint in relations with the Community involves the Council's 1991 decision to open up the common market to steel imports from Eastern Europe. According to WS representatives, the Community, with the German government's full support, took this action for purely political reasons – to promote the liberalization processes under way in these former Soviet satellites – and did not consult the EC's steel industries. Imports in 1992 from Czechoslovakia were up 300 percent over the previous year, while those from Poland increased by 200 percent and those from Hungary rose by 50 percent. The WS's prediction of a deleterious impact on prices has generally come true. The problem will attract continued concern from industry officials, since the prices for which Eastern European steel is sold bear no relation to production costs. The WS and most individual firms are aware that a certain level of imports from this troubled region is necessary to ensure reciprocal market access. Industry representatives have continued to press for import quotas and voluntary export agreements as a way of managing the situation and preventing a total disruption of prices on Western European steel markets.[44]

Despite these frictions, an indication of the steel industry's positive attitude toward Europe can be gleaned from their position on the extension of the ECSC treaty, which is due to expire in 2002. The WS has adopted the same position as the European Council: The treaty as a whole should not be extended, but key elements should be folded into the Treaty of Rome – e.g. the prohibitions on state aid and the mechanisms to ensure market transparency in capacity, investment, prices, and volume. The general industry view is that these ECSC components are more efficient and arguably more effective than existing state aid regulations operated by Directorate-General IV of the Commission. This pragmatic, instrumentalist view of international institutional arrangements is typical of general German industry attitudes toward the EU.

44. In August 1992, the European Commission announced that it would limit further imports of certain steel products from Czechoslovakia until year's end. The Commission acted on a request from the German government, supported by other member states, to activate the protection clause of the EC's association treaty with the Czechs.

CONSTRUCTION

When one thinks of big business in Germany, the construction industry rarely comes to mind. The sector is dominated by medium to large size firms, and there exists nothing on the order of the American behemoth Bechtel. Indeed, the typical German construction firm is overshadowed by its French and British neighbors. Still, the size of the German sector is impressive. Spending on construction in the EC in 1992 totaled DM 1.32 trillion. The German market, which is dominated by German firms, accounted for 29 percent of this total.[45]

The German construction industry is represented by two associations. The *Hauptverband der Deutschen Bauindustrie* (HDB) represents the larger companies (50-100 employees and up), which number approximately 4,200. Smaller construction firms are represented by the *Zentralverband der Deutschen Baugewerbe* (ZDB). An HDB representative remarked that the division of the industry into two associations is for the most part salutary, since it enables the HDB to pursue the distinctive interests of larger firms, including among other things the European Community. The impact of Europe on the German construction industry is a function of firm size; for the ZDB, the EU is not much of a concern, while for the HDB, it is becoming increasingly important. Nevertheless, some issues have led to tensions and disagreements between the two BIAs.[46]

The HDB reacted quickly to the collapse of the Wall in 1989, putting in place an all-German membership structure by October 1990. Unification has not caused significant political strains within the industry. The mini-boom in the construction industry generated by unification has led to more than enough work for firms across all of Germany.[47] The HDB has managed to escape the east-west membership tensions that have plagued industry associations in other sectors, such as shipbuilding or agriculture. Furthermore, the privatization of the eastern German *Baukombinate*, conducted by the *Treuhandanstalt*, has not generated conflicts within the industry on the order of the

---

45. Hauptverband der Deutschen Bauindustrie (ed.), *Die deutsche Bauindustrie in Europa* (Wiesbaden, 1992), 6-7.
46. Reflecting the industry's roots in the small, craft-oriented firm sector (*Handwerksbetriebe*), some of the HDB's *Landesverbände* are so-called *Doppelbändeverbände*, belonging simultaneously to the HDB and the ZDB. Thus, issues that divide the HDB and the ZDB can create internal tensions within the former. An HDB representative described this as "an unfortunate situation that had to be tolerated."
47. In 1991 and 1992, German investment in construction achieved growth rates of between 3 and 4 percent. Across the rest of Europe, construction investment had either plateaued or was heading downward.

steel industry, for example.[48] In the end, the privatization process could have an impact, albeit a modest one, on the structure of the industry, and therefore the internal distribution of interests. The firms that have been privatized by the THA are on average larger than the typical large western German firm. HDB representatives point out that large size per se is not a problem – after all, size constitutes the principal distinction between their organization and the ZDB – and that eastern German firms in any event will have to lay off additional personnel to meet competitive exigencies, thus shrinking in size.

Of the major industries covered in this chapter, the construction industry has been affected least and latest by the European common market. This arises in part from the nature of construction activity. For most construction firms, whether German, British, or French, the relevant radius of activity is no more than 80–100 kilometers from the base office. Construction firms, unlike automobile manufacturers or machine tool producers, do not make a product that can be shipped to markets and is subject only to the constraints of straightforward transportation costs. Rather, they must bring the workers and materials to the construction site. This places tangible limits on the reach of firms, and their overall susceptibility to the effects of the common market.

German firms, especially the larger ones like Holzmann, increasingly have factored the EU into their business calculations. They have been active in setting up operations in other EU countries and the EFTA countries. The HDB considers the industry to be "well prepared." The issue of *Standort Deutschland* plays only a modest role for the construction industry. In the end, a construction firm – be it French, German, or Dutch – must build on site. As an industry official explained, "production locations are not substitutable."

The HDB has begun to pay more attention to Brussels in recent years. To pursue the industry's interests at the European level, the HDB initially worked from Bonn; in other words, the association chose to cultivate its contacts with members of the European Parlia-

---

48. One privatization case that drew a skeptical response from the HDB and its western members involved the future of the six firms that made up the Elbo Bau Unternehmensgruppe, Rostock. The struggle pitted interests in Mecklenburg-Vorpommern and Brandenburg, supported in Bonn by Transport Minister Günther Krause, who favored privatizing the six as a group, against those who wished to privatize the firms individually; the latter group was led principally by FDP interests in Bonn and the *Länder* in question. A group privatization would have created the largest construction concern in Germany. Supporters saw this outcome as a plus for this region of Germany, while detractors feared the emergence of a business concern that was both inefficient and politically powerful. By mid-1992, the prospects for a group privatization had dimmed as interested buyers (notably Bouygues S.A. of France) withdrew from negotiations with the THA after getting a close look at Elbo's books.

ment, the Commission, and the German permanent delegation without the benefit of a permanent office in Brussels. This situation had its drawbacks in the eyes of HDB officials. The European umbrella association for the construction industry, the *Fédération Internationale Européenne de la Construction* (FIEC), is hamstrung by divergences of interests within its membership, and is therefore rather ineffective. These shortcomings led the HDB in September 1992 to establish an independent office in Brussels. An association official characterized the decision as long overdue: "In general, we have been sleeping where the issue of contacts with Brussels is concerned; in this regard, perhaps the HDB is no different than many other German industries."

In Brussels, the HDB seeks to ensure the continuing access of its members to the broader EU market. Thus, it has been active on the question of harmonization of technical standards, and recently has begun to push for the introduction of formal qualification standards for German construction firms. Some EU members like Italy, where professional standards have been in existence for years, have used them as a mechanism to exclude foreign contractors. A *Präqualifikation* (advance qualification) system would give German firms automatic access to these markets via the principle of mutual recognition.[49] The HDB has rejected calls for an EU industrial policy, yet it supported the scheduling of the new *Länder* as regions under the EU structural funds.[50] This entitles the eastern *Länder* to considerable financial assistance for public infrastructure projects from which the German construction industry will benefit.

In contrast to some of the other industry groups covered in this chapter, the HDB maintains a much more defensive posture vis-à-vis European integration. As one representative said, "we in the HDB are Euro-skeptics." From such grand issues as EMU and social policy to the more mundane aspects of public procurement regulations, environmental guidelines, and contracting law, the HDB warns against the burgeoning bureaucracy in Brussels. The HDB has been especially critical of EU regulations governing bids for public contracts, which must be announced on an EU-wide basis if the contract

---

49. Interestingly, the ZDB is against *Präqualifikation*, holding to the traditional view that the current *Meisterprüfung* is sufficient proof of a contractor's competence. The problem arises in that it is difficult to conceive how one could draw up a regulation for the German construction industry that would exempt the smaller firms; an all-German, all-industry regime seems the only solution. The ZDB looks upon this as an unwarranted intrusion and unnecessary, since for them European contracts are simply not as important. Such tensions find a reflection within the HDB through the *Doppelbändeverbände* previously mentioned.

50. These are defined as lagging regions in which per capita GDP is 75 percent or less of the Community average.

is to exceed 5 million ECU (approximately DM 10 million). In the opinion of HDB officials, the Commission ignores the limited reach of the vast majority of construction firms in the EU. The HDB argues that the Commission should instead concentrate solely on those areas in which the goal of opening the European construction market carries some meaning:

1. contract bidding in border areas;
2. large construction projects, on the scale of the Frankfurt Airport, where in effect permanent construction sites are created; and
3. specialty construction like subway systems, large sewer projects, and tunnels.

The current EU guidelines have led to sizable administrative burdens for German firms, not to mention the potential for unwitting transgressions of EU regulations.[51]

The unification of Germany has sharpened issues associated with the internal market. A 1992 IFO study commissioned by the main industry association estimated the construction requirements of the new *Länder* at a phenomenal DM 2.37 trillion from 1993 to 2005. This will overtax not only the public sector's ability to finance the massive project, thus raising the issue of private funding for public infrastructure, but also the capacity of the indigenous construction industry to meet these needs. Any shortfall in the latter will have to be met by foreign companies, most likely from other EU countries.[52]

MECHANICAL ENGINEERING

With almost 1.2 million employees, the mechanical engineering industry is Germany's largest. Many of its firms are world leaders, renowned for the quality of their products and their ability to tailor output to the specific needs of customers. The industry is extremely export dependent, shipping almost two thirds of its output to foreign markets. Between 1980 and 1991, German exports of mechanical engineering products accounted for just over 20 percent of total world exports in this sector. 1991 ushered in the sector's first recession in over a decade; by the end of 1992, more than 30,000 jobs had been lost. While much

---

51. One HDB official mentioned a case in which the Land of Sachsen did not carry out a public procurement announcement to the letter and had the European Commission called down on its head by a monitoring agency attached to the French embassy in Bonn.
52. IFO-Institut für Wirtschaftsforschung (ed.), *Baubedarf Ost: Perspektiven bis 2005* (Munich, 1992).

of the blame can be attributed to the international economy – export markets were not expected to pick up again until 1993 – the industry faced structural challenges as well. Competition from Asian firms, especially the Japanese, has intensified in recent years, which has prompted calls from within the industry for a concerted move toward larger firm sizes as a means of coping with the external threat.[53]

This highly variegated industry is represented by the *Verband Deutscher Maschinen- und Anlagenbau* (VDMA). The Verband is not only the largest membership organization in the BDI, but also the largest sectoral BIA in all of Europe; it represents about 3000 firms. Its organizational structures at the local and regional levels played an active role in helping members, either individually or jointly, to cope with the technological and trade challenges of the 1980s.[54] The Verband responded quickly to unification, establishing two regional offices (*Landesstellen*), one in Berlin and the other in Dresden, to serve as liaisons with and to provide services for its eastern members, which number around 200.

Unlike many other industries, the mechanical engineering industry profited only moderately from the mini-boom created by unification. In the face of numerous investment hurdles, many eastern German manufacturing firms had to postpone the purchase of expensive capital equipment. Once the eastern German firms held by the *Treuhandanstalt* were privatized, VDMA officials expected little or no change in the final structure of the industry. The typical German machine tool firm remains small to medium in size. No structural conflicts of interest between eastern and western members have arisen, although this did not prevent tensions from emerging over certain issues in the immediate aftermath of unification.[55]

One of these concerned export assistance. Firms in the new *Länder* were oriented primarily to former COMECON markets, and the

---

53. Although the sector can boast of many large member firms, such as Krupp and Mannesmann, analyses of the mechanical engineering's prolific success in the postwar period have focused on the innovation and flexibility generated by the industry's base in small and medium-sized establishments. See G. Herrigel, "Industrial Order and the Politics of Industrial Change: Mechanical Engineering," in: P. Katzenstein (ed.), *Industry and Politics in West Germany: Toward the Third Republic*, 185–220.
54. Ibid.
55. Some firms in the new *Länder* were unhappy with the limited range of services provided by the VDMA, and contemplated either withdrawal from the national association or the creation of regional associations to promote inter-firm cooperation in areas like product innovation and R & D. One such organization formed in Chemnitz – the *Interessenverband Chemnitzer Maschinenbau e.V.* – and quickly attracted 15 members. See "Maschinenbau-Verband: Ost-West-Gegensatz oder bloßer Wettbewerb?" *Frankfurter Allgemeine Zeitung*, 24 July 1992, 12.

VDMA came out in support of export credits for these eastern countries to keep new members in the east afloat. Generally speaking, western German firms supported this preferential treatment, but there were signs of their patience wearing thin. Yet another debate involved the privatization efforts of the *Treuhandanstalt* in the mechanical engineering sector. The industry union, IG Metall, proposed in 1992 that the THA should seek to privatize firms larger than those that currently exist in the old *Länder* to improve their competitiveness against the Japanese in the market for standardized products.[56] The VDMA rejected this approach, arguing that the flexibility and innovation attached to smaller firms had proven their worth in the past. It openly encouraged and supported the creation of an industrial structure in the eastern *Länder* that mirrors the one in the west. The industry association also came out against subsidy programs for the industry, which drew objections from eastern members.

The *Standort* debate sweeping Germany certainly has drawn the attention of the industry, yet the VDMA has not played a central role in the war of words. The typical list of burdens affects the industry negatively, perhaps more so because of the smaller size of the average firm, but this has not led to a wave of decisions to abandon German production locations. VDMA officials characterize their members as highly conservative on the question of alternative production sites. The industry simply cannot dispense with the skilled labor and inter-firm connections that *Standort Deutschland* provides.

This conservatism can also be seen in the industry's reaction to the Single European Act. Most firm-level adjustments to the implementation of the SEA have taken the form of increased investment and innovation research at home and an expansion of distribution networks in other EU countries. Foreign direct investment has played a much smaller role in the industry's adjustment strategies. According to the industry association, its members are well prepared for the barrier-free market.

On questions relating to the EU, the VDMA has worked out of its headquarters in Frankfurt and from its Brussels office, established in 1972. Despite what industry officials see as a growing avalanche of

---

56. "Die IG Metall fordert Holdings im ostdeutschen Maschinenbau," *Frankfurter Allgemeine Zeitung*, 4 June 1992, 16. IG Metall's proposal piqued the interest of the Chancellor in mid-1992, one of several indications that the government, facing what many eastern Germans were describing as the "deindustrialization" of the former GDR, was growing more willing to experiment with less orthodox, more interventionist economic policies for the five new *Länder*. See "Möllemann fordert Niedrigsteuergebiet im Osten," *Frankfurter Allgemeine Zeitung*, 2 September 1992, 11.

initiatives emanating from the Brussels bureaucracy, there are no present plans to expand their operations at the Community level. Many of the VDMA's members have their own representations in Brussels, but so far, this has not caused coordination problems, at least in the eyes of officials.

The VDMA is very active in Orgalime (*Organisme de Liaison des Industries Métalliques Européennes*), the European umbrella association. As the largest national association represented in Orgalime, the VDMA carries the most weight, and has used it to keep protectionist measures off the association agenda. There are efforts under way, supported by the VDMA, to strengthen Orgalime, particularly in view of the fact that the mechanical engineering industry is not particularly well organized in many EU countries. The VDMA has also devoted more attention in recent years to improving coordination among national associations.

Unlike other German BIAs active in Brussels, the VDMA has not adjusted its standard lobbying strategies to the evolving institutional situation in the Community. As a result, there is a general sense within the organization that it has begun to lose touch with the flow of developments in Brussels. A general initiative is currently under way to address these shortcomings; the attempt to coordinate with other national mechanical engineering associations is part of these efforts. According to VDMA officials, this rethinking is vital because Brussels has become an increasingly opaque and bureaucratized decision-making arena.

The VDMA represents a very orthodox set of positions in Brussels. It backed the multifaceted objectives of Project 1992, and pays especially close attention to the harmonization of technical standards in its product areas to facilitate internal market access for its members. It also supports the opening of public procurement markets in the EU. In general, like other German BIAs, it supports the deregulatory thrust of Community initiatives in internal market policy, but resists vigorously those actions that constitute re-regulation in Brussels; the transitional arrangements attached to the VAT harmonization constitute one such example. It vigorously opposes any moves toward an interventionist EU industrial policy; one official expressed his "horror" at what he saw as the Bonn government's complicity in opening the door to an EU industrial policy during the negotiations at the Maastricht summit.

In international economic affairs, the industry association represents a very liberal position, pushing hard for a successful conclusion to the GATT negotiations and resisting attempts to close off the EU market to Japanese imports in its product areas. Regarding the latter, the VDMA is concerned that the Japanese will take advantage of the completion of the internal market to step up their assault on German export markets. But as an official explained, "we cannot put our firms under a bell jar to protect them from the outside world – one only has to look to eastern Germany and the former COMECON countries to see the consequences of that misguided approach. We need the Japanese as a stimulus." The VDMA has also called upon the EU to increase its political and economic support for the countries of Eastern Europe.

"HIGH TECH" INDUSTRY:
ELECTRONICS, MICROELECTRONICS, AND COMPUTERS

Although some of Germany's largest and most successful firms – e.g. Siemens – can be found within these branches, the high tech industry has been overshadowed by its American and Japanese competitors, many of which are producing on site in Europe.[57] In some fields, such as computers, German producers have failed to keep pace with the world leaders, although their overall performance in many cases has been quite respectable.[58]

Germany is by no means alone in this regard – high tech in Europe has generally been a disappointment, particularly for political leaders who fear an ever-widening technology gap. All of Europe has become embroiled in a debate over the implications of foreign dependency in strategic fields like semiconductor research and production. Of the sectors covered in this paper, German high tech firms have come out most consistently for an interventionist industrial policy, operated at both the national and the EU levels, as well as protection from third country imports of these strategically important products. Since the end of 1991, the industry has found itself in the economic doldrums, a function of the worldwide drop-off in economic activity. Of the 1.1 million employed in the high tech sector at the beginning of 1992, about 22,000 had lost their jobs by the begin-

---

57. See G. Junne, "Competitiveness and the Impact of Change: Applications of 'High Technologies'," in: P. Katzenstein (ed.), *Industry and Politics in West Germany: Toward the Third Republic*, 249–74, and K. Flamm, "Semiconductors," in: G. Hufbauer (ed.), *Europe 1992* (Washington, D.C., 1990), 225–92.
58. An exception was Nixdorf computer company, which folded in the early 1990s. The firm has since been taken over by Siemens and reorganized under the name of Siemens Nixdorf Informationssysteme, now the twenty-seventh largest corporation in Germany. On the general condition of the German computer industry, see "Computerhersteller im Wettlauf mit dem Preisverfall," *Süddeutsche Zeitung*, 11 May 1992, 24.

ning of March. Sales, profits, and employment were not expected to pick up until 1993 at the earliest.

The 1,400 firms in the industry are represented by the *Zentralverband der Elektrotechnik- und Elektronikindustrie* (ZVEI). The association has succeeded in organizing the new *Länder*, virtually all of the approximately 100 eastern German firms currently operating in this sector are members. The ZVEI operates two *Landesstellen* in the eastern *Länder*, which have articulated effectively the specific needs of firms in the region. New members took advantage of a variety of special services provided by the association.

The ZVEI arranged partnerships between western and eastern member firms to assist the latter in carrying out the most basic of business tasks. No new internal membership conflicts have been generated by unification. Overall prospects for the electronics industry in the new *Länder* were gloomy, according to association officials. Only a few firms had been privatized by the THA by 1993, and most of the remaining concerns faced liquidation. With the completion of privatization, officials expected no visible change in the structure of the industry as compared to its pre-1989 contours.

For the industry, both unification and market pressures from the EU have sharpened the terms of the debate on the health of *Standort Deutschland*. According to industry officials, there has already been an impact on the electronics sector; labor intensive production and even some capital intensive production have been relocated in Spain, Portugal, and increasingly the Far East. The association recognized that many of the itemized weaknesses of the German *Standort* lay beyond the grasp of the public authorities. However, it argued that German policymakers must realize that they too act within a competitive environment. In other words, they must pay attention to what other countries are doing in the fields of taxation and regulatory policy, and take care not to place indigenous firms at a disadvantage through their actions.[59] Recent shifts in the focus of the government's technology policy toward a more praxis-oriented approach received the enthusiastic support of the industry association, although it remained skeptical that these can offset the mounting production costs in Germany. The ZVEI rejected the calls for project-related industrial policies in the high tech field, many of which came from within its own ranks.[60]

---

59. See the speech by the then ZVEI president and Siemens chief Karlheinz Kaske, "Internationale Wettbewerbsfähigkeit: Wie es zu schaffen ist," ZVEI Symposium "Internationale Wettbewerbsfähigkeit der deutschen Elektroindustrie," Frankfurt, 11 June 1992 (ZVEI press circular).
60. A case in point involved the decision by the government to reject demands from Siemens and IBM-Germany for sectoral assistance to construct a production

The European common market is crucial for the German electronics industry. The ZVEI estimates that its members export approximately 50 percent of their output, 75 percent of which remains in the EU. That being said, member firms largely have completed the necessary strategic adjustments to the internal market initiative. One source of influence, the effects of which are still unfolding in the industry, involved the Commission's efforts to open up public procurement markets (e.g. telecommunications) to European-wide competition. According to the ZVEI, this will bring both risks – notably increased competition in the previously shielded home market – and far greater opportunities for German firms elsewhere in the EU. To reap the benefits, German firms have formed strategic alliances with other European firms to access these rather Byzantine foreign public procurement markets.

To pursue its interests in the Community policy process, the ZVEI opened an office in Brussels in 1990. The office employs two staff members, who engage in the standard range of activities: information gathering, early warning, and networking. The office's functions are growing in importance, although the functions themselves are not expanding. Rather, the staff is generally in the business of putting experts from the Frankfurt headquarters in touch with the relevant personnel in the Commission or other actors in Brussels. Many member firms, such as Siemens, Bosch, Phillips, and AEG, maintain their own lobbies in Brussels. There have been no coordination problems to speak of. The ZVEI is also a member of Orgalime, which is employed when the association finds it necessary for tactical reasons to put across a "European" industry position to the Commission.

Recent institutional changes in the Community, particularly the extension of qualified majority voting in the Council, have prompted the ZVEI to adapt its standard lobbying strategies. Above all, this has involved closer contacts with other national electronics associations. The rationale provided by association officials parallels those voiced elsewhere in the German business community. Regardless of how closely the ZVEI and the Bonn government coordinate their positions, there is now the chance that Bonn can be outvoted in the Council. To protect its interests, the ZVEI increasingly must network not only with members of the European Parliament, but also with other national industry associations. "We have to motivate them to influence their governments on the issue in question." This is the only way that the ZVEI can improve its chances of being on the winning side. Lobbying strategies proceed on two fronts now: in relation to Bonn

---

facility for their joint "64-Megabit Superchip" project. See G. Lütge and E. Niejahr, "Mißklänge im Mega-Sextett," *Die Zeit*, 29 May 1992, 27.

and other national industry associations. Consequently, the political tasks facing the ZVEI are becoming more complicated.

The ZVEI monitors a range of EU issues for its members, including the harmonization of technical norms and standards for products. An avid supporter of the philosophy of deregulation behind the Single Market initiative, the ZVEI has voiced its concern recently over the increasing bureaucratization of Community affairs. On trade, the association maintains a liberal position, and opposes efforts by the French to close off parts of the market in electronics to protect home producers. According to an industry official, "we cannot allow this to happen, since it would place in jeopardy our access to crucial markets in third countries." On the issue of existing high tariff walls around the EU for products like semiconductors, the association is handicapped because its members are divided on the issue: Producers are in favor of continued and even increased protection, while chip consumers are in favor of openness. As a result, the ZVEI takes no official position on the issue. Unification has created some minor new accents in ZVEI positions – an increased focus on Eastern Europe as a trading partner, in view of its importance to member firms in the new *Länder*, and support for assistance programs to promote the political and economic liberalization processes under way there.

The ZVEI opposes any move toward an interventionist EU industrial policy, even though many of its members are inclined to accept direct subsidies for production. According to officials, a European industrial policy should focus on the competitive playing rules, and refrain from direct involvement in investment and production decisions. Applying the theme of subsidiarity, the ZVEI argues that Brussels should specify its conception of industrial policy in such a way that national governments would be unable to depart from it in any way. On EMU, the association simply does not see the need, especially in view of the many dangers. As to the widening of the EU, the association was in favor of a rapid inclusion of the EFTA countries because these are politically, economically, and institutionally compatible with the current EU average. Membership for the Eastern Europeans, however, cannot be forced.

Summary

The preceding analyses of peak and sectoral business associations since unification reveal a consistent pattern: The EU, as both economic and political entity, is growing in importance. As a large "home" market, the common market is indispensable, which accounts for Germany industry's widespread support for the manifold objectives of Project 1992. European Union, the new phase of integration, has received the support of most sectors of German industry largely for the economic gains it would bring. As a would-be polity, the Community is a source of considerable advantages. It underpins the common market with a variety of regulatory and distributive policies, and offers German firms either the reality or the possibility of a level playing field on which to compete. Via the EU, German industry is able to address the business practices of competitor firms or member governments and, certainly of increasing importance, to seek European-wide harmonization as a means of changing national policies – e.g. environmental regulations – with which it disagrees.

What is interesting about German industry's generally positive assessment of the EU is its continuity with the past. Apart from certain aspects of the *Standort* debate, unification has had few noticeable effects on the interests, objectives, and strategies of German business in Europe. German industry is asking its government and Union officials to tighten the purse strings in Brussels, and it is placing more emphasis on Eastern Europe as a target of EU political and economic initiatives. While significant, these shifts, each of which represents in effect an intensification of a prior policy preference, hardly constitute a revolution. In this sense, industry in a united Germany is no different from government in a united Germany where the continuity of its European commitments is concerned.[61]

These commitments, which are underpinned by a sober appraisal of the benefits and costs of further integration, are difficult to square with the image of German business as a European hegemon-in-waiting. Indeed, the tangible concerns expressed by the vast majority of BIA officials about the opaque and nettlesome Brussels bureaucracy belie the notion that the EU is an easily controlled institution and that German business is an eager and capable controller. The Union is too complex and autonomous and German business is too variegated in strength and interest to support the simple hegemony thesis.

There is a small, gray cloud on this generally sunny horizon. Virtually every BIA covered in this study expressed its profound concern with the trend toward greater *dirigisme*, interventionism, and bureaucratization. There was every reason to expect that the defeat of the Danish referendum on Maastricht in June 1992 and the razor-thin French *oui* to the treaties in September would lead to a more transparent Community process. But this would hardly address the distressing situation that many German BIAs already faced at the EU level *as organizations.*

---

61. See Anderson and Goodman, "Mars or Minerva?"

Industry associations, which are there to safeguard the interests of their members, are on the verge of becoming overwhelmed by the sheer volume of activity in Brussels. The EU apparatus is gaining responsibilities and, moreover, is changing institutionally in such a way that more is demanded of European interest groups if they wish simply to keep pace with, let alone influence, the decision-making process. For example, witness the changes in BIA strategies prompted by the extension of qualified majority voting in the Council of Ministers. Many German industry associations have already lost their monopoly of representation in Brussels as the larger member firms set up offices in response to what they see as a decline in the quality of service provided by the European and national umbrella associations.

German industry associations face a difficult challenge. They must upgrade their organizations, both at home and in Brussels, simply to cope. Yet they must ask their members for the money to fund new buildings, additional personnel, and research capabilities at a time when membership skepticism of the utility of association activities has reached an all time high.[62] Should the associations fail to convince their memberships of the urgency of the task, the fallout would be unevenly distributed. Business associations would no doubt continue to pursue their members' European interests, but at a diminishing level of performance. The only member firms able to compensate would be those large corporations capable of and willing to maintain their own offices in Brussels. In recent years, the Commission – ever starved for informational resources and ever vigilant for key political allies – has demonstrated a willingness to bypass the cumbersome Euro-groups and national umbrella associations, and instead work directly with individual corporations.[63] Since the success of the German economy has not rested solely on the performance of Daimler-Benz and Siemens, but on thousands of innovative small- and medium-sized firms; and since continued economic success increasingly is bound up with the flow of Community affairs, the transformation of Brussels' interest group scene into a club for the truly wealthy would be a most unwelcome development for German industry as a whole.

---

62. See for example K. Broichhausen, "Politik für die Industrie, keine Industriepolitik," *Frankfurter Allgemeine Zeitung*, 2 July 1992, 15. This rocky state of affairs within the business community, itself the product of the strains of unification, was underscored by the sudden resignation of BDI president Heinrich Weiss in September 1992. After enduring months of criticism from within BDI ranks over his leadership style and lack of pull in government circles, he stepped down with several months remaining in his first term of office.

63. See B. Kohler-Koch, "West German Lobbying in Brussels," unpublished manuscript, 1992.

TABLES

Table 1.1 Production and Employment in Major Industrial Nations from 1984-1990

United States

Year	Retail Sales Volume	Industrial Production	Unemployment Rate	Vacancy Rate Indicator	Composite Leading Indicator
1984	95.3	98.3	7.4	96.0	98.3
1985	100.0	100.0	7.1	100.0	102.7
1986	105.7	100.9	6.9	97.8	107.9
1987	108.3	105.9	6.1	105.0	109.8
1988	112.2	111.6	5.4	106.2	114.3
1989	114.7	114.5	5.2	99.4	113.3
1990	114.2	115.7	5.4	84.3	108.8

Japan

Year	Retail Sales Volume	Industrial Production	Unemployment Rate	Vacancy Rate Indicator	Composite Leading Indicator
1984	96.7	96.4	2.7	100.5	93.9
1985	100.0	100.0	2.6	100.0	96.4
1986	106.4	99.7	2.8	94.3	105.3
1987	113.5	103.1	2.8	108.3	115.2
1988	122.7	112.9	2.5	135.9	122.5
1989	132.7	119.9	2.3	147.0	125.7
1990	141.9	125.3	2.1	149.7	123.0

Germany

Year	Retail Sales Volume	Industrial Production	Unemployment Rate	Vacancy Rate Indicator	Composite Leading Indicator
1984	99.2	96.4	7.1	83.4	99.9
1985	100.0	100.0	7.2	100.0	103.7
1986	103.6	102.4	6.4	136.4	103.1
1987	107.4	102.7	6.2	149.4	103.8
1988	110.5	106.4	6.2	164.7	109.7
1989	113.6	111.6	5.6	218.9	112.0
1990	122.8	117.4	5.1	261.4	113.6

France

Year	Retail Sales Volume	Industrial Production	Unemployment Rate	Vacancy Rate Indicator	Composite Leading Indicator
1984	99.3	99.3	9.7		97.4
1985	100.0	100.0	10.2		101.1
1986	102.4	101.2	10.4		107.2
1987	104.5	103.1	10.5		107.3
1988	107.9	107.3	10.0		112.0
1989	109.6	111.2	9.4		111.4
1990	110.1	112.4	9.0		105.5

Italy

Year	Retail Sales Volume	Industrial Production	Unemployment Rate	Vacancy Rate Indicator	Composite Leading Indicator
1984	95.4	98.5	9.3		101.1
1985	100.0	100.0	9.6		103.6
1986	107.6	103.2	10.4		110.3
1987	113.4	106.8	10.9		112.5
1988	109.7	114.2	10.9		117.4
1989	117.4	118.7	10.9		115.6
1990		117.9	9.8		112.8

United Kingdom

Year	Retail Sales Volume	Industrial Production	Unemployment Rate	Vacancy Rate Indicator	Composite Leading Indicator
1984	95.6	94.8	11.7	93.7	100.7
1985	100.0	100.0	11.2	100.0	102.4
1986	105.2	102.4	11.2	116.1	105.3
1987	110.7	105.7	10.3	141.2	109.6
1988	117.7	109.6	8.5	144.3	108.5
1989	119.9	110.0	7.1	124.2	106.1
1990	120.4	109.2	6.9	97.8	102.3

Source: *Financial Times*, 29 April 1991

Table 1.2 Exports of Major Industrial Nations as a Percentage of GDP from 1913-1987

Country	1913[1]	1928[1]	1938[1]	1950[1]	1958[2]	1960[2]	1970[2]	1980[2]	1987[2]
Germany	19.3	14.4	5.4	8.5	15.1	19.0	21.2	26.5	28.7
U.K.	23.4	17.2	9.2	16.9	23.0	20.0	22.5	27.2	26.3
Italy	9.7	8.8	6.3	7.9	11.6	14.6	15.4	21.8	19.7
U.S.	6.6	6.0	3.7	3.8	4.3	4.9	5.6	10.2	7.6
Japan	14.3	14.5	14.9	8.4	11.8	11.1	11.3	14.9	13.2

Notes: [1] Goods only
[2] Goods and Services

Source: Weidenfeld, H. and H. Zimmermann (eds.), *Deutschland-Handbuch* (Bonn, 1989), 623.

Table 1.3 Percentage of World Export Shares of Major Trading Nations in 1991

Country	%
United States	12.0
Germany	11.4
Japan	8.9
France	6.1
United Kingdom	5.3
Italy	4.8
Holland	3.8
Canada	3.7
Belgium/Luxemburg	3.3
Hong Kong	2.8
Taiwan	2.2
Former USSR	2.2

Source: Die Zeit, 24 April 1992

Table 1.4 Germany's Exports/Imports in Current Prices (Mill. Marks) and by Volume (1913 = 100) from 1880-1985

Year	Current Prices		Volume	
	Exports	Imports	Exports	Imports
1880	2,923.0	2,813.7	22.4	25.5
1885	2,854.0	2,922.6	25.9	31.8
1890	3,335.1	4,162.4	29.8	44.0
1895	3,318.0	4,119.0	31.7	52.0
1900	4,611.2	5,768.6	44.7	63.2
1905	5,731.6	7,128.8	58.2	75.1
1910	7,474.7	8,926.9	77.4	88.3
1913	10,097.5	10,750.9	100.0	100.0
1923		6,150.1		
1925	9,284.0	12,429.2	66.4	82.3
1930	12,035.6	10,348.7	92.2	86.0
1932	5,741.1	4,652.8	55.6	62.5
1935	4,178.0	4,156.2	51.5	60.8
1940				
1945				
1950	8,363.1	11,373.9	34.3	47.4
1955	25,716.8	24,461.1	85.6	99.4
1959	41,062.4	35,485.7	120.6	153.7
1960	47,900.0	42,700.0		
1965	71,700.0	70,400.0		
1970	125,300.0	109,600.0		
1975	221,600.0	184,300.0		
1980	350,300.0	341,400.0		
1985	537,100.0	463,800.0		

Sources: Hoffmann, W.G. et al. (eds.), *Dar Wachstum der deutschen Wirtschaft seit der Mitte des 19. Jahrhunderts* (Heidelberg, 1965), 520ff.; Statistisches Bundesamt (ed.), *Datenreport 1985* (Bonn, 1985), 240; *Die Zeit,* 21 February 1986.

Table 1.5 Structure of Germany's Exports by Region from 1958-1985 (%)

Region	1958	1985
European Community	35.8	47.4
Other Industrialized Nations	37.2	34.7
Developing World	21.4	12.4
Comecon Countries	5.1	5.2

Source: Weidenfeld/Zimmermann, 629.

Table 1.6 Structure of West Germany's Exports and Imports by Major Trading Partners from 1900-1985 (Mill. Marks)

Country	1900	1913	1925	1930	1938[a]	1950[b]	1960[c]	1971[c]	1985[c]	1989
Exports										
France	278	790	462	1,149	217	614	4,202	16,975	64,000	
Netherlands	396	694	996	1,206	448	1,164	4,210	14,522	46,300	
U.K.	912	1,438	937	1,219	351	361	2,147	5,449	46,000	352,668[d]
Italy	127	395	423	484	301	486	2,847	11,451	41,800	
Belgium/Lux.	253	551	264	601	227	677	2,890	11,581	37,000	
Russia/USSR	325	880	251	431	32	0	778	1,608	10,500	29,306[e]
U.S.	440	714	604	685	149	430	3,723	13,140	55,600	46,624
Imports										
France	306	583	558	519	144	691	3,998	15,919	49,300	
Netherlands	215	333	743	561	198	1,246	3,638	15,769	58,300	
U.K.	841	876	944	639	283	489	1,956	4,413	37,200	258,660[d]
Italy	196	318	496	365	246	507	2,631	12,692	37,200	
Belgium/Lux.			416	325	194	405	2,441	11,638	29,100	
Russia/USSR	717	1,425	230	436	47	1	673	1,277	13,600	25,143
U.S.	1,021	1,711	2,196	1,307	405	1,735	5,974	12,420	32,300	38,265

Notes: [a] Reich territory as of 31 December 1937
[b] Fed. Rep. excluding Saarland
[c] Fed. Rep. including Saarland
[d] European Community
[e] Socialist States

Sources: Kocka, J. and B. Mütter (eds.), *Wirtschaft und Gesellschaft im Zeitalter der Industialisierung* (Munich, 1984), 142 ff.; *Die Zeit*, 28 March 1986; Smyser, W.R., *The Economy of United Germany* (New York, 1992), 197.

Table 1.7 Germany's Exports as a Percentage of GNP from 1910-1980

Year	%
1910-1913	17.8
1925-1929	14.9
1930-1934	12.0
1935-1938	6.0
1950	9.3
1960	17.2
1970	23.8
1980	26.7

Source: Smyser, 195.

Table 1.8 Structure of West Germany's Imports and Exports by Sector from 1962-1987 (%)

Sector	Imports			Exports		
	1962	1973	1987	1962	1973	1987
Agriculture	23.0	13.1	7.6	1.0	1.4	1.2
Food products	9.9	9.1	6.5	1.7	3.5	4.3
Mining	10.7	9.8	6.9	4.7	1.9	0.7
Basic raw materials	28.3	28.9	26.8	26.9	26.9	24.4
Capital goods	15.0	22.5	34.2	55.8	54.6	57.0
Consumer goods	13.0	16.6	18.0	9.8	11.8	12.4
Totals	100.0	100.0	100.0	100.0	100.0	100.0

Source: Weidenfeld/Zimmermann, 623

Table 1.9 Germany's Exports by Selected Commodity Groups from 1975-1988 (Mill. Marks)

Group	1975	1980	1988
Road vehicles	30,009	52,837	102,669
Mechanical engineering products	43,122	57,599	87,463
Chemical products	27,457	46,222	78,434
Electrical products	21,362	34,359	63,782
Iron and steel	17,395	18,693	22,092
Textiles	8,048	12,158	19,830
Iron, steel and sheet metal goods	6,045	9,896	16,011
Non-ferrous metals and semi-finished goods	3,959	9,928	12,221
Precision and optical goods; clocks and watches	4,317	6,638	10,803
Aerospace	1,178	5,147	10,624

Source: Deutsche Bank

Table 1.10 West Germany's Exports as a Percentage of Production by Major Branches in 1989

Branch	%
Shipbuilding	62
Air and space	59
Office equipment	53
Automobiles	48
Machine tools	45
Chemicals	44
Iron and steel	37
Precision mechanics, optics	36
Electronics	31

Source: Smyser, 196

Table 1.11 Percentage of Germany's Share of EC Production by Major Branches in 1988

Branch	%
Office equipment	48
Chemical goods	24
Machinery	24
Motor vehicles	23
Precision machinery; optics	18
Electronics	17
Textiles	16
Iron and steel	14

Source: Smyser, 213

Table 1.12 West Germany's Patterns of Foreign Investment by Region from 1981-1989 (Bill. Marks)

Region	FRG Assets Abroad		Foreign Assets in FRG		Balance	
	1981	1989	1981	1989	1981	1989
EC States	204	705	227	519	-23	186
Other Industrial States	193	474	150	340	43	134
Others[1]	168	278	122	155	45	123
Total	564	1,457	498	1,014	66	443

Note: [1]OPEC, Developing Countries, CMEA states, etc.

Source: Smyser, 200.

❖ 220 ❖

Table 1.13 The 50 Largest Industrial Enterprises in West Germany in 1988

Rank		Name	Branch	Turnover		Profit (Mill. Marks)		No. of Employees	
1988	1987			Mill. Marks	Change (%)	1988	1987		Change (%)
1	1	Daimler-Benz	Automobiles	73,495	8.9	1,702	1,782	338,749	3.8
2	3	Siemens	Electrical/Electronics	59,374	15.4	1,391	1,275	353,000	-1.7
3	2	VW	Automobiles	59,221	8.4	780	598	252,066	-3.2
4	5	VEBA	Energy/Chemicals	42,646	10.0	1,188	1,030	84,715	13.6
5	4	BASF	Chemicals	42,449	9.0	1,410	1,051	134,834	0.8
6	7	Hoechst	Chemicals	40,964	10.8	2,015	1,528	164,527	-1.9
7	6	Bayer	Chemicals	40,468	9.0	1,909	1,544	165,700	0.8
8	9	Thyssen	Steel	29,220	3.9	680	270	128,690	-4.5
9	10	Bosch	Electrical/Electronics	27,675	9.1	554	825	167,780	4.4
10	8	RWE	Energy	25,584	-1.4	766	779	76,298	4.8
11	12	BMW	Automobiles	24,467	25.7	n.d.[1]	n.d.[1]	65,812	4.8
12	11	Ruhrkohle	Mining	20,650	1.9	-110	38	120,341	-4.0
13	15	Mannesmann	Machines	20,422	22.6	292	134	121,782	7.5
14	14	Ford	Automobiles	19,247	13.1	545	810	49,530	5.2
15	13	Opel	Automobiles	17,462	1.6	505	479	52,325	-4.5
16	18	Metallgesellschaft	Metal Manufacturing	15,235	14.3	155	100	25,132	3.0
17	16	M.A.N.	Machines	14,962	0.0	202	163	62,025	1.5
18	17	Krupp	Steel	14,737	4.5	-202	42	63,391	-2.8
19	19	Degussa	Metals	13,605	16.1	146	121	32,419	5.3
20	22	Preussag	Oil	11,425	9.6	117	102	25,526	-14.0
21	20	IBM Deutschland	Electronics	11,372	-1.5	645	545	30,712	0.6
22	27	Bertelsmann	Publishing	11,325	23.6	362	207	41,961	-0.1
23	26	Henkel	Chemicals	10,252	10.8	352	292	35,943	3.5
24	31	Salzgitter	Steel	9,802	19.0	90	65	38,020	0.8
25	21	Deutsche Shell	Oil	9,540	-10.2	32	246	3,474	-4.2

(continues)

Table 1.13 (continued)

Rank		Name	Branch	Turnover		Profit (Mill. Marks)		No. of Employees	
1988	1987			Mill. Marks	Change (%)	1988	1987		Change (%)
26	30	VIAG	Holding	9,471	12.2	219	191	33,427	2.1
27	25	Ruhrgas	Energy	8,614	-9.7	430	513	8,322	29.1
28	29	Deutsche Philips	Electrical/Electronics	8,602	0.4	-19	109	35,100	-2.5
29	24	Esso	Oil	8,536	-11.5	126	63	2,626	-12.4
30	32	Hoesch	Steel	8,345	13.7	58	49	33,800	3.0
31	28	Deutsche BP	Oil	8,247	-6.6	327	143	5,521	-0.6
32	44	Continental	Tires	7,906	55.1	195	139	45,907	8.6
33	23	Feldmühle Nobel	Chemicals	7,901	-19.4	159	151	33,469	-22.0
34	33	Deutsche Unilever	Food	7,574	5.3	203	217	24,053	-0.2
35	35	MBB	Aerospace	7,120	16.8	100	5	39,886	3.7
36	34	Klöckner	Steel	6,121	8.0	0	-390	27,672	-2.0
37	37	Beyernwerk	Energy	5,818	1.2	252	233	9,561	0.5
38	36	Philipp Holzmann	Construction	5,810	0.2	30	23	22,770	-3.0
39	39	VEW	Energy	5,755	5.3	170	167	7,948	-1.6
40	51	ZF-Friedrichshafen	Machines	5,570	20.4	94	36	32,616	6.8
41	46	Asea Brown Boweri	Electrical/Electronics	5,467	10.2	35	20	34,151	-0.6
42	45	Nixdorf	Electronics	5,347	5.4	26	264	31,037	5.4
43	50	Schering	Chemicals	5,272	12.1	158	144	24,685	3.0
44	38	Saarbergwerke	Coal/Energy	5,224	-6.1	-85	-296	24,977	-13.2
45	48	Deutsche Babcock	Machines	5,150	6.7	40	45	22,451	1.5
46	53	Deutsche Nestlé	Food	5,085	4.1	103	113	17,161	14.6
47	47	Batig	Holding	4,873	-0.8	200	140	23,842	-3.2
48	n.V.	Enka	Chemicals	4,854	9.0	150	80	30,700	1.0
49	49	Hochtief	Construction	4,701	0.0	52	51	26,351	-6.7
50	54	Linde	Machines	4,667	12.9	126	118	21,222	8.0

Notes: [1] n.d. = no data available

Source: Die Zeit, 11 August 1989.

Table 1.14 The 100 Largest Industrial Enterprises in Europe, 1993

				TURNOVER			PROFITS		NO. OF EMPLOYEES	
Rank	Name	Country	Branch	Mill. Marks	Change (%)	in Europe (%)	Mill. Marks	Mill. Marks	Abs.	Change (%)
1	Royal Dutch Shell	NL	Oil	157,298	15.1	49	7,474	8,435	117,000	-7.9
2	Daimler-Benz	D	Automobiles	97,737	-0.8	65	615	1,451	366,736	-2.6
3	Brit. Petroleum	GB	Oil	86,780	5.1	73	1,532	-1,261	84,500	-20.1
4	Siemens	D	Electrics	81,648	4.0	73	1,982	1,955	391,000	-5.3
5	IRI	I	Holding	79,273	-0.8	92	-10,768	-5,944	366,471	-8.4
6	VW	D	Automobiles	76,586	-10.3	77	-1,940	147	253,108	-7.4
7	Unilever	NL	Food/Chemicals	69,100	1.4	54	3,379	3,554	294,000	2.4
8	Nestlé	CH	Food	64,355	5.4	46	3,164	2,919	209,755	-3.8
9	Veba	D	Energy/Oil/Chemicals	61,294	0.0	95	1,013	1,043	131,485	1.3
10	Elf aquitaine	F	Oil	61,209	4.6	90	321	2,106	94,300	7.3
11	Fiat	I	Automobiles	57,426	-0.2	n.d.	-1877	704	260,951	-3.7
12	ENI	I	Chemicals/Energy	56,712	8.2	84	441	-1,037	106,391	-14.2
13	Philips	NL	Electrics/Electronics	52,364	0.5	54	1,052	-522	252,214	-2.1
14	Electricité de France	F	Energy	51,350	-0.6	100	621	546	118,146	-0.4
15	Renault	F	Automobiles	49,560	-7.8	85	270	1,579	139,733	-4.7
16	Asea Brown Boverie	S/CH	Electrics	46,844	-4.4	56	119	823	206,490	-3.1
17	Hoechst	D	Chemicals	46,047	0.4	53	756	1,182	172,483	-2.9
18	Alcatel-Alsthom	F	Electrics/Telecom.	45,632	-3.3	68	2,316	2,494	196,500	-3.2
19	RWE	D	Energy	45,111	2.7	88	1,048	1,047	113,642	7.6
20	Peugeot	F	Automobiles	42,450	-6.4	93	-412	995	143,900	-4.6
21	Bayer	D	Chemicals	41,007	-0.5	51	1,372	1,563	151,900	-2.9
22	BASF	D	Chemicals	40,568	-3.3	63	858	613	112,020	-9.1
23	Total	F	Oil	39,545	-0.8	50	-933	900	49,772	-2.7
24	B.A.T.	GB	Tobacco/Paper	36,666	10.9	50	3,131	2,648	190,000	-4.0
25	ENEL	I	Energy	35,880	4.5	100	2,313	2,873	105,835	n.d.

(continued)

Table 1.14 (continued)

Rank	Name	Country	Branch	Turnover Mill. Marks	Change (%)	in Europe (%)	Profits Mill. Marks	Mill. Marks	No. of Employees Abs.	Change (%)
26	Thyssen	D	Steel	33,502	-6.3	80	-994	350	136,975	-7.4
27	Bosch	D	Electrics	32,469	-5.7	82	426	512	164,506	-7.2
28	BMW	D	Auto	29,016	-7.1	69	516	726	71,034	-3.4
29	Repsol	E	Oil	28,888	16.2	n.d.	1,095	1,094	18,797	-4.3
30	Mannesmann	D	Machines	27,963	-0.2	71	-513	63	127,695	-6.6
31	British Aerospace	GB	Air and Space	26,717	7.8	62	-574	-2,558	87,400	-14.7
32	ICI	GB	Chemicals	26,399	-11.8	47	447	-1,561	87,100	n.c.
33	Metallgesellschaft	D	Metal Manufacturing	26,094	2.1	52	-1,969	64	43,292	-30.8
34	General Electric Comp.	GB	Electrical/Electronics	25,906	-0.3	77	1,476	1,571	143,000	-8.3
35	Pétrofina	B	Oil/Chemicals	25,882	0.7	77	364	224	14,696	-5.1
36	British Gas	GB	Gas	25,788	1.3	100	-1,331	1,308	79,358	-5.5
37	Ciba-Geigy	CH	Chemicals	25,353	2.0	54	1,992	1,690	87,480	-3.4
38	BTR	GB	Mixed	24,264	10.5	37	2,294	2,183	129,814	-3.9
39	Hanson	GB	Mixed	24,234	10.9	45	1,823	2,998	71,000	-5.3
40	INI	E	Mixed	24,057	-13.9	n.d.	-1,741	-426	129,435	-7.4
41	Ferruzzi	I	Food	23,990	-10.1	77	-2,545	-1,921	41,329	-20.2
42	Viag	D	Aluminum/Energy	23,734	-2.4	81	302	371	80,683	-4.6
43	Volvo	S	Automobiles	23,618	29.1	n.d.	-661	-1,236	73,641	22.5
44	Rhône-Poulenc	F	Chemicals	23,516	-1.4	77	971	1,025	81,678	-1.9
45	Ruhrkohle	D	Mining	23,408	-4.7	98	49	66	111,150	-6.1
46	Preussag	D	Steel/Energy	23,290	-4.8	81	193	440	73,319	-0.5
47	Usinor-Sacilor	F	Steel	21,982	-6.2	83	-1,890	-887	67,984	-19.5
48	Österr. Industrieholding	A	Mixed	21,759	-7.8	n.d.	-1,734	-1,123	64,859	-16.6
49	Electrolux	S	Electrical/Electronics	21,274	24.5	56	136	73	114,700	-5.4
50	Saint Gobain	F	Mixed	20,882	-3.3	74	375	781	92,348	-8.0

(continued)

Table 1.14 (continued)

Rank	Name	Country	Branch	Turnover Mill. Marks	Turnover Change (%)	Turnover in Europe (%)	Profits Mill. Marks	Profits Mill. Marks	No. of Employees Abs.	No. of Employees Change (%)
51	Krupp-Hoesch	D	Steel/Machines	20,504	-9.7	80	-589	-250	78,376	-11.6
52	Danone (ehem. BSN)	F	Food	20,464	-1.0	91	990	1,153	56,419	-2.8
53	M.A.N.	D	Machines	18,972	-1.0	71	230	418	62,720	-2.4
54	Statoil	N	Oil/Gas	18,889	2.0	n.d.	792	627	14,560	1.5
55	Michelin	F	Tires	18,476	-5.3	55	-1	-4	124,575	-4.7
56	Thomson	F	Electronics	18,421	-11.1	56	n.d.	7	99,900	-0.9
57	Pechiney	F	Metals	18,396	-3.6	57	-286	60	57,450	-5.8
58	Bouygues	F	Construction	17,859	-2.5	n.d.	158	257	90,000	n.c.
59	Bertelsmann	D	Publishing	17,170	7.6	72	662	569	50,437	3.4
60	Sandoz	CH	Chemicals	16,904	4.7	42	1,918	1,679	52,550	-1.5
61	Schneider	F	Mixed	16,456	-8.5	62	76	7	91,458	-5.9
62	Roche	CH	Chemicals	16,025	10.5	36	2,812	2,145	56,082	-0.4
63	SmithKline Beecham	GB	Chemicals	15,305	18.1	30	2,091	2,079	51,900	-2.1
64	Degussa	D	Chemicals	14,901	16.3	55	121	121	32,094	-4.0
65	Aerospatiale	F	Aerospace	14,843	-2.7	n.d.	-445	-676	43,913	-4.8
66	Akzo	NL	Chemicals	14,696	-2.0	67	493	591	60,700	-2.9
67	Norsk Hydro	N	Energy/Oil/Gas	14,529	7.4	82	698	442	32,455	-4.6
68	Gasunie	NL	Gas	14,510	-3.1	100	71	71	1,860	-6.4
69	Ruhrgas	D	Gas	14,349	-0.5	100	729	796	11,574	-2.7
70	Gaz de France	F	Gas	14,338	0.2	100	310	468	25,801	-1.1
71	Henkel	D	Chemicals	13,867	-1.7	78	385	402	40,470	-4.2
72	Ericsson	S	Cables/Telecom.	13,376	33.9	56	616	157	69,597	5.1
73	Allied Lyons	GB	Drinks and Food	12,773	-4.0	78	750	718	71,713	-8.9
74	Philipp Holzmann	D	Construction	12,465	0.0	78	106	91	43,798	0.3
75	CEA	F	Nuclear Energy	12,289	7.4	n.d.	364	283	42,617	7.1

(continued)

Table 1.14 (continued)

Rank	Name	Country	Branch	Turnover Mill. Marks	Turnover Change (%)	Turnover in Europe (%)	Profits Mill. Marks	Profits Mill. Marks	No. of Employees Abs.	No. of Employees Change (%)
76	RTZ	GB	Mining	11,973	4.5	37	795	785	59,975	-12.2
77	British Steel	GB	Steel	11,846	-6.4	94	-358	-102	42,100	-18.4
78	l'Oréal	F	Cosmetics/Chemicals	11,723	6.9	76	803	723	32,261	1.1
79	Solvay	B	Chemicals	11,682	-4.1	68	167	480	43,163	-4.8
80	Dalgety	GB	Food	11,240	12.1	41	202	240	15,417	-4.1
81	Thorn Emi	GB	Electronics	11,054	12.6	67	412	248	49,433	-8.0
82	Bass	GB	Brewing	11,052	3.3	89	817	1,057	81,105	-3.6
83	Ass. British Foods	GB	Food	10,890	10.9	89	581	471	49,968	-3.4
84	Stora	S	Paper	10,716	6.1	86	138	-298	33,641	-13.5
85	Hilldown Holdings	GB	Food	10,384	14.1	61	293	61	43,251	-2.1
86	Pirelli	I	Tires	9,733	12.1	56	-101	-196	42,132	-7.9
87	BICC	GB	Cables	9,728	7.4	61	181	72	39,151	-2.4
88	Tate & Lyle	GB	Sugar	9,478	13.3	41	417	369	15,834	-6.9
89	Continental	D	Tires	9,369	-3.3	69	65	133	50,974	0.8
90	Cadbury Schweppes	GB	Holding	9,249	10.5	62	713	658	39,066	-6.8
91	Arbed	L	Steel	9,187	1.9	83	-225	-162	44,130	-9.6
92	Olivetti	I	Electronics	9,066	7.3	81	-459	-822	35,171	13.0
93	Lafarge Coppée	F	Building Materials	8,882	0.0	62	579	428	30,572	3.1
94	Rolls Royce	GB	Aerospace	8,735	-1.2	39	144	-556	49,200	-10.5
95	RMC	GB	Building Materials	8,710	1.9	89	328	295	27,635	5.0
96	United Biscuits	GB	Food	8,554	10.5	56	166	308	39,352	1.7
97	Bull	F	Electronics	8,246	-6.4	71	-1,479	-1,378	31,735	-9.8
98	BOC	GB	Gas	8,035	13.0	28	551	289	40,266	4.0
99	Vauxhall	GB	Automobiles	7,700	3.4	n.d.	314	380	10,554	-4.4
100	VEW	D	Energy	7,595	12.5	100	194	160	11,782	n.c.

n.d. = no data   n.v. = not comparable
Source: Die Zeit, 21 October 1994.

Table 2.1: **Growth in Current Value of World Foreign-Direct-Investment Outflows, Exports, and GDP, 1983-1989, as Compound Annual Growth Rate for 1983-1989 (%):**

World foreign-direct-investment outflows	28.9
World exports	9.4
World GDP	7.8

Source: United Nations, (ed.), *World Investment Report 1991* (New York, 1992).

Table 2.2: **Outflows of Foreign Direct Investment from Five Major Industrial Nations, 1985-1989, (A) in bill. US $; (B) in %:**

			A			B
Country	1985	1986	1987	1988	1989	1985-89
France	2.2	5.4	9.2	14.5	19.4	8.0
Germany	5.0	10.1	9.2	11.2	13.5	7.8
Japan [a]	6.4	14.5	19.5	34.2	44.2	18.8
U.K.	11.1	16.5	31.1	37.0	32.0	20.2
U.S. [b]	8.9	13.8	28.0	13.3	26.5	14.3
Total	33.7	60.2	97.1	110.2	135.6	69.1
Developed Countries	52.1	84.7	132.6	155.4	187.1	96.8
Developing Countries	1.2	1.7	2.4	5.9	8.9	3.2
Total	53.3	86.5	135.0	161.3	196.1	100.0

[a] Data for Japan do not include reinvested earnings.
[b] Excluding outflows to the finance (except banking), insurance and real estate sectors of the Netherlands Antilles.

Source: United Nations, (ed.), *World Investment Report 1991* (New York, 1992).

Table 2.3: German Foreign Direct Investments, 1980-1989 (Bill. Marks):

Marks			% Increases		
1980	1985	1989	1985/80	1989/85	1989/80
84.5	147.5	195.7	74.6	32.7	131.6

Source: Deutsche Bundesbank

Table 2.4: German Foreign Direct Investments by Country, 1980-1989 (Bill. Marks):

	1980	**1989**
France		17.5
U.K.		12.9
Netherlands		11.5
Spain		10.5
Belgium		9.9
Total EC	33.8	84.4
Former Soviet Bloc	0.1	0.5
US/Canada	24.3	61.4
Developing Countries	15.1	20.1

Source: Deutsche Bundesbank

Table 2.5: National, Joint, and International Participations (Including Take-overs and Fusions) in the EC, 1986-1990:

Branch	National Operations				Joint Operations				International Operations				Total			
	1986/1987	1987/1988	1988/1989	1989/1990	1986/1987	1987/1988	1988/1989	1989/1990	1986/1987	1987/1988	1988/1989	1989/1990	1986/1987	1987/1988	1988/1989	1989/1990
Foods and Drinks	39	25	35	41	11	18	27	44	2	8	14	17	71	85	107	148
Chemicals, Ceramics, Plastics	52	51	76	102												
Electr., Office machines	38	32	37	38	27	38	56	75	6	15	14	35				
Machine tools	33	25	23	20	6	4	18	16	2	7	8	10	41	36	49	46
Computers	21	24	31	25	8	5	17	13	2	9	7	14	31	38	55	52
Metal Manuf.	2	2	3	1	—	1	—	1	—	—	1	0	2	3	4	2
Automobiles	15	28	16	29	4	9	13	28	—	3	6	7	19	40	35	64
Paper, Wood products	15	3	7	11	6	9	6	13	—	3	1	8	21	15	14	32
Mining	17	24	32	28	7	6	26	30	1	4	3	21	25	34	61	79
Textiles, leather	8	9	11	10	1	2	5	8	—	1	3	1	9	12	19	19
Construction	4	11	11	4	2	2	7	8	—	1	2	1	6	14	20	13
Others	13	21	20	19	3	12	19	17	3	—	1	3	19	33	39	39
	6	10	7	15	—	5	3	4	1	7	3	7	7	22	13	26
Total	211	214	233	241	75	111	197	257	17	58	62	124	303	383	492	622

Source: European Commission, (ed.), *Bericht über die Wettbewerbspolitik, 1986-1990,* (Brussels, 1991).

List of Contributors

Jeffrey J. Anderson: Associate Professor of Political Science, Brown University, Providence RI

Volker R. Berghahn: Professor of History, Brown University, Providence RI

Peter Hayes: Professor of History, Northwestern University, Evanston IL

Margit Köppen: Member of the IG Metall Executive, Frankfurt

Reinhard Neebe: Research Fellow, Department of History, Bielefeld University

Simon Reich: Associate Professor at the Graduate School for Public and International Affairs, University of Pittsburgh PA

Harm G. Schröter: Research Fellow, Department of Economic History, Free University Berlin

Robert Mark Spaulding, Jr.: Assistant Professor of History, University of North Carolina, Wilmington NC

UNITING GERMANY
Documents and Debates, 1944-1993

Konrad H. Jarausch *and* **Volker Gransow**
Translations from the German by **Allison Brown** *and* **Belinda Cooper**

The unification of Germany is the most important change in Central Europe in the last four decades. Understanding this rapid and unforeseen development has raised old fears as well as inspired new hopes. In order to make sense out of the bewildering process and to help both expert and lay readers understand the changes and the consequences, an American historian and a German social scientist put together this collection of central texts on German unification, the first of its kind. An invaluable reference tool.

"The first comprehensive documentation in English of the German reunification...a good chronological range of sources...The editing is not only expert but also user-friendly...belongs in all serious academic and major public libraries." **Choice**

Konrad H. Jarausch is Lurcy Professor of European Civilization at the University of North Carolina, Chapel Hill. His many publications include *The Rush to German Unity* (1994) and *Students, Society, and Politics in Imperial Germany* (1982); **Volker Gransow** is teaches in the Department of Political Science at the Freie Universität Berlin. One of his more recent publications is *The Autistic Walkman* (1985)

304 pages; glossary, bibliog., index; ISBN 1-57181-010-2 hardback **$64.00/£46.00**
ISBN 1-57181-011-0 paperback **$18.95/£13.95**

INTERNATIONAL POLITICAL CURRENTS
A Friedrich-Ebert-Stiftung Series; General Editor: **Dieter Dettke**

Volume 1:

TOWARD A GLOBAL CIVIL SOCIETY

Edited by **Michael Walzer**

The demise of Communism has not only affected Eastern Europe but also the countries of the West where a far-reaching examination of political and economic systems has begun. This collection of essays by internationally renowned scholars of political theory from Europe and the United States explores both the concept and the reality of civil society and its institutions.

Michael Walzer has been a permanent faculty member at the School of Social Science, Institute for Advances Study in Princeton since 1980. He is an editor of *Dissent* and a contributing editor of *The New Republic,* and has published among numerous works *The Company of Critics* (1988) and *Interpretation and Social Criticism* (1987).

344 pages; ISBN 1-57181-054-4 hardback **$39.95/£31.00**

165 Taber Avenue • Providence, Rhode Island 02906
Phone: 401-861-9330 • Fax: 401-521-0056 • E-mail: BerghahnBk@aol.com

GERMANY'S NEW POLITICS
Parties and Issues in the 1990s

Edited by **David Conradt, Gerald R. Kleinfeld, George K. Romoser, Christian Søe**

Four years after unification, Germany has just completed what has been called the "super election year": no less than nineteen elections, culminating in the Bundestag vote on October 16, 1994. Four years after unification, the elections of 1994 reveal the state of German unity and the interplay of new forces in post-Cold War Europe. This book analyses the elections for specialists as well as for students, placing them in the wider context of political and economic developments in Germany in the 1990s. An appendix with full data on previous Bundestag elections and relevant charts on party developments enhances the value of this volume which students, scholars and the general reader interested in German affairs will find indispensable.

336 pages; tabl., statistics ISBN 1-57181-032-3 hardback ca. **$42.00/£30.00**
ISBN 1-57181-033-1 paperback ca. **$15.00/£11.50**

OSTHANDEL AND OSTPOLITIK
German Foreign Trade Policies in Eastern Europe from Bismarck to Adenauer

Robert Mark Spaulding, *Department of History, University of North Carolina at Wilmington*

For the first time a vitally important aspect of German-East European relations is examined.

"Long eclipsed by the scope of the Atlantic economy, obscured by Anglo-German rivalry, and nearly destroyed by the post-1945 division of Europe, the flow of goods across East Central Europe has been, nonetheless, an immensely significant pattern of European economic exchange. For Germany, the Osthandel was both a blessing and a curse; its bounty provided much of the raw material for the rise of German economic and political power in Europe while its lure tantalized German ambitions to the point of madness." (From the Introduction). Based on rich archival material, this wide-ranging study documents and analyses for the first time a vitally important aspect of German-East European relations over a seventy-year period. It spans the years from the very first trade treaty between the German and Russian empires to the postwar establishment of full commercial relations between the Federal Republic and the Soviet Union. A brief Epilogue probes the continuities of German policy in the period from 1960-1990.

July, ca. 512 pages, 15 tables, 36 figs., bibliog., index
ISBN 1-57181-039-0 hardback · ca. **$79.00/£55.00**

165 Taber Avenue • Providence, Rhode Island 02906
Phone: 401-861-9330 • Fax: 401-521-0056 • E-mail: BerghahnBk@aol.com

EUROPE AFTER MAASTRICHT
American and European Perspectives
Edited by **Paul Michael Lützeler**

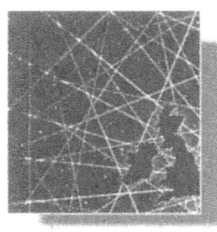

During the era following the Second World War world peace was largely assured through American-European cooperation on the political, military, and economic level. This status quo was upset by the ratification of the Treaty on the European Union (Maastricht Treaty) which will, whatever obstacles still remain, inevitably lead to closer cooperation among (west) European countries and to a shift in Europe's position within world politics. This raises a number of questions that are discussed in this volume by an international team of experts from Europe (east and west), Russia and the United States.

Paul Michael Lützeler is Rosa May Distinguished University Professor in the Humanities at Washington University of St Louis; Director of the European Studies Program; Director of the Center for Contemporary German Literature and Chairman of the Senate Council. His most recent publication is *Die Schriftsteller und Europa. Von der Romantik bis zur Gegenwart* (1992)

320 pages; 10 tabl., bibliog., index; ISBN 1-57181-020-X hardback **$29.95/£23.00**

JAPAN AND GERMANY IN THE MODERN WORLD
Bernd Martin

With the founding of their respective national states, the Meiji Empire in 1869 and the German Reich in 1871, Japan and Germany entered world politics. Since then both countries have developed in strikingly similar ways: the Japanese, after experimenting with American, English and French models of modernization, finally opted for the Prusso-German example which they followed from 1881 to 1945, when they restructured not only the Meiji constitution but also the entire administration, the modern legal system, the education system from the village school to the Imperial University, the Imperial Army and last but not least the social system. It is not surprising therefore that these two countries became close allies during the Second World War, although in the end this proved a "fatal attraction." The developments in both countries since the war have again shown remarkable similarities. Yet this fascinating parallelism has been largely neglected in Western scholarship. This volume by one of Germany's leading Japan specialists will fill this gap.

Bernd Martin is Professor of Modern History at the University of Freiburg/Br. Although he is well known for his work on Japan, his interests extend to the history of modern Southeast Asia, and he frequently lectures, in addition to Japan, in China, Taiwan, South Korea and Thailand. He has published numerous books and articles on modern Germany and Southeast Asia.

256 pages; ISBN 1-57181-858-8 hardback ca. **$39.95/£28.00**

165 Taber Avenue • Providence, Rhode Island 02906
Phone: 401-861-9330 • Fax: 401-521-0056 • E-mail: BerghahnBk@aol.com

www.ingramcontent.com/pod-product-compliance
Lightning Source LLC
Chambersburg PA
CBHW071156070526
44584CB00019B/2815